Praise for

Love Outpouring

In *Love Outpouring* Scott Flynn has provided a marvelous overview of nonduality. The book begins with a definition of Love Outpouring as "A spontaneous outward expression of laughter, tears of joy or awe-nessing, corresponding to a sense of deep love and gratitude for the One who shines as the mystery of life; yourSelf." This spirit is consistently exhibited throughout the book.

Even though Scott draws upon works in the areas of science, psychology and spirituality, the main point of the book is practical. The book is peppered with inspirational quotes and practical exercises designed to point the reader beyond understanding to a direct experience of nondual Reality.

He asks questions rather than provides answers, knowing that the Answer cannot be put into words. A sense of joy and love fills the pages, making it clear that the author knows the Reality of which he speaks. I highly recommend this book as an important contribution to the literature of nonduality.

Thank you for writing this book!

Marshall Davis, author of a multitude of influential nonduality books such as *Unitive Awareness*, *Experiencing God Directly* and *Living Presence*, and the host of *The Tao of Christ* podcast

T0190678

Love Outpouring

Experiencing Ever-Present Happiness
by Illuminating and Eliminating the
Difference between Who You Are and
What You Have Mistaken Yourself to Be

Love Outpouring

Experiencing Ever-Present Happiness
by Illuminating and Eliminating the
Difference between Who You Are and
What You Have Mistaken Yourself to Be

Scott Flynn

MANTRA
BOOKS

London, UK
Washington, DC, USA

CollectiveInk

First published by Mantra Books, 2024
Mantra Books is an imprint of Collective Ink Ltd.,
Unit 11, Shepperton House, 89 Shepperton Road, London, N1 3DF
office@collectiveinkbooks.com
www.collectiveinkbooks.com
www.mantra-books.net

For distributor details and how to order please visit the 'Ordering' section on our website.

Text copyright: Scott Flynn 2023

ISBN: 978 1 80341 560 4
978 1 80341 579 6 (ebook)
Library of Congress Control Number: 2023937558

A CIP catalogue record for this book is available from the British Library.

Design: Lapiz Digital Services

UK: Printed and bound by CPI Group (UK) Ltd, Croydon, CR0 4YY
Printed in North America by CPI GPS partners

The author of this book does not dispense medical advice or prescribe the use of any technique as a form of treatment for physical, emotional, or medical problems without the advice of a physician, either directly or indirectly. The intent of the author is only to offer information of a general nature to help you in your quest for emotional and spiritual well-being. In the event you use any of the information in this book for yourself, which is your constitutional right, the author and the publisher assume no responsibility for your actions.

We operate a distinctive and ethical publishing philosophy in all areas of our business, from our global network of authors to production and worldwide distribution.

Table of Pointers

Prologue i—A Direct Invitation   1
    What words represent   4
Prologue ii—An Outpouring to the Reader   8

INTRODUCTION TO SELF-UNDERSTANDING   15

Chapter 1—Love Outpouring—An Introduction   17
    A unitive model of Reality   18
    From madness to love   21
    Isolation experiment   25
    Getting out of the ego-vehicle   27
    Ego-blocking   28
    From love to love   29
    Cessation   32

Chapter 2—Inherent Understandings of the Nondual
    Perennial Message   37
    What is being asked of you   37
    Crossing the barrier   42
    Dissolving the ego-piece   44
    What is being utilized of yours   48
    What is being pointed to   49
    What the message is not   50
    What is not being denied   52
    No expectations   54
    What is the value of this?   56
    Resting IN and AS yourSelf   57
    Why the message is so challenging to translate   59
    Sources of the message   60

SECTION 1: SELF-KNOWLEDGE   67

Chapter 3—What Is Self-Knowledge?   69
    Jñāna-knowledge   69

Chapter 4—A Metaphor: Who You Are   76

Chapter 5—What Does It Mean to Know-Inherently
               and Experience-Directly?   80

Chapter 6—What Is Totality?   84
    Blasphemy   88
    A courageous question   90

Chapter 7—What Is Real?   95
    The nondual understanding   96
    Living the dream   100
    The flow of Reality   101
    Illusion of distance   102
        Space-Distance   102
        Time-Distance   103
    The dimensionless point   104

Chapter 8—What Is Ego?   108
    The elephant's trunk   115
    Forgetfulness, evil and love   115
    The weight of the world   118
    Time, space and contrast   119

Chapter 9—What Is Self?   124
    Expressions of Self   127
        Structure Attributes   128
        Essence Attributes   129
    Other non-objective essences   132

A letter written by yourSelf, from yourSelf, through yourSelf, to yourSelf   133

Chapter 10—Sharing yourSelf with the World   137
    Perplexing-wonder   137
    Our purpose and mission   140
    Our shared Being   141
    Seeking wholeness   142
    Love without otherness   143
    Shared by all   144
    Society can't change itself   145
    You ARE love (Bhakti)   148

SECTION 2: SELF-INVESTIGATION   151

Chapter 11—What Is Self-Investigation?   153
    Self-investigation   154
    The Direct Path   156
       Neti Neti   161
       Self-Inquiry   165
    Vasanas   171
    Arising thoughts   171
    Self-body-bond   172
    Daily practice   174
    Running the show   175
    Physical phenomena   176

SECTION 3: SELF-POINTERS   181

Chapter 12—What Is the Mysterious Wonder of Awe?   183
    AWE-er 1: Who is the real problem-solver?   185
    AWE-er 2: Is matter a fact?   186
       No existence   187

Planck time   188
Volumeless matter   190
AWE-er 3: The Hard Problem of Consciousness   192
AWE-er 4: What are we made of?   195
Physical non-permanence   195
Who is living who?   198
AWE-er 5: Is your daily life more complex
             than the game of chess?   200
Cessation statement   203

Chapter 13 — Science, Philosophy and Self   206
David Bohm, PhD (1917–1992)   207
Jiddu Krishnamurti   209
Albert Einstein (1879–1955)   212
Childlike genius   212
Genius meets mystic   215
Erwin Schrodinger (1887–1961)   219
Bernardo Kastrup, PhD   222
Donald Hoffman, PhD   226
Spacetime denied   228
Free will   229
Beingness   232

Chapter 14 — Western Religion and Self   235
Brother Lawrence (1614–1691)   237
Meister Eckhart (1260–1327)   242
Diversity of Oneness   246
'I AM' sharing   251
Self-psalm   253
Die to Self   254

Appendix   257
    Acknowledgments   257
    Quote Sources   257
    Bibliography   271
About the Author   274
Note to Reader   275

Only those who have dared to let go can dare to re-enter.
Meister Eckhart[1]

Love Outpouring:

A spontaneous outward expression of laughter, tears of joy or awe-nessing, corresponding to a sense of deep love and gratitude for the One who shines as the mystery of life; yourSelf.

> This [Self-realization] often causes such joys and raptures inwardly, and sometimes outwardly, that I am forced to make an effort to moderate them to prevent their appearances to others.
> **Brother Lawrence**[2]

Love Outpouring:

A physical form of expressing and sharing your deep love and gratitude for the One who shines as the mystery of life. This can be expressed and shared via kind actions, compassionate words, beautiful gestures, servant-leadership, conscious-business, and various loving media such as podcasts, videos, blogs, talks, poetry, art, music or print—like the book you have in your hands. But the greatest expression of Love Outpouring is to just simply BE yourSelf AS yourSelf.

My deepest outpourings go out to:

Rupert Spira,
for clearly pointing me directly back to mySelf,
the One-Reality of ever-present happiness.

Michael James,
for relentlessly reminding me to turn my attention inward and
clearly showing me the meaning of 'Love Without Otherness.'

Marshall Davis,
for clearly reminding me what I have inherently known
since I was a child: He and I are One.

All other,
sages, saints, seers, pointers, chiefs, mystics, gurus, scientists,
poets, artists and humanitarians who unceasingly continue to
illuminate the beauty and love inherent in humanity
and enhance the vibrancy and wonder of the mystery of life.

Prologue i

A Direct Invitation

The phrase 'Know ThySelf' is one of the oldest pointers to the paradoxical nature of Reality: the Truth of Existence. The phrase dates back to as early as 2000 BC when it was inscribed in the ancient Egyptian Coffin Texts and more notably to 600 BC when the phrase was carved into the stone foyer at the Temple of Apollo at Delphi in Greece. 'Know ThySelf' is a timeless reminder of what it truly means to be a human being and is the foundation of the perennial message pointed to throughout *Love Outpouring*. The message has forever been an open and available summons for humanity to know the inherent nature of their own Being, yet unfortunately, most of us are reluctant to take this ageless wisdom up on its beautiful and loving offering.

Of every direct perception, however luminous it may be,
we should know that to the majority of the readers of its expression
it will appear nonsensical, to a minority a mystery,
and to a very few a faint reflection
of a luminosity that glimmers within themSelves.
Wei Wu Wei[1*]

There are no one-stop shops—in the form of books, videos, podcasts, seminars and/or retreats—that contain or convey clearly and/or precisely the perennial message of antiquity; it is impossible to create such a comprehensive delivery vehicle. The reason is that the message cannot be known conceptually or intellectually, and consequently it cannot be described accurately and precisely in any sort of medium. At best, the perennial message can only be portrayed by pointing to what it is not, and THAT which remains IS the answer. The perennial message is an inquiry into the nature of yourSelf (the answer), namely THAT WHICH REMAINS after the inquiry has illuminated and eliminated everything you are not.

Any such attempt to articulate the perennial message is therefore just that—a graceful attempt, or more sincerely, a loving invitation, to communicate the unimaginable and unnamable song of the universe. This book is one of those loving invitations. It is an attempt, by yourSelf for yourSelf, to explain in a general sense the fundamentals of the Truth of Existence, with the mission of significantly reducing or possibly even eliminating your human suffering. Once read, it is then up to you to determine if you want to take the message further and know yourSelf more clearly.

This book is a message of love from yourSelf with its purpose being for you to experience-directly and know-inherently your true ever-present nature of peace, happiness and love. Interpreting the book in any other way than this is a misunderstanding.

Due to the counterintuitiveness of the message, the book may be written off by most as ridiculous and absurd, or even radical and dangerous; which is all true for an ego, yet strangely enough the book is a long-awaited swan song for your Heart. To be clear, this is not a self-help book, but more in line with a collection of Self-pointers to significantly reduce and possibly even eliminate ego altogether, which mysteriously leads to absolute boundless freedom and happiness.

To be direct, this book has absolutely nothing to offer to an individual person (ego, self). Hoping to find, gain or become something new from the contents of this book will only lead to disappointment. If successful, this book will lead to a loss, if anything. In fact, if what is being pointed to here is actually heard and followed through to the end, the loss will be your ego; yourself. Yet this loss, paradoxically, is precisely what you have been seeking your entire life: the loss of you (ego) IS the rediscovery of yourSelf AS permanent peace and contentment.

We are talking of something entirely different,
not of self-improvement, but of the cessation of self [ego]."
Jiddu Krishnamurti[2]

Therefore, because of the potential of the perennial message to alter your understanding of the Truth of Reality and thereby change your perception of Who You Are, in which to realize your true nature of permanent unconditional love and acceptance, you may want to reconsider even reading the book if you are not open to this possibility.

There is an Eastern metaphor stating that once someone has experienced directly the sweet nectar of their Self, they will be evermore caught in the jaws of the tiger. A tiger's clench is inescapable, and so is the warmth and love of yourSelf. One taste of it and you will evermore long to return to, and rest in, its eternal, fulfilling, silent wholeness.

What you seek is seeking you.
Rumi[3]

What's perplexing, though, is that *Who* is reading these words right now is what the perennial message is pointing to; You already ARE, and have eternally been, the answer to this book. You have never not been Who You Are, yet most likely you have mistaken yourSelf as something 'other than' Who You Are. Now the question is: Do you have the openness, willingness and courage to find out the beautiful meaning behind the ancient phrase 'Know ThySelf' and to answer and experience the ultimate question of life: 'Who Am I?'

What words represent

Due to the nature of the content pointed to throughout *Love Outpouring*, namely the nature of You, there is no truly accurate linear way to format and present the material depicted herein. The reason is that the infinite and eternal do not have a beginning, an end, or anything that resembles a center, which is why you just have to jump in and go from 'here and now.'

Furthermore, due to the paradoxical nature of the material, regardless of the efforts to clearly describe what is being pointed to, the clarity of the message is constantly falling apart: all pointers, metaphors or analogies break down at a certain point. Any attempt to shore up weak areas of a pointer, metaphor or analogy only creates new holes that need to be re-shored up. This is why it is impossible to precisely articulate the perennial message in words or language. To understand it at all you have to learn how to BE the message—the entire premise of the book.

At times, words or phrases have to be fabricated or accentuated in such a way as to emphasize the point(er). For example, the phrase "the relentless pursuit of effortlessness" means feverishly trying to obtain the quality of an actionless-act of being effortless, which to an ego is a tad bit ridiculous to say the least. How can you work your butt off without exerting effort to obtain the goal? Yet, this is precisely the point. The message requires no outward efforts from you, only the cessation of efforts, to experience ever-present happiness (the goal).

Therefore "the relentless pursuit" means to repose into and Be-Knowingly the absence of internal exertion, effort or urge, that is, internal motionlessness. Yet, and here is the incomprehensible part, life still happens and flows after you experience the internal motionlessness of Self, even though You are both mentally and physically silent, still and empty.

Tigger: Just how do you do it, Pooh?
Pooh: Do what?
Tigger: Become so effortless.
Pooh: I don't do much of anything.
Tigger: But all those things of yours get done.
Pooh: They just sort of happen.
The Tao of Pooh[4]

There could be countless nonsensical words or phrases in this book that may not have meaning in mainstream conversation, but have great point(er) qualities herein. When describing what it means to repose into the indescribable unnamable Self, there may need to be at times whimsical pointers that bridge the gap between the form (ego) and formless (Self). Some whimsical pointers you will encounter are: subjectness,[§] objectlessness, dimensionless-space, denselessness, and destinationless-destination.

Fully capitalized words represent their literal meaning. For instance: You ARE the love you seek means you ARE literally love itSelf, and therefore no seeking for it is required. You are not the concept or idea of love, nor do you 'have' love: you ARE actually (literally) the inherent quality of it. Fully capitalized words are meant to guide you to their very source, so that you can experience and become their meaning directly AS yourSelf.

The distinction between lower-case and upper-case words such as 'self and Self,' 'yourself and yourSelf,' and 'you and You,' is monumental. It is literally the difference between misery and happiness respectively. 'self', 'yourself' and 'you' represent the ego, also depicted throughout as 'mind.' The ego is the greatest sleight-of-hand master ever imagined. It will do whatever is in its apparent power to make sure you stay forever unhappy, which is exactly what keeps it apparently existing. Whereas the Self's true nature is happiness, the ego's true nature is suffering.

The ego knows that its existence is inversely proportional to your experience of happiness. The stronger the ego, the less happy you ARE, and vice versa. The more you become acquainted with the message contained in the book, the more transparent and less powerful the ego will get and the more and more present the Self—that is, love, peace and happiness—will get. Synonyms for Self, yourSelf, You and God (Brahman, Nirvana, Allah, Tao, and so on) are: Consciousness, Awareness, Presence, Being, Existence, Heart, Knowing, Divine, Totality, Truth, Atman, One-Reality, Reality, Universal-Mind, THAT/THIS, and 'I' or 'I Am.' It is suggested that you pick out a few Self synonyms that you are most comfortable with to begin your investigation.

Hyphenated words suggest that the words contained in the hyphenation are all inherent properties of what is being pointed to, meaning more than one quality embodied in the same essence; or, stated slightly differently, many inherent qualities contained AS one subject. From an English language point of view, hyphenated words are most likely the combined verb qualities of the noun or pronoun.

Notes

* The micro-biography of a quoted individual will be presented only when that individual first appears in the book, via a note. The quote sources are provided in the Appendix, corresponding to the chapter and the quote's superscript number within that chapter.

** Brackets [ ] are inserted in quotations throughout the book wherever it was deemed appropriate to clarify the synchronicity of the person's insights with respect to the perennial message, with the intention of giving the reader the clearest opportunity to see/hear what the quote is pointing to.

§ The suffix -*ness* means the quality of being that adjective. For our purposes, it typically means to literally rest IN and AS the actual meaning of the word; BE its meaning.

1 Terence James Stannus Gray (1895–1986) was a producer who created the Cambridge Festival Theater in Cambridge, England. Later in life, under the pen name Wei Wu Wei, he published several highly regarded books on nondual philosophy, primarily from a Taoist point of view.

2 Jiddu Krishnamurti (1895–1986) was a modern Buddha-like figure, in the sense that at a young age Krishnamurti denounced his privileged life, in which he was indoctrinated to be the new World Teacher of the Order of the Star in the East (OSE), a sister organization to the Theosophical Society of Madras, India, and instead dedicated his life to seeking and sharing Truth with the world. From 1929, when Krishnamurti denounced the OSE, until his death in 1986, he spent his life illuminating the need for a revolution in the mind of every human being.

3 Jalaluddin Muhammad Rumi (1207–1273), known simply as Rumi, was a thirteenth-century Persian poet, scholar, theologian and mystic. Rumi is still regarded today as the most recognized and cherished Sufi mystic of his tradition.

4 *The Tao of Pooh*, published in 1982, is a book written by Benjamin Hoff. It is an introduction to the Eastern philosophy of Taoism. The book utilizes the beloved Winnie-the-Pooh stories to explain the underlying principles of Taoism, which are intended to intrigue the Western mindset into further investigation.

Prologue ii

An Outpouring to the Reader

In early 2016 a close friend handed me a little blue paperback book and said, "I think you might be interested in this." It was a copy of Tony Parsons' book, *The Open Secret*. Little did I realize at the time that Tony's book would confront my deepest beliefs and send me on a trajectory into the depths of the nature of Reality, into the wisdom and love of eternity's interwoven fabric of unity: launching me into a thorough investigation to answer the question 'Who Am I?'

> *The day that question [Who Am I?] arises in the mind*
> *is the greatest day of one's life, for once it is born,*
> *it does not succumb until it is satisfied.*
> **Sant Kirpal Singh Ji**[1]

While reading *The Open Secret*, a message that points to the paradoxical nature of Reality, I honestly did not know what the author was trying to convey. To this day I am surprised that I even finished the book. But there was some distant place within me, a place I could not put my finger on, that whispered to me the importance of what the message of the book was pointing to. The whisper was a dormant yet oddly familiar 'Knowing' within me that longed to further know itSelf. The longing soon became known as love longing for itSelf; my longing for mySelf.

Not knowing where to turn next for more insight into the subject, I reached back out to my friend for another referral. He suggested yet another little blue paperback book, *Awakening to the Dream* by Leo Hartong. Leo's book is a beautiful soft introduction into antiquity's nondual message of Know ThySelf. This book was the clincher that sent me on the path to Self-realization.

Even though Leo's book was the catalyst, it did not give me complete clarity on the subject. For the next several years I aimlessly and sometimes frustratingly, yet still enthusiastically and curiously, tried to uncover what exactly the perennial message was depicting. Then, one random day in the summer of 2020 while watching just another random, yet graceful, nonduality video, I heard it. To be more accurate, I directly experienced the message as it presented itSelf to me. The experience was so real, clear and unmistakable as to what the perennial message of nonduality was pointing to: mySelf, and more importantly it allowed me to understand and embody what Self actually is.

The video was from a Rupert Spira presentation I located on the Science and Nonduality website. Rupert teaches a lineage of inescapable Self-knowledge that originated in India known as Advaita Vedanta, which utilizes a Self-inquiry practice to experience Self inherently, known as 'the Direct Path.' It is the inescapable Self-knowledge of Advaita coupled with the direct-experience of Self-inquiry that has allowed me to answer the question 'Who Am I?' and has inspired me to share what was revealed in *Love Outpouring*.

Yet, one of my most beautiful and refreshing discoveries was that this message is not just rooted in Eastern culture, but is also the root of all great religions, philosophies and spiritual/mystical teachings, along with the brilliance of quantum physics, neuroscience and psychology. Even though the perennial message is rooted in all of these institutions, the message itSelf has zero affiliation with any of them—which is the most profound and reassuring recognition of all. Because of this 'zero affiliation' discovery, I was left free and unbound to explore in a new light all of the beliefs, judgments and biases that had unknowingly kept mySelf in bondage, which has allowed life to be freshly experienced, untethered from mental suffering.

A free mind [Self] is one which is untroubled and unfretted
by anything, which has not bound its best part to
any particular manner of being or devotion
*and which **does not seek its own interest in anything**.*
Meister Eckhart[2]

Since 2016 there has not been a day gone by when I have not read, watched, listened to, contemplated, attended, shared, written about, investigated and/or inquired into the nature of Reality: the Truth of Existence. I have turned over just about every perennial nonduality rock possible. The more I investigate into the nature of 'Who Am I?' (the Truth of Reality), the more it reveals itSelf as its own message of love. It has asked absolutely nothing from me, yet its love has been, and continues to be, constantly present and available for me to rest into. The message is dimensionless, eternal and infinite; it has no income, yet has One outcome: ever-present peace-happy-love.

I have nothing but love for the perennial message depicted in this book, for it was the message itSelf that reminded me of the love that I have for mySelf and humanity. The perennial message goes against everything we have been taught, especially in the Western hemisphere; and for all those who have crusaded over millennia to keep the secretless lineage alive, I am deeply grateful. It has given me the courage to openly admit to an inherent-Knowing that I've had contained within me since childhood, that:

Regardless of your ideologies or actions,
labeled as either good or evil or right or wrong,
there is one thing that I know for absolute certainty:
that before I ever meet you or know anything about you,
I love you unconditionally AS mySelf.

This book is dedicated to the inherent nature from which these words have arisen; the eternal source that lies within each one of us. The words in this book are not my words, nor my teachers' words, nor their teachers', but words from antiquity. They are your words, our words, the universe's words. They are You calling yourSelf back home to yourSelf.

What is contained in the words of *Love Outpouring* is unbelievable, unknowable and undesirable to the one you have mistaken yourself to be, your ego. But to the One who has made it this far into the book—your Heart, yourSelf—it is an intimate open-armed homecoming of unconditional permanent peace. Your task, which at first may appear to be impossible, is to trust what is being pointed to here and curiously fall in love with it.

All information within these words has been, currently is, and will evermore continue to be my experience of the perennial message. It has become obvious that our minds perpetually keep us in a state of separation-imprisonment, in which labeling the perennial message as unattainable, extremely complicated and downright non-existent is the ego's primary tactic to perpetuate humanity's bondage and suffering.

After observing my ego's diabolical strategies, and therefore purposely engaging in the elimination of my ego via Self-inquiry, it has become clear that the perennial message has all along been pointing to the Truth, which is this: If the illusion of the ego is seen through to the Oneness of your Heart, then Nirvana, Heaven, Brahman, Consciousness, Peace will be witnessed on Earth. Therefore, the experience of ever-present happiness is not a clear-silent-still state of mind (ego); it is the absence of one altogether.

In closing, if mySelf longs for anything 'other than' itSelf, it longs for You to have the willingness and courage to dismantle all of your societal and upbringing conditioning and be led by your Heart (Self) to what is being pointed to in this book. The message is brutally simple: Know yourSelf AS yourSelf and rediscover the peace, love and happiness that IS the true nature of all 8 billion of us.

> *We rarely hear the inward music,*
> *but we're all dancing to it nevertheless.*
> **Rumi**[3]

May the little blue paperback book in your hands unlock the same bottomless curiosity that my first two blue paperback books did for me: may *Love Outpouring* be your silent whisper that warmly and curiously caresses you into the unfathomable unconditional love and acceptance that You eternally already ARE—yourSelf.

> *Wisdom tells me I am nothing.*
> *Love tells me I am everything.*
> *And in between the two my life flows.*
> **Sri Nisargadatta Maharaj**[4]

Love Outpouring,*
Scott

PS:

> *May you absolutely and non-metaphorically*
> *lose your never-content ever-fluctuating maddening ego (self),*
> *and experience-directly and know-inherently*
> *the permanent beautiful sanity of your ever-loving Heart (Self).*

Notes

* The word 'Outpouring' is a dedication and a gratitude offering to David Carse and his 2005 book, *Perfect Brilliant Stillness*. David set a beautiful example of 'sharing yourSelf with the world' by not copyrighting his book, making his experience and knowledge of the perennial message free and available to humanity. 'Outpouring' illuminates the immense gratitude that arises within as yourSelf experiences itSelf directly.

1 Sant Kirpal Singh Ji (1894–1974) was an Indian spiritual master in the tradition of Nirgun Bhakti (Devotion to Formless Love). He was the President of the World Fellowship of Religions, which has representatives from all the main religions of the world. In 1962 he became the first non-Christian to receive the Order of Saint John of Jerusalem for his spiritual and humanitarian work.

2 Johannes Eckhart (1260–1327), respectfully known as Meister Eckhart, was a theologian, philosopher and mystic. Due to his brilliant use of imagery and metaphysical passion to depict a 'single Oneness' between Self and God, Eckhart is still considered today to be one of the most earnest and radical thinkers ever associated with Christianity. There is an entire section in Chapter 14 dedicated to Meister Eckhart.

4 Sri Nisargadatta Maharaj (1897–1981) was a Self-realized Indian sage in the tradition of Advaita Vedanta, the Hindu philosophy of 'One without a second.' He is still regarded today as one of the most profound perennial-knowledge teachers of the twentieth century.

INTRODUCTION TO
SELF-UNDERSTANDING

Chapter 1

Love Outpouring* — An Introduction

We all long to be happy, and since we have experienced happiness, we know that it exists. But happiness's intermittent and fleeting characteristics draw us to the conclusion that ever-present happiness is unattainable. *Love Outpouring* shows us, through our own direct-experience and inherent-Knowing, that this is a misunderstanding and that ever-present happiness is always available; it is our true nature — it is **who we are**.

> *We all live with the objective of being happy;*
> *our lives are all different and yet the same.*
> **Anne Frank**[1]

We have been conditioned our entire life to believe that to be happy we need to reach out into the world to become and acquire attributes 'other than' ourSelf; career, wealth, status, reputation, material objects, and so on. In this reaching and acquiring 'other than' ourSelf, we falsely identify ourSelf AS these 'other than' attributes. This false identity creates a sense of separation from the wholeness of ourSelf, generating our human suffering. Misdiagnosing our suffering problem, we then reach back out into the world for more 'other than' attributes to fill our void of separation and suffering, when all we are seeking is to return to the unconditional love, happiness and wholeness of ourSelf.

Retracting your reach back from the world and returning to the wholeness of Self is conducted by illuminating and eliminating the difference between who you are (Self) and what you have mistaken yourself to be (egoic-attributes 'other than' yourSelf). This 'illuminating and eliminating' dissolves your agitated 'other than' egoic-attributes, leaving only a permanent aware peaceful Presence that re-illuminates the vibrant wholeness of life that has always been; all to re-establish an eternal wondrous-awe that has not been witnessed since childhood.

This 'illuminating and eliminating' to experience yourSelf directly AS ever-present happiness is done by relinquishing all your misconceived notions of your egoic 'other than' yourSelf attributes, so as to experience-directly the intimate inner-peace you have never lost; yourSelf. Therefore, ever-present happiness is not freedom *for* your egoic-self; it is freedom *from* your egoic-self, in which you win by losing, gain by discarding, and Self-fulfill by ego-emptying.

Love Outpouring is a gracious suggestion to have you abandon your identification as an ego and adopt the identification as your already present and available Self. Adopting yourSelf over your ego allows for everything in life to continue to happen, yet with a renewed fresh awe-ness of wonder. You have written yourSelf this book for the purpose of giving yourSelf the permission to fall back in love with yourSelf and allow yourSelf to unavoidably shine your love-light upon the world as brightly as possible—the greatest gift you or anyone can share with humanity.

A unitive model of Reality

As we peer out into the world we can't help but wonder why there is so much inner-human suffering (such as depression, anxiety, fear, stress) and outer-societal conflict (war, racism, violence, hate and so on) when we know-inherently that the mass majority of civilization only wants to live in peace and harmony. The perennial nondual message proposes that the internal-human turmoil and the external-global friction that we relentlessly and perpetually witness originates from the very fabric of society's (mis)understanding of the current model of Reality.

By no fault of our own we have been conditioned to believe that the current paradigm of reality goes something like this: 13.8 billion years ago, an extremely large physical event happened known as the Big Bang; over the course of several billion years, the physical components of the Big Bang condensed into the cosmos we know today; a couple of billion years ago, life crawled out of the primordial ooze; and a few million years ago, apes stood upright on two feet and developed a brain, giving rise to conscious-individuals who have cultivated today's civilizations. This current paradigm of reality can be labeled as the 'matter-first model.' For it states that first matter came into existence; then much later, Consciousness arose out of that matter (brain-matter), which gave matter-based individuals the ability to flourish as a society.

Yet, and here is the bewildering part, there is absolutely no evidence for the matter-first model of Reality. Still today, Western academia has zero proof that matter itself even exists, or has zero verification that individuals (egos) are real, or has zero plausible explanations as to how Consciousness arises out of brain-matter—zero evidence on all three accounts! To state this more directly, quantum physicists, neuroscientists and psychologists have never found your body (matter), your mind (ego) or your Consciousness (Existence). All their attempts to locate these apparently vital components of life lead them to a realm of no-thingness; of Oneness: an underlying dimensionless Reality of eternal-infinite potential; a unified fabric of Absolute Being-Consciousness (discussed further in Section 3).

Believing in the matter-first model of reality is believing in a model of separation. The Western belief in the matter-first model of separation is the primary reason for the inner and outer disharmony experienced by so many throughout history, which continues more than ever today. The underlying understanding of the matter-first model is that we all have our own separate realities apart from everyone else's, in which each of our individual realities needs to co-exist with and maneuver through all other individuals' realities to survive.

Where the matter-first model is a paradigm of separation, the Eastern perennial nondual message, which could be described as a 'Consciousness-first model' of Reality, is a paradigm of unity. The nondual message maintains there is only One-Reality that exists, in which your Existence alone is the evidence for a One-Reality model. Since there is only a single Existence in a One-Reality model, and since You know You absolutely exist, then You, yourSelf, must be the One-Reality. This One-Reality paradigm is a Consciousness-first model of Reality where separation is non-existent and therefore only unity reigns AS the love of yourSelf.

The nondual Consciousness-first model of Reality could be viewed as directly-experiencing the West's evidence of a One-Reality derived from the findings of quantum physics, neuroscience and psychology by applying and practicing the nondual-wisdom of the East, all to witness the permanent wholeness and happiness to which both the Western and Eastern systems of knowledge point.

There is obviously only one alternative,
namely the unification [nonduality] of minds or Consciousnesses.
Their multiplicity is only apparent;
in Truth there is only one mind [One-Reality].
This is the doctrine of the Upanishads [Eastern Vedic texts].
Erwin Schrodinger[2]

Aligning with the Consciousness-first model ends our misunderstanding of being separate individuals and brings us back into alignment with the One-Reality, which terminates inner-human suffering and outer-global conflicts. For when it is inherently-known by you that yourSelf IS humanity's Self, you lose the ability to harm yourSelf or others, because you realize there are no others, only the unconditional unitive-love of the One-Reality appearing AS yourSelf.

Love Outpouring is a benevolent attempt to bring you back into alignment with the nondual Consciousness-first model of Reality—the One-Reality of yourSelf—so that you can break your spell of believing you are a separate isolated individual and instead experience-directly the ever-present unitive-happiness you have eternally been.

From madness to love

Considering society's incredible technological advances over the past 100+ years, especially since the turn of the twenty-first century, you would think that by now humanity would have left the medieval ages of human history and reached some sort of global institutional cohesiveness where we could actually call ourselves a civilized world. Yet this is clearly not the case, for how can it be when our economic, political, monetary, media, religious and educational institutions and their corresponding human mindsets (egos) continue to be inherently designed to decouple, and therefore separate us from one another and ourSelf? Simply stated, the global industrial mindset, even as well intended as it may be, is incapable of moving humanity closer to any sort of sustainable happiness.

The wake of the Covid-19 pandemic, the Black Lives Matter movement and the global-political and social-unrest upheaval of 2020 has only exacerbated the world's already emotionally irritated and physically exhausted psyches. Fortunately, out of this uprising, new surges of wellbeing policies, particularly seen in the Human Resource (HR) realms of corporate America and college universities, sprang into place to soothe the newly agitated worker/student sentiments and calm the accompanying polarized workplace/campus environments.

Sparked by the elevated 2020 social tensions, HR departments from around the globe have heightened their diversity, equity/equality and inclusion (DE&I) programs to capture and curb such restlessness, and they are still highly engaged today. The DE&I programs have luckily spread to create an awareness within mainstream society of such personal-bettering terms as Whole-Self, Authentic-Self and True-Self to help individuals understand themselves more clearly, with the purpose of experiencing higher states of personal satisfaction and wellbeing. Slogans such as 'Bring Your Whole-Self to Work' and 'Be Your Authentic Self' are still common tactics to keep the minds of the workforce and general public off the social turmoil and redirected onto themselves.

While the Whole, Authentic and True terms do have good intentions, they leave a large gap in their understanding and positive impact. Before Self can be Whole, Authentic or True, we need to first know and understand what this elusive Self is; the primal element of wholeness, authenticness and trueness. Therefore, it's not until Self is understood clearly that the true impact from DE&I programs, or any other such self-bettering programs being practiced around the globe, can be realized.

Skipping Self-understanding and jumping straight to becoming more Whole, Authentic or True leaves a void of confusion in the process of seeking wellbeing, exactly the opposite of what becoming Whole, Authentic or True was meant to accomplish in the first place. It is likened to leapfrogging over the first-person pronoun (I) and focusing primarily on the second- and third-person pronouns (you; he/she, they). Meaning, how can you accurately assess an object (anything 'other than' yourSelf, such as second and third persons) if you don't clearly know the subject (I, yourSelf) 'doing' the assessment? You can't, which leads to a distortion, an abstraction, of Reality, which is what has led to the bulk of the confusion and separation in the world. Skipping over the first-person pronoun of Self (I) has the same irrationality as eliminating the number 1 from the number line, then thinking you absolutely know and understand what a 2 and a 3 are.

We have become so disconnected from Self, the truest form of sanity, that we as a global collective have literally gone mad, yet sadly have illogically convinced each other that our madness is positive progress and that capturing Whole, Authentic and True is just around the corner. The most demented aspect of this collective insanity is the fact that it is not being led by convicted criminals or institutionalized lunatics, but by global leaders who are considered by our highest-ranking authorities to be somewhat intelligent and rational. Yet as we look around the world, it is not difficult to see our leaders' necrotic ego-minds seeping into all the cracks of our global society, especially into the ego-minds of the very citizens they took an oath to protect.

> *By far the greater part of violence that humans*
> *have inflicted on each other is not the work of criminals*
> *or the mentally deranged, but of normal, respectable citizens*
> *in the service of the collective ego.*
> *One can go as far to say that on this planet "normal" equals insane.*
> **Eckhart Tolle**[3]

The perennial message reunites us with our innate sane Self, collapsing the gap between sanity and insanity, the gap between who you are (Self, sane) and what you have mistaken yourself to be (ego, insane). This gap-collapsing is accomplished by relentlessly pointing yourself back to yourSelf, so that the 'definition' of Self is literally experienced and known directly by and AS You. This is about You witnessing directly the most intimate, loving and sane experience possible: the non-objective experience of experiencing yourSelf.

Illuminating the intimate experience of experiencing yourSelf is all intended to pull you out of, or keep you from falling deeper into, the downward-spiraling psychosis of global insanity, and instead have you experience directly the ever-present happiness you have innately alive within You. All with the purpose of consciously redefining "normal" to equal sane, so that humanity has some sort of a probability to live peacefully someday soon.

The most beautiful collective experience of this gap-collapsing—also known as the collapsing of the distance between Self and other—is that it renders you incapable of not knowing yourSelf as others and others as yourSelf. This union of Selfs is the greatest destructive force on the planet to eliminate the grotesque human cruelty and violence still so prevalent in the world today.

Self is the source of happiness, and therefore the relentless pursuit of Self is the means to experiencing permanently our true-sane nature of happiness. Happiness is the birthplace of creativity and love. Therefore, knowing our birthplace creates a felt-recognition of internal wholeness and completeness where the greatest potential for family, work, societal and global peace and happiness can be realized.

If one doesn't play a part in the creative whole,
he is not worth being called human.
He has betrayed his true purpose.
Albert Einstein[4]

Ever-present happiness is simply yourSelf directly experiencing itSelf. Experiencing yourSelf directly and clearly is the primal-original experience of every human, which, when remembered by you, is intimately-known as a permanent delightful warm homecoming. Therefore, the ultimate goal in life is to know and love yourSelf AS yourSelf unconditionally.

Ever-present happiness of Self is experienced when a felt profoundly-intimate 'absolute full-stop' of internal mental/ physical outward movement is directly witnessed by you, which is initiated by allowing your agitated-ego to withdraw back into its peaceful-sane-silent home of Self, so that only Self alone is experienced AS You: the entire premise of this book.

Permanent-happiness probably sounds completely unrealistic and unattainable, which it is to an ego, but when acknowledged by your Heart (Self) as real, even if just for a moment at first, you will evermore realize the Truth of this pointer.

Our conventional way of understanding reality has led us to the misunderstanding that if our ego were to vanish there would be nothing left of us, which is only a delusion of the Western-hemisphere mindset. What the perennial message has demonstrated for over 8000† years is that when ego is eliminated, all that remains is the beautiful foundational structure of the Universal-Mind (Self): You, ever-present happiness.

Isolation experiment

In a 2014 experiment conducted by the University of Virginia and Harvard University, psychologists examined the outcome of over 100 people, ranging in ages from 18 to 77 and from all walks of life, sitting in a plain undecorated room for 6 to 15 minutes doing nothing but isolated with their own mind. The objective was to determine why we find it so hard to be alone with ourselves and to determine just how far a person will go to distract themselves from the unpleasantness of their own silent solitude.

The findings were a bit shocking to say the least. In over 11 separate experiments, the psychologists showed that the applicants despised being left alone with themselves, regardless of their age, education, income, or the amount of time they spent on their smartphones or social media. To determine just how far someone will go to distract themselves from the agitation of sitting alone in silence, in a following experiment the researchers allowed the applicants to self-administer electric shocks to themselves as needed to distract themselves from the pain of doing nothing. The researchers were surprised to find that 67% of the men and 25% of the women gave themselves up to four shocks each in the given timeframe.

> *All men's miseries derive from not*
> *being able to sit in a quiet room alone.*
> **Blaise Pascal**[5]

It is apparent that the majority of us do not enjoy being isolated with ourselves and will make valiant efforts to obtain external distractions in order to keep our minds entertained on anything 'other than' ourSelf. We have been relentlessly trained over our lifetime by our teachers, parents, clergy and superiors to feel internally irritated when resting in the peaceful solitude of our own skin.

Needless to say, if we are not busy distracting ourselves from a place of solitude, meaning if our mind is not busy seeking contentment in entertainment, substances, relationships, careers, adventures, and so on, then due to the peaceful solitude, our preconditioned minds fall into a realm of agitation. This shines light on the fact that there is no such thing as a peaceful-still-silent mind; it's either busy keeping itself busy with distractions or agitated by silence.

Any sort of idle mind generates internal irritation, wherein tendencies then arise within us to mentally or physically move away from 'here' to be 'anywhere else but here'; hence the high fail-rates of sitting still for 15 minutes. The state of mind of 'never being fully content with here' is known as unhappiness.

Getting out of the ego-vehicle

The perennial message is truly about getting completely out of your current perception-vehicle, and getting into an apparently new perception-vehicle, that is, getting out of your ego-vehicle and into your Self-vehicle. The reason the Self-vehicle is an *apparently* new one' is because it has literally been your primary perception-vehicle for eternity, yet you have cloaked it with ego and forgotten about it, making it now only 'appear' to be new.

The problem is that a 'vehicle' of any type can't get out of itself and into something new. A 'vehicle' only has its own limited faculties to work with, and therefore lacks the capacity and desire to know and become something 'other than' itself, that is, to disassemble itself and get into another 'other-than'-itself vehicle.

> *It is not possible for the manifest [ego-vehicle]*
> *to search for the unmanifest [Self-vehicle].*
> *There is the unmanifest only in the absence of the manifest.*
> **Sri Nisargadatta Maharaj**[6]

Therefore the only way to create a new vehicle is to abandon the old vehicle by focusing primarily on the new vehicle. The now new vehicle will soon forget the original vehicle, making the original vehicle obsolete.

> *You never change things by fighting the existing reality.*
> *To change something,*
> *build a new model that makes the existing model obsolete.*
> **Buckminster Fuller**[7]

In general, this vehicle trade is what the intent of the message in this book is: to get out of the corrosive-vehicle of ego and into the wholeness-vehicle of Self. This is approached by noticing the beautiful qualities of Self relative to the ego, in which you rationally come to an understanding that you would prefer to experience the permanent beautiful loving qualities of Self relative to the relentless agitation recycling of the ego-mind, and you then lovingly and simply make the rational move.

Ego-blocking

Love Outpouring utilizes several different institutional classifications, engaged through Self-knowledge and Self-inquiry practices, for the purpose of making it impossible to escape what is pointed to throughout the book. Your ego will do everything in its power to deny and flee the perennial message, so the goal with the many classifications is to block your ego's escape in any direction it tries to turn and run. When the ego realizes there is no escape hatch from the jaws of the tiger (the Truth), it will become exhausted and collapse into its own home of Self, leaving only You.

The primary ego-blocking classifications contained within the book are historic/current scientific, religious and spiritual figureheads, physics, logic, mathematics, philosophy, poetry, and the arts. Not only are these utilized as blocking techniques, but they also aid in the dismantling of your mainstream way of 'perceiving life,' with the main intention to always be pointing you back to yourSelf.

The variety and multitude of these classifications is to provide the understanding that the message presents itself in all aspects of life; yet, oddly enough, these classifications remain completely unaffiliated with, and totally free from, any aspect of the perennial message or yourSelf.

Since everyone comes into this message with different backgrounds, conditioning and preferences, the diversity of classifications, quotes, stories, pointers and metaphors gives the reader the best possibility of seeing and experiencing what is being pointed to. In general, the diversity of the classifications is meant for you to find congruence within the message to help pull you out of your ruts of belief, judgment and bias, and into the vast world of bottomless awe: yourSelf.

From love to love

Since there is only One-Reality, then by the definition of One, the author's Self must also be yourSelf, and therefore *Love Outpouring* is actually a book written by yourSelf, from yourSelf, through yourSelf, to yourSelf. *Love Outpouring* is your gift to yourSelf; a hand written reminder to yourSelf to lovingly remember itSelf—a warmhearted invitation from your infinite Self to persuade its finite egoic-self to return home to the immense-eternal-peace of itSelf.

The message in this book is the essence, the whisper, within You; the essence you have known since birth; the essence felt within yourSelf as the utmost intimate remembrance of unconditional love and acceptance. This book is this essence calling itSelf back home to itSelf; it is love calling itSelf back home to itSelf, and You ARE this love. This essence asks only one effort of you: to remember, while in return it promises to surrender eternity to You. You ARE literally eternity returning itSelf back to itSelf, so that eternity can learn from itSelf.

Not only do we transform as eternity unfolds in us,
but also eternity may transform as it returns to itSelf
in a richer way through our participation.
David Bohm[8]

This essence, the fragrance of your Heart, is the innocent childlike wonder that has been periodically sensed by you over your lifetime, but is accompanied with the unsatisfying feeling of not being able to put your finger on where the sensation has originated from within you. This sensation, the essence of permanent youth, is yourSelf, is You—and when honest with yourSelf You intimately, inherently, know this. This essence is the so-familiar taste you have experienced intermittently over the course of your life—in your teens, twenties, thirties, forties, and so on—but have not yet been able to place it or hold on to it for more than a few moments. *Love Outpouring* is your attempt to call yourSelf back to your inherent-Knowing, the felt innocence of your youth, which has always been eternally available, waiting for you to melt back into its open ever-loving arms.

YourSelf is the perfume of your Heart, the same essence that is generated by youthful memories of running through the sprinklers, playing hide-n-seek, cloud gazing, being frightened by the boogie-man, learning to ride a bike, playing house or building cardboard forts. You ARE this perfume. This perfume has never abandoned You, forgotten You or un-loved You; you have only unknowingly mistaken it as unreal and ignored its calling. The nondual perennial message is the whisper that has been on the tip of your tongue for decades now, the intimate calling of you back to yourSelf to experience-directly and know-inherently the essence of ever-present happiness, the perfume so innately interwoven into the fabric of your Being.

We all inherently know directly from childhood that unconditional love and acceptance is the underlying nature of life, but we have lost the courage to be honest with ourSelf and allow this to remain the Truth. Because of this, negative emotions—worry, anxiety, fear—are the outcomes of our loss of courage to let love reign as the Truth. This Truth is the cradle of undoubtable assurance that everything is going to be OK, regardless of the circumstances. The solution is beyond simple: relinquish all resistance to your misconceived notions of yourself and regain what you have never lost—You.

As you read the book, try not to read it from the place of your mind (ego), which is a place of concepts and ideas, but from the place where this innocent essence is located: your Heart (Self). The Heart is the location from which this book was authored, the place that is being spoken to, and the only place that could possibly understand what is being pointed to here. So don't try and remember with your mind what you have read, for it is somewhat impossible; just be open to allowing your Heart the availability to listen to and hear what is being depicted and messaged.

> *When you fish for love,*
> *bait with your Heart, not your brain.*
> **Mark Twain**[9]

Your Heart is the ever-present and aware, all-encompassing IS-ness of Existence; the unnamable, eternal and infinite substratum of Reality. This substratum is a place the ego says is non-existent and unreal. Don't let your ego fool you again and whisk you away into another fanatical rollercoaster ride of broken promises such as "I swear I will make you feel whole, complete and content if you ignore the nondual perennial message," which, if your ego is followed, will only lead you farther and farther away from the place that will actually permanently deliver...yourSelf.

You have written this book to break your egoic-self wide open. To return to being completely exposed and vulnerable as a lost lamb while remaining coupled with the aspect of the impenetrable essence of a lion. I/Self/You promise I will never leave your side no matter how challenging or fearful the path may become. I AM / You ARE / the book IS a message from yourSelf to yourSelf calling yourSelf back home to rest into eternal ever-present peace, love and happiness...yourSelf.

> *May God break your Heart so completely*
> *that the whole world falls in.*
> **Mother Teresa**[10]

Cessation

This book is a message of content-embodiment, where you transfigure yourself to innately-One AS the content contained in the message itself; You 'BE / ARE' the content...the ever-close non-objective experience of yourSelf. YourSelf experiencing itSelf AS itSelf is the direct witnessing of ever-present peace-happy-love encapsulated in completeness.

You take the blue pill, the story ends,
you wake up in your bed and believe whatever you want to believe.
You take the red pill, you stay in wonderland,
and I show you how deep the rabbit-hole goes.
Morpheus, in *The Matrix*[11]

Regarding the rabbit-hole quote, the perennial message is actually a paradoxical twist on the quote, in which the message is redirecting you to the fact that you (ego) are the rabbit-hole itself, in an attempt to transfigure you back into Reality (Self). The transfiguration is analogous to your ego being asleep to the dream of life, in which the nondual message is eagerly, yet lovingly, trying to awaken your ego to the dream, so you can experience-directly life's wondrous nature as yourSelf. Look at the table below; which pill would you prefer to take?

Blue Pill (rabbit hole, ego, mind)	Red Pill (Reality, Self, Heart)
Permanent:	**Permanent:**
Separation, suffering, seeking, insanity, matter-first model	Unity, peace, love, happiness, silence, stillness, emptiness, contentness, wholeness, fulfillment, satisfaction, awe, sanity, consciousness-first model
Permanent cycles:	
Discontent, irritation, resentment, frustration, fear, doubt, confusion, agitation, satisfaction pursuits	**Permanent cycles:** None

The overall nondual message is the opportunity to move yourself from the Blue Pill box to the Red Pill box; to transcend what you have mistaken yourSelf to be (ego), to who you actually already are (Self): taking the Red Pill is awakening to the beautiful dream of life.

The perennial wisdom seeps into the space of our mental and physical contractions and unconsciously dissolves them to reveal our true nature of boundless expansion and happiness. Once expanded, *Love Outpouring* solidifies the direct Self-experience by investigating within, where you rediscover the permanent source of the peace, love and happiness that you have evermore longed for...yourSelf.

Love takes up where [conceptual-]knowledge leaves off.
Saint Thomas Aquinas[12]

Notes

* Outpouring is an intrinsic verb. An intrinsic verb is inherent to the noun. Since love is shared, it therefore innately has a flowing quality, hence it outpours; that is, outpouring is inherent to love.

† According to Delhi University's Sanskrit Department, the Hindu Vedic texts date back to 6000 BC.

1 Annelies Marie "Anne" Frank (1929–1945), between the ages of 13 and 14, wrote her now-famous diary while in hiding from the Nazis during the German occupation of the Netherlands in World War II. Her diary, which was published as a book after her death, *The Diary of a Young Girl*, is one of the world's most recognized and beloved books. At the age of 16 Anne was murdered by the Nazis at Bergen-Belsen concentration camp, Germany. It is apparent from Anne's writings that she saw good in all people, regardless of their ideologies and actions.

2   Erwin Schrodinger (1887–1961) was an Austrian physicist who developed the fundamental understanding of quantum theory, which awarded him the 1933 Nobel Prize in Physics. Erwin was a devotee of the Vedic Upanishads and was open about his understanding that Consciousness could not be accounted for as an object, and since it is absolutely fundamental, it cannot be accounted for in terms of anything else.

3   Eckhart Tolle is a spiritual teacher born in Lunen, Germany, and the author of two number-one bestsellers, *The Power of Now* and *A New Earth: Awakening to Your Life's Purpose.* At the center of Eckhart's teachings is the transcendence of ego into a conscious enlightenment he envisions as the next frontier in humanity's evolution.

4   Albert Einstein (1879–1955) was a quantum physicist who holds the title of the Father of Modern Cosmology. He became widely aggrandized and pedestalized after creating and proving his famous equations on the General Theory of Relativity. Albert was a brilliant scholar and a wholehearted humanitarian, and is highlighted in his own section in Chapter 13.

5   Blaise Pascal (1623–1662) was a French mathematician, physicist, philosopher and Catholic theologian. Among many brilliant discoveries, Blaise is mostly recognized for the International System unit of pressure, known as a pascal (Pa). One pascal is equivalent to 1 newton (N) of force applied over an area of 1 square meter (m^2), $Pa = N/m^2$.

7   Richard Buckminster Fuller (1895–1983) was an American architect, systems theorist, writer, designer, inventor, philosopher and futurist. He was most recognized for the

geodesic dome, like the one at the Disney World Epcot Center in Florida. Buckminster's mission was to discover what a single individual could contribute toward changing the world and benefiting all humanity.

8   David Joseph Bohm, PhD (1917–1992) was an American-Brazilian-British theoretical quantum physicist. The Dalai Lama has referred to Bohm as his 'science guru' and Bohm was depicted by Albert Einstein as his 'spiritual son.' What made Bohm such a significant influencer was that he allowed his quantum findings to lead him to the Truth, regardless of the current mainstream ways of thinking. There is an entire section in Chapter 13 dedicated to Bohm.

9   Samuel Langhorne Clemens (1835–1910), pen name Mark Twain, was an American writer, humorist and lecturer who was known as the Father of American Literature. Ernest Hemingway once commented that all modern American literature comes from one book by Mark Twain called *The Adventures of Huckleberry Finn*.

10   Saint Teresa of Calcutta (1910–1997), also known as Mother Teresa, the Living Saint, was a missionary nun who was one of the greatest humanitarians of the twentieth century, receiving the 1979 Nobel Peace Prize for her altruism. In 1950 she founded the Missionaries of Charity in Calcutta, India, which set up soup kitchens, leper colonies, orphanages, and homes for the dying destitute, and also educated the poorest of the poor and fed the homeless.

11   *The Matrix* is a 1999 movie starring Keanu Reeves and Laurence Fishburne. It depicts our current reality as we know it as an illusion generated by a computer simulation

which we are asleep to, and suggests that underlying the simulation there is a real physical world that we need to wake up to.

12   Thomas Aquinas (1225–1274) was an Italian Dominican friar and priest who was a radical influential philosopher and theologian of the Catholic Church. Thomas has been described as the most influential thinker of the medieval period and the greatest of all the medieval philosopher-theologians.

Chapter 2

Inherent Understandings of the Nondual Perennial Message

What is being asked of you

In general, what is being asked is to be open to the possibility of another way of perceiving and experiencing Reality. There are some big pills to swallow here, as you might have picked up from prior pointers. Some, at first, may be too undigestible to get past the gag reflex. If so, it's OK—it's part of the process. What is suggested is to come back later to the pointers that are too overwhelming and that confront your ego-conditioning in a way that is too unbelievable.

It is suggested, though, that you read the book in the most consecutive fashion that works for you. The information has been formatted to build on itself in what has been witnessed to be the clearest way possible; but, if necessary, skip the chapters or sections that give you trouble, then return to them.

As a brutally honest, yet unconditionally loving reminder, the answer to knowing yourSelf does not lie in this book, so don't rush through it expecting to find the answer herein. Spend as much time as possible in the One non-space within You to which all the chapters within the book point. If the answer to life was contained in this book, that would mean the answer to the Truth of Existence—namely the Truth of You—would be found outside of yourSelf, which is illogical. You ARE the Truth of You...You ARE the answer you are expecting to find in this book.

The message is presented from many different points of view throughout the book, so there is a good chance you may find the clarity you need in other chapters. The reason for the diverse pointer redundancies is that you (and the rest of us, for that matter) are a really-really good forgetter. You, with the help of others, have diligently trained yourSelf over the course of your lifetime to know and be anything/everything 'other than' yourSelf, which has led to a persistent Self-forgetfulness.

To be nobody-but-yourSelf
– in a world which is doing its best, night and day,
to make you everybody else –
means to fight the hardest battle which any human being can fight;
and never stop fighting.
E.E. Cummings[1]

This forgetfulness is not a location or life problem, but a remembrance problem. You do not have to run off to some foreign land, visit a secluded island or live in a cave to remember yourSelf. If you are not willing to remember and rediscover happiness here-and-now at your current location, you will most likely not be willing to do so in these other places as well.

Sometimes reading/hearing the same topic and pointer presented in several different ways can trigger a sense of understanding. What is for sure is that beliefs, biases, judgments, concepts, objects and 'personal-ego' conditioning will need to be confronted and abandoned as 'not You,' prior to experiencing the benefits of ever-present happiness.

The only sign of progress is perseverance.
If you persevere it means you have love.
Love is the Mother of true-knowledge.
Without love we cannot succeed to know ourSelf.
Michael James[2]

No one but you can persevere and no one but you will know if you are persevering or not. This is not about anyone else, but you. Let this be repeated. Only you can make the relentless motionless efforts to know yourSelf directly and to experience ever-present happiness. As explained above, teachers, books, videos and so on can only point you to yourSelf, but at some point these pointers will need to be abandoned and you will be on your own. It may sound selfish at first glance, but in Reality it is the ever-loving effortless-effort of Self-realization that brings the greatest love, peace and happiness to yourSelf and to humanity.

> *The way to reform the world is to reform oneSelf*
> *in such a way that Reality shines in the Heart.*
> **Sri Ramana Maharshi**[3]

> *Sanctify yourSelf and you will sanctify society.*
> **Saint Francis of Assisi**[4]

Everyone's personal conditioning is different and therefore everyone's path to their true nature will be unique, yet everyone's true nature (Self) is equivalent. It is not this book's job to determine your path; its job is to give you enough credibility in the subject that your love for the Truth charts its own trajectory to effortlessly embark on the eternal journey of antiquity. It will most likely be a fascinating ride with many eye-opening (I-opening) blind corners and inspiring uncertainty; this again is OK—it is part of the script.

Because of the message's unfamiliar content, understanding and embodying the material may take many repeated investigations, contemplations and inquiries to solidify. As your Heart (Self) gains more understanding of the material, that is, as your ego fades to the background, it is suggested to come back and reread unclear sections to capture their content. The reason you may not understand them at first is that you will try to comprehend and remember the material with your mind (ego), which is OK. But the mind is limited and finite and is not capable of understanding and interpreting the infinite Self. It may take many trials to inherently-know the difference between ego and Self; if so, let it be so.

Besides your Existence and your love of being happy, there are no prerequisites to knowing yourSelf. In fact, every human IS their own direct conduit back to themSelf, which is what allows you to constantly know and be aware of yourSelf.

Quick question: Are you not aware of yourSelf at this very moment? And if you're not, who is? This is how intimate and available the answer to 'Who Am I?' is.

Levels or rankings with regards to your intelligence, imagination/creativity/cleverness, social status, wealth and career have nothing to do with you knowing yourSelf. Neither does your race, gender, sexual preferences, nationality, or culture have anything to do with you achieving ever-present happiness—which puts everyone on the same playing field. And most importantly, your happiness does not depend on any other person's circumstances. The ego will tell you all day long why others were able to achieve enlightenment and why you will fail because you don't have the life they have. Learn to understand that the ego's job is to make sure you don't hear what is being suggested within these words. Watching the ego kick, scream and fight for its illusory life will soon become joyful entertainment, as you witness it squirm from the profound peace of your Heart.

Therefore, be kind to yourself, rest in awe of the simplicity and the absence of demands and requests of the perennial knowledge, let it play out organically, and most of all enjoy the rediscovery of the love you have inherently contained within You. (In Sanskrit there is a term for new Self-discoveries: *Sphurana*, a non-conceptual experience of a new, clear and fresh knowledge of one's Existence.)

There is really no soft way to introduce someone to this message; the message of eliminating your ego and illuminating yourSelf. To many it will be very confronting material at first; if so, let it be as it is. Most will also not 'get it,' which is rightly so. Rest assured, no one (ego) has ever 'got it'; it 'can't be gotten.' So let it be as it is, for it can't be known conceptually, intellectually or mentally in any way. This is because what the message is pointing to is too infinitely large for the limited finite ego to get its mental-arms around in order to know it and label it as something.

[The perennial message is...]
An understanding, which has nothing to do with comprehension
A knowing, which has nothing to do with knowledge.
David Carse[5]

You can only BE what is being pointed to, which can only be inherently-known and directly-experienced. Let the message speak to you and allow it to take you directly to the place to which it points and which resides within you: your Heart (Self). Strive to knowingly-understand how to allow the message to become an inherent property WITHIN and OF you. If persistent, you will see the paradox that lies within this pointer, that in 'becoming' the inherent properties of this message you will realize you already ARE these inherent properties and therefore no 'becoming' had to take place at all.

You cannot become what you already are.
You cannot be what you are not.
Rupert Spira[6]

At first, because of our conditioned mental reflex to turn everything 'other than' ourSelf into an object and label it, you will try to make this message into something new, like a new topic or subject, a new way of living, or a new religion or spiritual practice. If so, let it be. This 'new something' is the apparent path your ego takes to return home to itSelf. Yet you will soon come to realize directly that nothing new has to come into existence; nor do you have to become anything different than you already are in order for you to experience the perennial message.

If the material frustrates, angers or upsets you in any way, take this as a huge positive indicator that your ego has heard clearly what this teaching is pointing to, and is rebelling in fear. Why fear? Because if this understanding is fully embodied, the ego will no longer exist. The paradox of the matter is that when Self-realization is experienced, it will be clearly seen that the ego never existed to begin with, and therefore no real ego-annihilation ever happened.

How wonderful that we have met with a paradox.
Now we have some hope of making progress.
Niels Bohr[7]

The beauty of it all is that as the ego dissolves into Self, suffering dissolves into happiness. Restated: As the ego perishes into the untethered stillness of your Heart, the Self rises AS unbound silence and shines as genuine eternal permanent serenity; your true nature.

Crossing the barrier

The Tao that can be told is not the eternal Tao.
The Name that can be named is not the eternal Name.
Lao Tsu[8]

These are the first two lines of the *Tao Te Ching*, a classic Chinese teaching written over 2500 years ago. These verses are considered by most literary scholars to be some of the most profound yet practical pointers to a life of eternal happiness. The title *Tao Te Ching* translates as 'The Book of the Way and of Virtue,' where *Tao* means the essential, unnamable 'Way' of the universe, *Te* means inner integrity, and *Ching* means book. The Tao Te Ching is a beautiful lesson that there are no words, examples, phrases, experiments or metaphors that can clearly and accurately describe the perennial nature of the universe – the message of what is being suggested and pointed to throughout *Love Outpouring*. All pointers break down at some point as their descriptions cross the manifestation-Existence barrier: *the point in which finite-form (manifestation) retracts back into the infinite-formless (Existence) by means of your **ego** sinking back into your**Self***.

Bridging the manifestation-Existence barrier is understanding how to disassemble your mind (ego) and allow it to retract back, and rest in, your Heart (Self). It's about dissolving your chattering monkey-mind and living in the silent-aware intimate-freedom of yourSelf. Therefore, experiencing sanity, that is, the other side of the manifestation-Existence barrier, is not about developing a clear egoic-mind, it's about eliminating the egoic-mind altogether. Sounds scary, doesn't it? Only to an ego is it scary; it is heaven on Earth to your Heart (Self).

In reality, the manifestation-Existence barrier is the only hurdle that stands in the way of realizing what the message contained in *Love Outpouring* is pointing to. The paradox, which is one of many throughout the teachings, is that once this barrier is crossed it will be seen as having never existed in the first place. Let it be known that every saint, sage, seer, scientist, chief, master, or anyone else who has Self-realized and experienced the ever-present happiness within us all, has overcome this imaginary roadblock; following their lead is highly encouraged.

Therefore, in the attempt to bring you back across the barrier (from ego to Self) to the Oneness that is permanently available here-and-now, there are many frequent attempts in several different forms to remind you of yourSelf. For example, you will be reminded countless times and in many different ways that you ARE permanent peace-happy-love and unconditional acceptance-wholeness-unity, which are two ways of stating the same thing. You will also constantly be reminded that the solution to end your mental-suffering lies within You and can only be experienced through Self-investigation. Even a few quotes have been repeated, so as to aid in folding you back into an understanding. Just remember, the ego reading these words does not want to hear what is being pointed to, so if it gets repetitive at times, let it be as it is. Let the ego get tired of hearing it repeated, at which point the ego will surrender and the message can be known-inherently by your Heart.

Due to the Oneness of yourSelf, the message is therefore not a subject-object message (that would be duality), it is a subject-subject message (nonduality). It is subject knowing subject, subject knowing only itSelf; yourSelf only knowing itSelf. Because of the subject-subject fundamental-ness of the message, the message seems to continuously be folding itSelf back into itSelf as it reveals itSelf.

The difference between ego and Self is subtle, yet monumental in its magnitude of happiness-impact, and it is the misunderstanding that generates the apparent manifestation-Existence barrier that is so seemingly unbelievable and scary for the ego to cross. Where it gets perplexing, and therefore only *seemingly* unbelievable and scary, which you will soon come to realize, is that your ego has only imagined its own existence and therefore was never anything real to begin with.

Dissolving the ego-piece

You may not realize it all the time, but you are permanently aware. The ego is a cloak that veils your permanent Awareness, dulling Awareness's splendor. The ego arises into apparent-existence by moving away from its home of Self and tags on to Awareness.

Ego never completely severs its connection from its home of Self; it just extends itself from Self and manifests as life and the world. Awareness is a co-inhabitant of ego when ego extends from Self. The ego never has been, nor ever will be, a real stand-alone independent entity. The ego is just a semi-transparent unreal veiling of Awareness falsely claiming to be the 'doer' of the manifestation and life, when all along the actual underlying Truth of the ego's reality is Awareness alone. Awareness is therefore the actual 'doer' of the manifestation and life; the ego is just a non-existent impostor. The manifestation of life as you (ego) know it therefore consists of two pieces: 1) a real-piece (Awareness) and 2) an unreal-piece (ego). Having two-pieces creates duality; your job is to understand and rest in one-piece (One-peace), nonduality; Awareness alone.

The nondual message is the acknowledgment of the ego's false existence and the retraction of the unreal ego-piece of the manifestation back home to Self through a practice known as Self-inquiry. This retracting of the unreal ego-piece is the crossing of the manifestation-Existence barrier, where the unreal ego-piece dissolves into Self...leaving only the real Awareness-piece of the manifestation. The crossing is the effortless-effort of moving from duality (two-pieces) to nonduality (One-piece; that is, Oneness).

A simplified diagram:

A young child (pure Self) as it ages, and due to its conditioning, crosses the Existence-manifestation barrier ($\rightarrow$) into being an adult (ego).

Child (Self) = Existence (Awareness-piece) $\rightarrow$ Manifestation (ego+Awareness-piece) = Adult (ego)

As the result of Self-realization via Self-inquiry, the Existence-manifestation barrier process is reversed, leaving an apparent adult with a childlike sense of worldly wonder.

Adult (ego) = Manifestation (ego+Awareness-piece) → Existence (Awareness-piece) = Adult (Self): Childlike Wonder

Self-realization is when the ego-piece dissolves into Self, leaving pure Self (Awareness) alone. Because there is no ego left to be aware, Self (subject) then becomes solely aware of its own Existence (subject knowing subject), which is the objectless (non-conceptual) direct-experience of ever-present happiness; that is, objectlessness of Being, or its synonym: subjectness.

Oddly enough, there is no 'person (ego)' after Self-realization to experience objectlessness, only the non-objective experience of 'I Am'; only 'I' experiencing and knowing itSelf AS 'I': You knowing yourSelf AS yourSelf. In spiritual circles, Self-realization, Self-attentiveness, Self-remembering, Self-abidance, objectlessness and subjectness (and countless other Self-Knowing-itSelf words) would be referred to as enlightenment, liberation, or awakening. The direct experience of knowing yourSelf, no matter what label you place on it, is the ultimate destinationless-destination of every sentient Being on planet Earth. Self is the home of peace-happy-love.

As the ever-Presence of Self moves to the forefront of your Awareness via the practice of Self-inquiry—that is, as you reverse back across the manifestation-Existence barrier (from ego to Self)—it will be seen that there never existed a barrier in the first place. It will dawn on You that there never was a 'before' Self-realization, 'during' Self-realization, or 'after' Self-realization; there has always just been what has always been...You (yourSelf). And since it is recognized that the ego never existed to begin with, then there never was anyone to become enlightened, liberated or awakened in the first place. It is realized that enlightenment, liberation and awakening were merely illusory ideas of the non-existent ego. This makes it clear that there is no such entity as an enlightened, liberated or awakened person (ego); only in the absence of a person are these qualities experienced. This can't be comprehended by the finite ego; it is an infinite mystery that is only understood by knowing yourSelf—the perennial paradox.

> *The Great Way is gateless,*
> *approached by a thousand paths,*
> *pass through this **barrier**,*
> *You walk freely in the universe.*
> ## Zen koan[9]

Why is it a destinationless-destination? Because there is absolutely no distance from yourSelf to yourSelf. You are always yourSelf and you take yourSelf with you no matter where you go.

Try this simple experiment regarding no-distance:* Stand up and put your feet together and let your arms rest by your side. Now, take a step closer to yourSelf. How far did you have to travel and how much effort did you have to exert? The answer is zero.

This is a direct example of the zero-distance needing to be traveled, and the zero-effort needing to be exerted, to experience the always-available ever-present happiness of your Being (Existence, Self). So what is it that appears to make Being-happiness so hard and complex? It is the ego. It will do everything in its power to prevent you from hearing what is being discussed here. *Love Outpouring* is an attempt to expose and give guidance on the zero-requirements to Be-yourSelf.

Continuing the experiment: Now try moving away from yourSelf by taking a step away from yourSelf. You can't. No matter where you go, you take yourSelf with you.

This is an extremely reassuring point, because once you experience the peace-happy-love that you ARE, then this AREness is all You know, and You take this loving-AREness with you into all of life's situations and circumstances. As you become more and more acquainted with your AREness, the pull of life's situations and circumstances, generally labeled as positive or negative, become weaker and weaker and the peace-happy-love of the AREness within you becomes stronger and stronger...and you experience it inherently: it is a Self-observed experience of itSelf (subject knowing subject).

At some point it will dawn on you that it's not necessarily the Oneness of the ever-present happiness of the manifestation of life that is so enamoring, it is the sheer perplexing-awe that the manifestation is even happening at all (childlike wonder).

What is being utilized of yours

What is being utilized of yours (ego) is three primary attributes: your openness to the possibility of what is being pointed to in the message, your willingness to understand the message, and your courage to engage into it. Nothing will be pointed to that cannot be experienced-directly and known-inherently by you; that is, no beliefs or hypotheses are utilized. The pointers throughout may reference concepts and ideas, but only for the purpose of helping you to understand your true nature. At its core, what is really being utilized of Yours (Self) is the direct-inherent-acknowledgment of the infinite-Being that is perceiving these words right now.

What you are looking for is already in you.
You already are everything you are seeking.
Thich Nhat Hanh[10]

What is being pointed to

What the message is pointing to is You, yourSelf. The message's intention is to be constantly pointing yourself back to yourSelf. Looping you back, and back, and back, with ever-decreasing smaller loops until the loops collapse to zero and you are resting IN yourSelf AS yourSelf, to a point where there is nothing but yourSelf alone. It is the subtle yet profound difference between conceptual-knowing (ego, mind) and inherently-Knowing (Self, Heart) in the process of looping back that dissolves suffering and leads to happiness-realization.

The Heart is the origin of ALL that is inherently-known, it is the 'Knowing' of the known; your Heart is yourSelf. Get comfortable with yourSelf (yourHeart) being the ever-present 'Knowing' of ALL; it is the primary understanding of the entire message. The mystery is that You will not know how You know ALL from your Heart and not your ego-mind, but somehow You will inherently know it to be the Truth. Your Heart IS the mystery of life, and therefore so are You.

Allowing yourself to knowingly-know, and therefore embody life from your Heart-perspective, will free you from your apparent psychological bondage and unlock the ever-present availability of peace-happy-love.

To realize the mystery of this One-essence,
is to be released from all entanglements.
When all things are seen without differentiation,
the One Self-essence is everywhere revealed.
Seng-ts'an[11]

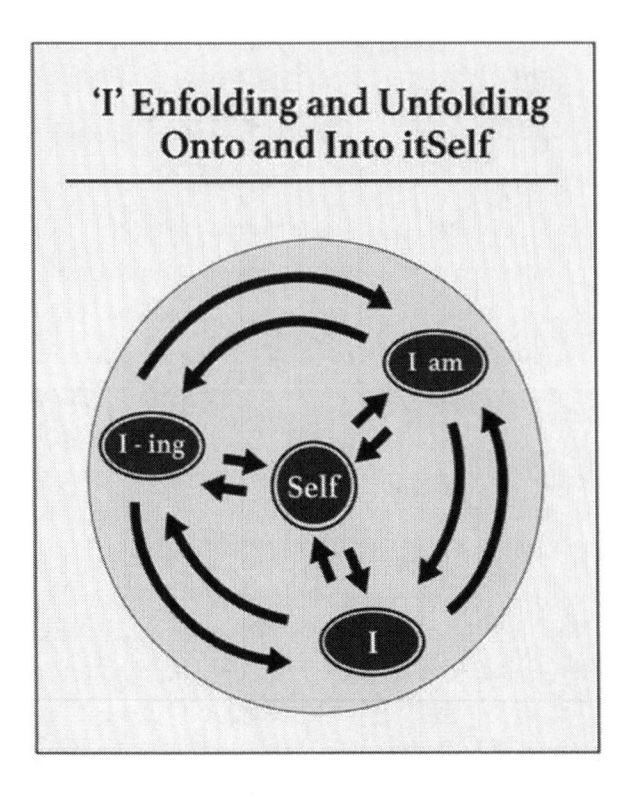

'I' Enfolding and Unfolding Onto and Into itSelf

In knowing yourSelf AS your Heart alone, your mind (ego) will be completely absent of ego-based thoughts, and therefore so will the thought-belief of separation and its subsequent suffering. Yet all of your faculties will remain intact, and life will flow as it always has; how comforting and yet oddly simultaneously perplexing!

What the message is not

We have been misled throughout the majority of our life to believe that the human intellect has the ability to rein in and control the wild-Heart of Consciousness. Any such control is not the message of eternity, and therefore not the message of this book. In fact you could say the message is the absence of control, which leaves You wide open, available, and completely exposed and vulnerable, yet paradoxically completely impenetrable.

Truth is a pathless land, and you cannot approach it
by any path whatsoever, by any religion, by any sect.
The moment you follow someone, you cease to follow Truth.
Jiddu Krishnamurti[12]

Therefore religion, spirituality, mysticism, philosophy, physics, psychology, cosmology, theology or any other organized structured human institutions or knowledge systems are not considered here. Belief systems, mind control, mind/ body faculties, mindfulness, meditation or yoga practices, breath work, chanting, mantras, yogic postures, therapy or creating a healthy mind and body also do not have a place in the perennial message. You could maybe say it is about well-Being, minus the 'well' part, because 'well' is an inherent property of Being, a tautology.† What is left then? Simply put, all that is and all that has ever been...yourSelf.

Concepts and ideas are incapable of expressing Reality as it is.
Nirvana [the One-Reality] is the extinction of all concepts.
If you are able to free yourself from these concepts,
anxiety and fear will disappear.
Thich Nhat Hanh[13]

The words and message in this book are not the Truth and will never be the Truth. They are truthful in their own right, but again are not specifically the Truth. They only point to the Truth. Truthful-knowledge is highly useful, for it dissolves false-knowledge, which allows you to approach what is true in a more direct path, while the intelligence within truthful-knowledge knows that it too, at its origin, is false. Once truthful-knowledge has dissolved all that is false, it then devours itself, leaving only the Truth...You. The dissolution of false-knowledge in Sanskrit is known as the Path of Jñāna (pronounced *n-ya-na*) and is explained in more detail in the next section, 'Self-Knowledge.'

The requirements of this message should be a massive relief, for absolutely no new actions or efforts are being asked of you. You are most likely exhausted from trying to add new aspects to yourself to satisfy your bottomless pit of desire, in the hopes of someday getting to an end and being done. Achieving-achieving-achieving, becoming-becoming-becoming, acquiring-acquiring-acquiring; but the future always arrives somewhat shorthanded and unfulfilling, and therefore leaves you still longing for more. *Love Outpouring* suggests there is a different way to perceive life, a possibility of ending your exhausting mental cycles of 'more.'

There may at first appear to be a decision made by you to engage in the apparent journey of nonduality. If this is the case, then you are encouraged to engage into this apparent decision. If earnest perseverance into the matter is pursued, you will quickly realize that you yourself did not make the initial decision, that it was by Grace alone pulling itSelf back home to itSelf that the 'first apparent decision' arose. You ARE this Grace (Heart, silence) pulling (calling, drawing) yourself back home to yourSelf.

There is a huge silence inside each of us
that beckons us into itSelf,
and the recovery of our own silence
can begin to teach us the language of heaven.
Meister Eckhart[14]

What is not being denied

Nothing in your perceived reality is being denied or rejected by the nondual perennial message. Said in a more open way: all that is known, all of life, is unconditionally accepted AS IT IS. The reason for this is that Self/You IS/ARE unconditional acceptance. Self never resists, denies or rejects life in any way whatsoever. For eternity, Self has shown up every day with wide-open arms of unconditional love and acceptance for the resistantless embracement of happiness, Self's primary inherent property.

So what this means for the previous topics of **'What the message is not'** is that we are not denying, manipulating, judging or rejecting any of them in any way, we just are not interested in any of them; they are not what is being pointed to here. So let them be as they are. It doesn't mean that the **'What the message is not'** topics can't be utilized as precursors to knowing yourSelf—they may be very helpful in the initial stages; it's just that at some point you will need to let them go and to lose your identity with them and your attachment to them. AND it doesn't mean that you can't come back to them once it is understood what Self is, but initially your identity with them and your attachment to them will need to be abandoned. The reason is that these topics are things 'other than' yourSelf. Knowing yourSelf is so foreign to the ego, yet so incredibly intimate to your Heart, that you have to first jettison the apparent identity/attachment extremes of 'otherness' to experience Self directly.

Even the ancient phrase 'Know thySelf' is misleading. At first, we take the word 'know' as a conceptual-intellectual knowing, something that the mind can understand, apply and gain, which again only moves us away from the experience of Self. The word 'know' is actually meant as an inherent-innateness Knowing, only a 'Knowing' we can BE, because we already ARE thySelf and we inherently-Know it. 'Know thySelf' is antiquity's original tautology.

This also goes for anything else that is known. For instance, all mind activity (thoughts, images, ideas, memories and conceptual-intellectual-knowledge), perceptions (sight, sound, smell, taste and touch), and bodily parts and sensations (arms, legs, heads, core, feelings, sensations and emotions) are not what is being pointed to here. We again are not denying, manipulating, judging or rejecting their apparent existence; we are just not necessarily interested in their apparent reality. They will, though, be used as objects and tools in helping to point you back, and back, and back to yourSelf.

Any of life's activities are not being rejected or denied either. A living still needs to be made, dishes need to be washed, relationships need to be attended to, children need nurturing, illness still needs to be healed, and the dog still needs to be walked and fed. Life still happens. It just happens without the perpetual ego-judging as to whether life is satisfying or not, and without the resistant bodily sensations generated by the unsatisfactory ego-judging psychology. In the words of Paul Hedderman, author of the book *The Escape to Everywhere*, "You travel lighter."

No expectations

An expectation is the thought, effort or desire that sometime in the future you will attain something that you don't currently have now. Expectation is yet another movement away from yourSelf. Self 'IS' and therefore is always available now; there is nowhere you need to go and nothing to achieve, acquire or accomplish to experience a life of permanent happiness. This is a perplexing concept to the ego. It has absolutely no idea what to do with such information. All the ego knows is objective-furtherment-betterment: how is it supposed to 'become' happy and loving if it can't reach out and obtain it? Here lies the crux of the apparent problem for the ego, that happiness is not found in objects, relationships, substances or experiences. It is actually located at the source of the ego; yourHeart, yourSelf. It is prior to ego that the eternal happiness for which you seek is located, which is only available in the 'here and now.'

Expectation is a subtle rejection of the now.
Francis Lucille[15]

The ego only knows things (objects) 'other than' Self and therefore doesn't have the qualifications to know happiness directly. Trying to attain ever-present happiness through objects, relationships, substances and experiences is futile. At best the happiness experienced through these objective-vehicles is fleeting and temporary. It is not suggested that objects, relationships, substances and experiences are not important to a life well lived; the message is saying absolutely that ever-present happiness cannot be directly-experienced by means of them.

Hope is another form of expectation. Most people hope that someday in the future it will be better than it is now. This leads us away from ourSelf in the hunt for something 'other than' ourSelf, denying the love in which we ARE now. This book is not a message of hope—a structured regime of rituals, such as religions or spiritual doctrines. These structured regimes give hope that happiness and salvation are just around the corner, especially if you are willing to work just a bit harder and believe just a tad deeper. The message in this book gives no hope for the ego to reach Heaven, Nirvana or Brahman located somewhere in the distant future. Only when it is known-inherently and experienced-directly that happiness is 'now,' will the salvation you're looking for reveal itSelf.

All hope abandon, ye who enter here.
Dante's epic poem *Inferno*[16]

Even as you contemplate, Self-investigate, pray and/or meditate as means to understand what is being pointed to here, do not take them to be doing-becoming-achieving vehicles, and by no means should expectations on possible outcomes be associated with contemplation, Self-investigation, prayer and/

or meditation. Simply put, contemplation, Self-investigation, prayer and/or meditation pointed to in the book are expectationless-actionless actions to experience-directly non-objective stillness, silence and emptiness. The act of actionless-activity continues the paradox: how do you gain everything you have longed for in life by the absence of activity? That is, how do you maximize success with zero effort? The answer is via Self-inquiry (discussed in Chapter 11).

What is the value of this?

When ALL that is known IS yourSelf, then literally, everything known by You IS yourSelf. And since yourSelf is complete-whole-peace-happy-love then this is ALL You know. Since the perception of the manifestation of life is known by You, then by logical deduction the manifestation MUST also Be You as well.

What I AM, perception IS.
David Carse[17]

You realize You have always been completely One and intimate with the manifestation, yet completely free from it. The manifestation is just the play of yourSelf, and since you love yourSelf, You therefore inherently love all of the manifestation unconditionally, regardless of its appearance. This leaves You incapable of hate and harm and of feeling hated and harmed, that is, You lose the ability to not love unconditionally, which happens unintentionally. This is the epitome of unconditional compassion for yourSelf and anything 'other than' yourSelf, namely Humanity, Earth and Cosmos.

What you ARE the world IS.
And without your transformation [Self-realization],
there can be no transformation of the world.
Jiddu Krishnamurti[18]

When You know yourSelf AS 'others' and 'others' AS yourSelf, the illusion of 'Self and other' (separation) collapses and suffering ends. This is Oneness (better stated, not-twoness); nonduality...Love Outpouring.

Lopon Tenzin Namdak Rinpoche was a Tibetan monk who was imprisoned, tortured and starved by the Chinese for 18 years. The Dalai Lama once asked Lopon if he was afraid during his hellish prison sentence. Lopon responded, "Yes, there was one thing I was afraid of. I was afraid I would lose compassion for the Chinese." Lopon's experience is an extraordinary example of the Self's inability to hate regardless of circumstances. Lopon's Self IS yourSelf; right now you have full access to dissolve into the bottomless compassion of Lopon's eternal unconditional love for Humanity.

Resting IN and AS yourSelf

As ego (you) rests into itSelf during Self-inquiry, it creates an ever-widening environment for the expansion of internal physical and mental phenomena. The boundaries in which 'me' (ego) was once familiar being contained begin to increase, and with them so does the feeling of your once solidified emotional, mental and physical identities. 'Me' becomes less-dense, until 'me' becomes denselessness itself, that is, infinite transparentness. Denselessness is the beginning of what is known as a direct-gain from actionless-action via the means of Self-inquiry. The actionless-action of Self-inquiry transfigures the once dense body and mind into a denseless body and mind; that is, by doing nothing (actionless: Self-inquiry) you gain something (action: transfiguring denseness into denselessness). As the body and mind begin to release their grip on all of the emotional and physical sensations that have kept you in bondage, you become less and less identified with bodily concepts and more and more familiar AS being ALL THERE IS.

This is the definition of resting IN and AS yourSelf, also known as Self-realization via Self-inquiry.

> *The game is not about becoming somebody,*
> *it's about becoming nobody.*
> **Ram Dass**[19]

This can be a bit unsettling to the ego. If so, let it be as it is—it's all OK, it's part of the gig. Notice the paradox in words. Earlier it was mentioned that the message will not ask you to become anything, yet here it is pointing you to become non-mental-body-activity; it is asking you to become no-thing, to embody not-a-thing, to be no-thing-ness...the actionless-activity of becoming the absence of something. This is known in Taoism as Wu Wei: 'action without action,' 'non-action,' 'effortless-action' or 'effortless-doing': the deliberate and principled decision to do nothing for a reason.

> *An example of Wu Wei:* An extended spring, like an extended slinky, does not need new energy put into it for it to return to its original relaxed form. The spring only needs the relinquishing of the original energy that extended it to begin with to allow it to withdraw back into its authentic cylinder-like shape. The relinquishing of the original energy is another way of saying effortless-effort (Wu Wei), where the original-shape is accomplished by the effortless-doing of relinquishing energy.

The Wu Wei example is highly correlated to the experience of resting IN and AS Self via Self-inquiry. As you relinquish your lifetime of outward energetic tendencies and retract back into Self, your original-shape of Self is regained by the effortless-doing of releasing the outward tendencies.

Once you have become well established in your original-shape of Self, in which 'original-shape' has the inherent quality of 'effortlessness' since all outward tendencies have been relinquished, and experience yourSelf AS 'effortlessness' itself, you then take your inherent 'effortlessness' with you wherever you go and the 'effortlessness' remains permanent no matter the circumstances (this is known as ever-present happiness).

'Effortlessness' is another way of saying 'One with Reality,' in which 'effortlessness' IS the absence of any mental or physical resistance when engaging in an effort or action. There is no effort to an action if there is no resistance to that effort, hence effortless-action; also known as the absence of resistance.

> *There is great happiness in not wanting,*
> *in not being something, in not going somewhere.*
> **Jiddu Krishnamurti**[20]

As we gradually, or in some rare cases spontaneously, dissolve into no-thing-ness we begin to realize and embody ourSelf: the dimensionless, eternal, infinite, non-objective experience of Consciousness itSelf.

Why the message is so challenging to translate

The English language is designed for there to be a subject (I, you, us) that references in some form or fashion an object (anything 'other than' I, you, us). Subject and its corresponding object are the baseline definition of duality, that is, Self and other. English does not have the capabilities to describe directly the subject alone, which would be subject discussing subject. Therefore almost every effort in language, especially the English language, is a movement away from yourSelf.

> *We are trapped by language to such a degree*
> *that every attempt to formulate insight is a play on words.*
> **Niels Bohr**[21]

The perennial message is only subject-based. It is subject describing itSelf, namely yourSelf describing itSelf. YourSelf doesn't need to move away from itSelf to define and know itSelf; it knows itSelf just by being itSelf. This is why, in the attempt to use language to point to the perennial message, we sometimes find strange and awkward descriptors to solidify the point. There are languages, such as Tamil and Sanskrit, that are designed to describe Self directly, with no pronoun. These languages have tremendous depth where each word seems to have its own vibrational liveliness and the ability to describe itSelf if needed. The English language is more lifeless, more like a noun: rigid, solid, dead. Whereas Tamil and Sanskrit, the world's two oldest languages still in use, are more verb-like: moving with the vitality of creation.

Sources of the message

The primary source of the message contained in *Love Outpouring* is of Tamil and Sanskrit origin, which is the basis of the Indian language and culture. The earliest Indian scriptures, known as the Vedas, contain multiple texts of scripture, in which one of its doctrines, known as the Upanishads, contains a scriptural teaching known as Advaita Vedanta.

Vedas → Upanishads → Advaita Vedanta

Advaita literally translates as 'not-two' or 'One without a second,' and Vedanta is perceived by the Indian culture as a 'point of view,' or most succinctly a 'Way of Being.' Advaita maintains that the Self is the One existing Reality (not-two) and is the single residence of peace, happiness and love, in which You ARE the One-Reality. Advaita, known as nonduality in English terms, is the message and pointer which *Love Outpouring* attempts to describe. Nonduality is the perennial message, which is a way of finding abundant wealth for yourSelf and humanity without the need to exploit anyone or anything.

The perennial message and *Love Outpouring* do not in any way suggest that nonduality (Advaita) is the only body of knowledge that can aid in pointing you back to yourSelf. There are countless pathways to point yourSelf home. The book will attempt to show you, in a holistic manner, the many different credible historic and modern sources to draw from, via all of the quotes and references herein.

The many other historic and modern trustworthy Self-discovery sources utilized throughout *Love Outpouring* are: Dzogchen Buddhism, Zen Buddhism, Taoism, Sufism, Christianity, Christian and Sufi Mysticism, statistics, philosophy and quantum physics, neuroscience and psychology. None of these sources has any more ever-present happiness force than any other, including Advaita. At some point you will need to abandon the message of all doctrines, texts, and pointers of any kind—including Advaita and the contents of this book—and turn within via Self-inquiry to experience the perennial message of Being alone...which is true-liberation, absolute-freedom.

Regardless of the origin of the nondual message, and your beliefs and ties to it, the ultimate goal is to realize ever-present happiness. Debating, arguing and disputing specific pointers as right or wrong only moves you further and further away from yourSelf. As mentioned in prior sections, if some of the pointers trouble you, move around them with the insight of keeping your eye (I) on yourSelf.

*The soul [ego] that is quick to turn to speaking and conversing
is slow to turn to God [Self].*
Saint John of the Cross[22]

You are highly encouraged, though, to question every pointer in this book, especially if your questioning's purpose is directed towards further understanding of the perennial Truth, and if your question's mission is to guide yourSelf back to itSelf. Do not take this book or any pointers within it to be true, for they are not, until you yourSelf have directly realized them AS yourSelf; the Truth. Simply put, don't take the book's word for it—see for yourSelf. This is not about anyone else but You, because only You can understand, realize and BE the Truth.

The important thing is not to stop questioning.
Curiosity has its own reason for existence.
One cannot help but be in awe when he contemplates the
mysteries of eternity, of life, of the marvelous structure of Reality.
It is enough if one tries merely to comprehend
a little of this mystery each day.
Albert Einstein[23]

Be careful of 'why questions.' In most cases, 'why questions' will only send you into a continuous spiral away from yourSelf. 'Whys' are the mind's devious way of keeping itself useful, moving you away from yourSelf and perpetuating suffering. 'Whys' are not necessarily discouraged; just beware of them. The better question to ask is "Who?" Who is the one asking the 'why question'?

Notes

*   Credited to Rupert Spira.

†   Tautology: the saying of the same thing more than once in different words. This entire book is a tautology.

1   Edward Estlin (E.E.) Cummings (1894–1962) was an American poet, author and playwright. He is often regarded as one of the most important American poets of the twentieth century. Edward was known for praying for strength to be his essential Self and repeated such

statements as "May 'I' be 'I' is the only prayer—not may 'I' be great or good or beautiful or wise or strong."

2   Michael James is a devout devotee of the beloved Sri Ramana Maharshi and is considered to be one of the most knowledgeable living scholars of Ramana's teachings. He first encountered Ramana's teaching in 1976 in Tiruvannamalai, India, while traveling abroad, and ended up living there for 20 years to learn the Path of Sri Ramana. Michael knows himSelf as the Absolute Reality, the one fundamental, essential, immutable, infinite, undivided and nondual Consciousness of our own Being, which all 8 billion of us experience as 'I Am.'

3   Sri Ramana Maharshi (1879–1950) is known as the most beloved and cherished Indian Hindu sage of the twentieth century. Ramana Self-realized at the early age of 16 and proceeded throughout his lifetime to write some of the most profound inescapable documents in history on the nature of Reality. His most notable works are *Nan Yar?* (Who Am I?), *Ulladu Narpadu* (Forty Verses on What Exists) and *Upadesa Undiyar* (The Essence of Spiritual Teachings).

4   Giovanni di Pietro di Bernardone (1181–1226), better known as Saint Francis of Assisi, was a mystic Italian Catholic friar, founder of the Franciscans, and one of the most venerated figures in Christianity. Francis later became associated with the patronage of animals and the natural environment.

5   David Carse is the author of the 2005 book, *Perfect Brilliant Stillness: Beyond the Individual Self.* The book is an intimate account of spontaneous spiritual enlightenment and its implications in a life lived beyond the individual ego. David set a beautiful example of 'sharing yourSelf with the

world' by not copyrighting his book, making his experience and knowledge of the perennial message free and available to humanity.

6   Rupert Spira is an English nonduality teacher, philosopher and author. His core understanding is based in the Indian Advaita Vedanta practice of the Direct Path to Self-Realization. He is known in the nonduality spiritual circles as one of the most enlightened Beings of modern times. He utilizes insights from Atmananda Krishna Menon, Sri Ramana Maharshi, Sri Nisargadatta Maharaj and Jiddu Krishnamurti, but his primary understanding was conveyed to him by his teacher Francis Lucille.

7   Niels Henrik David Bohr (1885–1962) was a Danish philosopher, humanitarian and physicist who made foundational contributions to understanding atomic structure and quantum theory, for which he received the Nobel Prize in Physics in 1922. Bohr is credited for creating the first model of the atom and making the claim that everything we call real is made up of things that cannot be regarded as real.

8   Lao Tsu, also known as Laozi (Old Master), was an ancient legendary Chinese philosopher and writer. He is the author of the immensely profound Tao Te Ching and the founder of philosophical Taoism. Lao Tsu was born in the Henan province in China some six centuries before the Christian era. His texts are still today of great importance to Chinese heritage and humankind as a whole.

9   Koans in Zen Buddhism of Japan are direct paradoxical statements or questions used as contemplative practices for

devotees. Solving koans is intended to fatigue the cognitive mind so as to end the egoic intellect.

10 Thich Nhat Hanh (1926–2022), Zen Master, was a global spiritual leader, poet and peace activist who was revered around the world for his pioneering teachings on mindfulness, global ethics and peace. Ordained as a monk at the age of 16 in Vietnam, Thich Nhat Hanh soon envisioned a kind of engaged Buddhism that could respond directly to the needs of society. He was fond of saying, "Our own life is the message."

11 Seng-ts'an is known as the Third Zen Patriarch of the Buddhist school of Chan in sixth-century China. He is most famous for his immensely profound Chan poem, 'The Hsin-Hsin Ming' (Inscription on Faith in Mind). He expressed his Self-realization by affirming that there is only One undefilable Reality.

15 Francis Lucille is a spiritual teacher in the Indian tradition of nonduality. Francis teaches the ancient wisdom of nonduality via Advaita Vedanta, Chan Buddhism, Zen, Taoism and Sufism. Francis' teachings are traditional, which means that the experience of our true nature has been transmitted from generation to generation by a lineage of sages. His understanding was transmitted to him by his master Jean Klein.

16 Dante's *Inferno* is a fourteenth-century AD epic poem depicting the journey through hell. It depicts the earthly realm of those who have rejected spiritual values by yielding to bestial appetites or violence, or by perverting their human intellect to fraud or malice against their

fellow human beings. Dante's poem has been attributed to the journey of nonduality and Self-knowledge, which Christian Moevs, Associate Professor at the University of Notre Dame, clarifies in his book, *The Metaphysics of Dante's Comedy*.

19 Ram Dass, born Richard Alpert (1931–2019), was an American spiritual teacher, guru of modern yoga, Doctor of Psychology and author. In 1967 in India, Alpert met Neem Karoli Baba, who became Alpert's guru. Baba gave Alpert the name "Ram Dass," which means "servant of God." Dass's 1971 bestselling book, *Be Here Now*, contained his account of his spiritual journey, as well as recommended spiritual techniques, and was intended to influence the Western mindset.

22 John of the Cross, born Juan de Yepes y Alvarez (1542–1591), was a Spanish Catholic priest and mystic, and a Carmelite friar. His poetry and writings on the soul are considered the pinnacle of mystical Spanish literature and among the greatest works of all Spanish literature. In 1926 he was declared a Doctor of the Church by Pope Pius XI, and is commonly known as the "Mystical Doctor."

SECTION 1

SELF-KNOWLEDGE

Chapter 3

What Is Self-Knowledge?

The practice of knowing yourSelf clearly and experiencing permanent peaceful-silence begins with Self-knowledge. The primary purpose of Self-knowledge is for you to have a reasonable understanding of how false-knowledge is dissolved to expose your true-Self, prior to initiating Self-investigation, which is explored in Chapter 11.

You could say Self-knowledge is understanding the mechanism in which false-ego-knowledge transcends into Truth alone; that is, how ego dissolves into Self. Knowing yourSelf is similar to attending university, where Self-knowledge is likened to the lecture portion of a college class, while Self-investigation is comparable to the lab portion.

The paradox about this college class is that the goal is not to learn anything new, it's about learning how to let go of burdensome false-knowledge, which is any knowledge 'other than' yourSelf. You succeed by surrendering, acquire by relinquishing, liberate by disbelieving, and realize Self-fulfillment by ego-abandoning.

Articulating Self-knowledge is correlated with the ego-vehicle metaphor earlier in the book, wherein the ego will not willingly dissolve itself. Only by diligently attending to the Self, by renouncing the false-knowledge you ARE NOT, will the ego withdraw and perish into the true-knowledge you ARE.

Jñāna-knowledge

Self-knowledge in Sanskrit is known as Jñāna (pronounced *n-ya-na*), where Jñāna refers to the Indian Vedic yoga practice of the 'Path of Knowledge' or the 'Path of Self-realization.' In

Indian culture, Jñāna is considered to be the highest practice of direct knowledge: direct pure-eternal-knowledge: You.

Since Jñāna is pure-knowledge it therefore has never come into Existence, meaning it is unborn and eternal, it is Existence itSelf. Jñāna uses its unbornness as a baseline to compare all other knowledge against. When Jñāna shines its light on that which is not itSelf, Jñāna's light dissolves it as false-knowledge, including in the end the knowledge of Jñāna itSelf; leaving only yourSelf (Awareness) standing alone. Jñāna's underlying Reality is infinite, eternal and dimensionless, which is unknowable to your mind, and is why in the end even the mental-concept of any 'Path of Jñāna' has to be eliminated as false-knowledge.

> Truth is eternal. [Conceptual-]Knowledge is changeable.
> It is disastrous to confuse them.
> **Madeleine L'Engle**[1]

Jñāna-knowledge locates, exposes and destroys false-knowledge, which then leads to the destruction of itself, leaving only the Truth (You). With the 'Path of Jñāna' there is an end to the relentless seeking for personal fulfillment and contentment. Once all false precepts of yourSelf have been eliminated, and only Self (Truth) remains, you will experience directly that yourSelf IS permanent fulfillment-contentment, ending your exhausting lifelong pursuit of such personal attributes.

The end of the pursuit does not mean that your life is over; in fact, just the opposite, it means that your life has just begun. After the thousand-pound weight of your ego, the ultimate false-knowledge, has been dissolved, the once perceived lead jacket of your ego is now but a transparent shadow, leaving you free and light to dance around the ballroom of life.

We all have two lives.
The second begins when we realize we only have one.
Confucius[2]

The end of seeking is therefore the beginning of life. It is the beginning of sinking deeper and deeper into the mystery of the manifestation and marveling at how it all works and plays out, and most importantly, realizing you yourSelf ARE this mystery.

The 'Path of Jñāna' is a unique form of seeking; it is a distanceless path to nowhere, a path that leads you right back to the One reading these words. Whereas prior to encountering the perennial message, all of your efforts were in the hopes of finding some lost piece of information that would complete you, information that you could add to yourself to make you whole, Jñāna is a path of subtraction, a 180-degree pivot in the approach to locating what you have never lost, Your wholeness and completeness. It is a path of information destruction in which more and more ego-destruction leads to a lighter and lighter ego-load to bear, until there is nothing left but the weightless-You.

Eventually, it will become clear to you that the Western way of seeking happiness is futile, that persistently gaining knowledge to strengthen your ego-mind to be happy is illogical, and that permanent happiness is only obtained when there is no information remaining to know; that is, in the absence of information, there is the absence of ego-knowledge and therefore the absence of ego-mind; leaving only the peaceful silent-vastness of yourSelf.

At first the 'Path of Jñāna' may appear to be the gaining of new knowledge; if so, let it be so. Falling in love with the message via books, videos, podcasts and so on will appear to be a new attribute of information, but you will soon see that it is the start of information elimination. By diligently trying to prove the perennial message itSelf false, due to your ego's built-in doubts about the absurdity of the message, it will start to become clear that the message is true. Only when it becomes obvious, meaning known-inherently, that the multiplicities of the manifestation of life cannot be known by your ego-mind, will true-peace be directly-experienced AS yourSelf. Directly stated: only yourSelf is true-knowledge that can be known for sure, and it is known only by yourSelf.

We perceive the world as we experience ourself. If we take ourself to be a physical independent separate object, we will perceive everything else in the world as the same. But if we experience ourSelf as unified Oneness, then the world will be perceived as Oneness as well, regardless of how the world is manifesting.

The primary purpose of Jñāna is to dispel your false beliefs and concepts* of how you perceive the world, how you take yourself and the objects in the world to be physically real, and to deliver the world back to You in its actual One formless-form. It is to remove you from the misconception that the multiplicity of objects you witness in the world are independent material-based 'things' with their own separate existences, and move you into the One-Reality where there is no separation among the multiplicity, therefore revealing that only One-Existence exists; in which this One-Existence is yourSelf. By knowing yourSelf directly you know the One-Existence, which equates to ever-present happiness.

Directly stated: the 'Path of Jñāna' is the dismantling of all the false precepts that Self needs an object 'other than' itSelf to know itSelf (also known as: fact-checking beliefs, ideas and concepts and abandoning the ones that are false). *Self knows itSelf just by being itSelf; therefore any object 'other than' Self is false-knowledge.* The 'Path of Jñāna' illuminates and eliminates false-knowledge, leaving only Self (pure-knowledge: Jñāna). One who has reached the end of the path, that is, is Self-realized, is known as a Jñāni (pronounced *n-ya-nee*): One who has direct permanent Awareness of One's Self alone.

The 'Path of Jñāna' is the basis of the subtitle of *Love Outpouring*: Experiencing ever-present happiness by *illuminating and eliminating [via Jñāna] the difference between who you are [Self] and what you have mistaken yourself to be [ego]*.

Folding back to the Meister Eckhart quote on the first page of the book: Only those who dare to have the courage to let go [via Jñāna] of *what* they believe they are, can dare to re-enter the kingdom of *who* they actually are.

Just as a wooden stick that tends to the stirring of a campfire is consumed into ash as it stirs, so are the false pretenses of yourself consumed and discarded in the 'Path of Jñāna.' As Jñāna stirs the mind and reveals its false-flames of ignorance,† dissolving them into ash, Jñāna then too is completely consumed by the fire as false, leaving only Truth: yourSelf.

Quick Jñāna pointer: Beliefs seem to be one of the easier false-knowledge attributes to start the Jñāna path.

Question: Why do you have to believe in the item in question for the item in question to be what it is?

- Do you have to believe you love your mother to love your mother? No
- Do you have to believe the Holocaust was horrific for it to be horrific? No
- Do you have to believe ice cream is cold for it to be cold? No
- Do you have to believe God is omnipresent for God to be omnipresent? No
- Do you have to believe you exist for you to exist? No

Name one thing you have to believe in for that thing to just be what it is. There are no beliefs required for the multiplicity of the manifestation of life to be happening AS IT IS; to simply be WHAT IT IS.

By abandoning all your beliefs do you actually change physically, mentally, emotionally, ethically, morally or spiritually? No, You remain You. When experiencing the absence of belief, you actually become unbound from the restriction of the belief, which paradoxically draws you ever closer than before to the item you once believed in.

The false-knowledge (ajñāna) being abandoned is only in regard to the beliefs and feelings that keep your ego apparently alive. Utility and practical knowledge remains, since it is what allows life to remain living; it is just not 'done' by an ego anymore. Self has an apparent quality of preserving its manifestation and has a set of rules which it plays by to do so. It becomes clearer as you sink deeper into the mystery of Self that life doesn't need an ego to manifest itSelf and live itSelf. Ego doesn't run the show—never has, never will; Self does.

Every chapter in the book is considered the 'Path of Jñāna' since the content of the messaging in the chapters is meant to dissolve the false-sense of you (ego) to reveal the true-sense of You (Self). Yet, understanding Self-knowledge via books, videos and podcasts is only a secondary tool of usefulness. Self-investigation is the primary instrument that eliminates false-knowledge. Self-investigation brings about the direct Self-knowledge of yourSelf, giving you complete understanding of Self so that you can contrast ego-knowledge against it. Having the ability to discern false-from-true arms you with the most destructive false-knowledge force in the cosmos, yourSelf. Directly-experiencing yourSelf allows you to quickly dissolve the irritative beliefs and ideas you have about yourself, lifting you out of the insane rabbit-hole of the ego and into the sane realm of Self.

*To recognize one's own insanity is, of course,
the arising of sanity, the beginning of healing and transcendence.*
Eckhart Tolle[3]

Notes

* False-knowledge is known as *ajñāna*.

† Forgetting yourSelf in Advaita Vedanta is what is referred to as ignorance. Ignorance has nothing to do with someone's intelligence, such as being stupid or dumb, but is the sheer act of overlooking (forgetting) your true nature of Self. Knowledge is the antonym of ignorance. Remembering yourSelf by eliminating ignorance is Self-realization.

1   Madeleine L'Engle (1918–2007) was an American writer of fiction, non-fiction, poetry, and young adult fiction. Her most famous book was *A Wrinkle in Time*, which won her the 1963 John Newbery Medal for excellence in children's literature. She believed that regardless of people's actions, all are loved, and in the end, all will be united with the Divine.

2   Confucius (551–479 BC) was a Chinese philosopher and politician who is traditionally considered the paragon of Chinese sages. He emphasized personal and governmental morality, correctness of social relationships, justice, kindness and sincerity. Confucius preached the Golden Rule, 'Do unto others as you wish them to do unto you.'

Chapter 4

A Metaphor: Who You Are

Imagine yourself alone in a large, completely empty warehouse the size of a professional football stadium. You quickly notice that the massive size of the warehouse represents something equivalent to infinite space. After becoming comfortable within the massive spaciousness, you then perceive how vast, permanent and absolutely silent and still the space within the warehouse is. You then become aware that the space within the warehouse represents an environment of immense-peace-silence. This scenario, being aware of infinite immense-peace-silence, in which the infinite immense-peace-silence represents yourSelf, is the experience of ever-present happiness.

Pointer: The infinite immense-peace-silence is literally 'who you are.' It IS yourSelf.

To further the metaphor, picture yourself in the same warehouse, but now it is consumed with operating manufacturing equipment and teeming with workers. Notice the chatter coming from the equipment, along with the bustle and semi-contentness of the workers. The manufacturing scenario represents the chattering-bustle of your ego, your life.

Pointer: The chattering-bustle manufacturing scenario is 'what you have mistaken yourself to be.' It's your ego.

Yet both the immense-peace-silence of the warehouse space and the chattering-bustle of the manufacturing scenario exist collectively; together they are one complete whole. Notice that the manufacturing scenario is contained within the immense-peace-silence of the warehouse, and therefore the manufacturing scenario is dependent on the immense-peace-silence of the warehouse for its existence. This is equivalent to your ego (manufacturing scenario) being contained within yourSelf (immense-peace-silence). YourSelf doesn't need your ego to exist, but your ego needs yourSelf for it to exist. If your ego (manufacturing scenario) went away, yourSelf (immense-peace-silence) would remain unchanged.

Notice the metaphor is depicting that you 'ARE space' (immense-peace-silence) and that you 'ARE NOT a physical object' (manufacturing scenario). Re-notice that the metaphor is suggesting that you ARE space, you DON'T HAVE space; that is, the immense-peace-silence 'space' is NOT an attribute of you that comes and goes—it's permanent. Stated differently with regard to your present moment, you are NOT the physical body-mind (form) reading this book, you ARE the immense-peace-silence (formless) space of the room you are in that is allowing the reading to happen within it. Simply put, You ARE formless space, NOT a physical body-mind form as you currently mistake yourself to be.

The solution to end suffering (manufacturing scenario) and experience ever-present happiness (immense-peace-silence) is not to try and fix the ego, it is to simply stop identifying as the ego and start identifying as yourSelf. As has become so obvious as we move through life, the ego cannot be permanently fixed but can only be managed, and at best temporarily upgraded, as it cycles through its relentless ups and downs of life.

To your ego, it may at first appear like suicide to stop identifying with it. The ego, in all of its arrogance and ignorance, actually takes itself to be the energy life-force in your body, along with being the director (the doer) of this life-force. This is a fallacy. It is actually the Self who is the life-force and director of the energy-animations of your body. Just as in the metaphor, yourSelf doesn't require ego-energy to exist, but your ego requires yourSelf-energy for its apparent existence. If your ego (illusory energy) went away, yourSelf (real energy) would remain unchanged and life would continue AS IT IS.

I am not asking you to commit suicide.
Whatever happens, remind yourself that only your
body and mind are affected, not yourSelf.
Sri Nisargadatta Maharaj[1]

Bettering the ego is actually the denial of life. This is due to our ego claiming that life is unjust and therefore 'our life' is the primary cause of our personal suffering. In Reality, our egos are unjust, which causes the illusion of an agitated life, when all along life is actually perfectly beautiful AS IT IS. Knowing yourSelf is clearly seeing that the grind of the manufacturing facility (ego, form) is only an illusion appearing *within* the real space of the immense-peace-silence warehouse (yourSelf, formless). In knowing yourSelf, it will be experienced that the immense-peace-silence (formless) and the manufacturing equipment (form) are not separate from one another, they are One peaceful whole.

Identifying as yourSelf instead of your ego is actually a celebration of life. Life continues to happen AS IT IS, but instead of experiencing life from the mental state of a chattering-bustle manufacturing facility (ego), life is witnessed and experienced from an aware-space of the immense-peace-silence warehouse (Self). When seen from the aware-space of the immense-peace-silence warehouse (yourSelf), neither the warehouse space nor the manufacturing equipment are denied; both are celebrated holistically in their own unique ways; they are One.

The experience of this aware-space is permanent and is all that is known by you, because it is 'who you are.' The most awesome part of it all is that you don't become this aware-space; you realize that you have always been this aware-space, you have just been cloaking it with your ego (via ignorance).

Chapter 5

What Does It Mean to Know-Inherently and Experience-Directly?

Love Outpouring will never ask you to believe in anything, assume something, acquire anything or become someone you are not. Any Self-realized knowledge will come directly in the form of inherent-Knowing and/or direct-experience, which are both prior to any knowledge or understanding that your mind can comprehend or intellectualize.

The lines of questioning below are direct pathways back to yourSelf that give you a brief taste of the 'Knowing' of yourSelf directly, which will establish a baseline of Self-understanding to contrast your ego against. Therefore, repeating these questions to yourself and honestly trying to hang out in the place they are pointing to for as long as possible, even if just for a moment at first, is of utmost importance and will provide the greatest Self-realization impact.

We have spent so much of our life covering ourSelf up that this place of peaceful-solitude within us has now become somewhat of a Fairy Land of Make-Believe, a realm too good to be true, and therefore we ignore its calling and deny its existence. So, remember to not believe or listen to your ego when it tells you that the place within you being pointed to with these questions is not real and does not exist. Be reassured, it is the only place that is real and exists, and this place IS You.

Ask yourself the question: Do I exist?

Notice that you paused for a moment...then you responded with an undoubtable "YES." The question did not even have to be second-guessed in the slightest. In fact if you know anything at all, you know for certain you exist. Even if you said you don't exist, there still had to be something that existed to know that you do not exist; the reality of the question is inescapable.

Now ask yourself the question: Where did I go within mySelf during 'the pause' to find the answer of "YES" to this question?

The answer is undescribable because the place is non-comprehensible, yet you absolutely know this place has to be real, because it delivered the answer of "YES" to the question "Do I exist?" Neither did you have to 'believe' it's true, or have to consult your mind for approval for your known-Existence to be actualized. This is what it means to Know-inherently (it is causeless Knowing). Inherent-Knowing is undeniable and inescapable direct-knowledge, and is the starting point for understanding the nondual perennial message; that is, the starting point for understanding the inescapable knowledge of yourSelf. The spaceless-place you went during 'the pause' is exactly the non-physical-place this entire book is feverishly trying to point you to: the silent-peaceful-emptiness of You, yourSelf, yourHeart, I, or I Am.

Have you ever had an experience that did not take place 'here and now'?

Try for a moment to step out of 'here and now' and experience anything 'other than here and now.' For you are incapable of not experiencing 'here and now' even if your life depended on it; you take 'here and now' with you wherever you go. This is an unavoidable example of what it means to observe a concept and experience it directly.

Quick question: How far is it from 'here' to 'now'? Zero distance, and therefore they are One, as are You with them. Here IS Now, and so ARE You.

Notice that no effort by any means, physical or mental, needed to be performed for this experience of 'here and now' to happen. You never leave yourSelf or the 'here and now' to witness this experience-directly. Therefore, experiencing-directly is the Self-embodiment of a concept or idea where there is no distance between you and the concept's innate properties.

> *The only source of knowledge is experience.*
> **Albert Einstein**[1]

So, for you to 'experience-directly' you do not need an object 'other than' yourself for this experience to take place; that is, you don't need to add a 'here and now' to yourSelf for 'here and now' to be happening. You, yourSelf, ARE the experience of 'here and now.' Direct-experiences are non-conceptual encounters of non-objectiveness: they are experiences of the subject (You) experiencing itSelf as the object; that is, subject experiencing subject: You (subject) experiencing yourSelf (subject) directly.

Notice how close both Knowing-inherently and experiencing-directly are to You. There is no space between You and them; no distance from You to them. You don't have to go anywhere to obtain them. They are One AS You. You ARE them. This is how close you ARE to yourSelf. This is how close you are to absolute wholeness and completeness—they ARE your very nature.

Quick metaphor: Picture a solid rubber ball. How far does the ball have to move away from itself to experience its own rubber-ness? The answer is: zero movement is required. You are the ball in this metaphor and yourSelf is the rubber. This is how close You are to yourSelf. As the ball and the rubber are inseparable, so are You and yourSelf. They are One.

How far does the ball (You) need to move away from itSelf to know its rubber (yourSelf) exists? Again, the answer is zero. The ball knows itSelf (as rubber) just by being itSelf.

Learn to trust the undeniable evidence of your inherently-Knowing and direct-experience, which should be the only test of Reality anyway, not some belief system or theory taught in church or school. That which is true must be verifiable, and the only verifiable Truth is that you exist. *Love Outpouring* utilizes the verifiable evidence of your direct experience of Existence to validate the Truth in the same way you would in a university class with a corresponding lab.

Self inherent-Knowing (Sections 1 and 3 of the book) — understanding the underlying nature of your Existence — would be likened to the lecture portion of the class; whereas Self direct-experiencing (Section 2 of the book) — investigating yourSelf directly — would be likened to the lab portion.

The dimensionless-place being pointed to within you with these questions is the immense-peace-silence that the metaphor in the prior chapter is linguistically endeavoring to convey in words. After reading the questions above and resting in the spaceless-space they point to, try to couple the truthful-knowledge of the metaphor with the Self-experience of the above questions. See if you can, to some extent, experience-directly the infinite immense-peace-silence of yourSelf, as it holds the placeless-space for you to read these words in, right 'here and now.'

Chapter 6

What Is Totality?

This chapter and the following chapter, 'What Is Real?', constitute the comprehensive picture of Oneness, of yourSelf. One could say that these two chapters strive to depict the overarching operations of the One-Reality, which could be considered the pinnacle of Jñāna-knowledge. They are an attempt to reveal how it is not possible for separation and suffering to actually be occurring, that separation and suffering are only appearances within the manifestation generated by ego, in which unity and happiness are the actual underlying Truth of Reality.

From the perennial nondual point of view, the Self is unborn and infinite; it is ALL THAT IS: Self IS the emptiness the big bang exploded into and IS what will remain after the universe collapses back into itself. Because of these innate attributes of unbornness and infiniteness, Self has no 'unoccupied' inside or outside space to distance itSelf from itSelf and therefore loses its ability to become something 'other than' itSelf.

Without the ability to distance itSelf from itSelf, Self therefore also loses the ability to create and know separation. Self is therefore the absence of separation and separation's deviant counterpart, suffering; leaving Self AS unified wholeness, completeness and happiness.

The essential quality of the infinite is its subtlety, its intangibility.
That which is truly alive is the energy of spirit,
and this is never born and never dies.
David Bohm[1]

Don't feel alone,
the entire universe is inside You.
Rumi[2]

Being unborn, Self therefore does not have a progression of Existence; it has ever-lived and therefore will never die. Self does not have a starting place, middle ground or end point. Understand that Self has *ever*-lived, not *fore*-ever lived. *Fore*-ever assumes an infinitely long timeline; *ever* is the absence of any timeframe whatsoever; that is, it is eternal. Self IS eternal Existence, unborn.

Having no beginning, middle or end, Self therefore has no boundaries. Better said, Self is the absence of boundaries, the absence of limits...it is therefore complete limitless-freedom. Being boundless, unlimited and free, it is therefore infinite. It has no inside or outside: how could it, since it is ALL THAT IS? Being infinite, with no outside, nothing can stand external or apart from Self. Being infinite, with no inside, Self cannot be internally divided, fragmented or compartmentalized. Being infinite, it is whole and complete, lacking absolutely nothing. Self IS immeasurable Existence; infinite-wholeness-completeness.

Ultimately, the entire universe has to be understood
as a single undivided whole, in which analysis into
separately and independently existing parts
has no fundamental status.
David Bohm[3]

Eternal and immeasurable Existence; that is, unborn-infinite-Being IS Totality. You, yourSelf, ARE Totality. Your AREness is Totality's ISness. Totality is not something You have, nor is it a property of You; it is too intrinsic to be a possession and too fundamental to be a feature. This is not something you can know or comprehend with your mind. Only your Heart, yourSelf, can Be this understanding. You are Being the immeasurable Existence of Totality right at this very timeless-moment, for how could you not...being that You, Totality, exist at this very timeless-moment—right?

Your ego, striving to 'know' Totality, will attempt to expand its limited-finite-self to a size larger than infinite Totality. Every attempt by your ego to get bigger than Totality to try and know it and make Totality a *thing* to comprehend and call its own perpetually leads to defeat. Failing to become larger than it, know it and label it, the ego will then announce that Totality does not exist and that it is not real. Yet You have ever-permanent direct access to Totality, to yourSelf, which is the same dimensionless-place that delivers the answer "Yes" when you ask yourSelf the question: "Do I exist?" or "Am I aware?"

Totality is not one, but Oneness: the undefinable 'Presence' of unborn infinite Existence. For there to be one of anything it has to stand apart from and be contrasted against something else, which then makes two things: 1) the thing, and 2) the contrast, which is duality. Totality cannot stand apart from anything else because it already IS everything/anything else, hence losing its ability to be anything 'other than' Oneness (itSelf). This is precisely why Advaita Vedanta refers to Oneness as 'One without a second.'

Therefore nothing exists apart or separate from Totality, including You. Logically then, Totality doesn't even exist. For what would Totality stand apart from in order to exist independently from it? The verb 'exist' comes from the Latin *existere*, which means 'come into Being,' and is derived from a combination of *ex*, 'out,' and *sistere*, 'take a stand.'

Totality can't 'come into Being' because it is already 'Being' itSelf. There is no space for it to 'come out of' to be able to 'come into' and independently 'take a stand.' From the viewpoint of nonduality, nothing actually exists independently; there is only Totality (Existence, Self) alone. Therefore Your Being is Totality's Being. Neither You nor Totality ever came into Existence and became independent; You-Totality have ever-existed non-independently.

When I say 'I am',
I do not mean a separate entity with a body as its nucleus,
I mean the Totality of Being, the ocean of Consciousness,
the entire universe of all that is known.
I have nothing to desire for I am complete forever.
Sri Nisargadatta Maharaj[4]

Totality, that is, yourSelf, does not have an attribute of 'distance,' and therefore it does not know the concept of separation; Self only knows and IS wholeness and happiness. Yet the ego, in an attempt to find happiness, becomes something 'other than' the wholeness of Totality, thereby creating a false-sense of separation within and apart from Totality, placing itself (ego) into a limited reality of bondage and suffering. In general, the ego leaves its loving happy home of Self (Totality) to seek love and happiness elsewhere, while placing itself in bondage and suffering to do so...silly ego!

The ego then runs around its entire life looking to improve on its false-sense of identity, continuously adding to its everlasting laundry list of self-betterment; all with the hopes and expectations of getting happy. The ego, never being able to find the perfect permanent identity 'fix,' even in the most ideal situations, accomplishments and acquirings, perpetually seeks fulfillment in anything 'other than' itSelf; when all it is seeking is its home of Self: Totality.

Bondage and suffering (bondage-suffering) *is* what maintains the ego's identity and only apparent existence. For the ego to preserve its apparent existence it has to constantly be distracting you from yourSelf, because it knows the moment you get a taste of yourSelf directly, its illusory existence is nearing an end. The end is when the ego dissolves back into its home of Totality, back into its home of Self, collapsing the apparent 'distance' between itself and Totality, ending separation: ending bondage and suffering. The beautiful paradox is: the more your ego dissolves back into yourSelf via Self-inquiry, the more ever-present happiness You experience-directly and know-inherently.

Blasphemy

If a finite-entity was ever able to step outside of infinite-Totality, that is, if a finite-entity was to remove itself from infinite-Totality and stand independently of it, it would become separate from infinite-Totality, redefining Totality's definition of 'infinite' into 'finite,' and therefore collapsing infinite-Totality into finite-Totality (creating duality). There would then be two independent existences (duality), 1) the finite-entity (regardless of how small) and 2) the finite-Totality (regardless of how large). But once anything becomes separate from infinite-Totality, infinite-Totality no longer is infinite-Totality; it becomes a finite-entity, and therefore there would now be two finite-entities and no infinite-Totality.

Being now two finite-entities, the original finite-entity would now be equal to, and possibly even greater than, the once infinite-Totality. An ego, believing itself to be an independent finite-entity that stands apart from the whole of infinite-Totality, ignorantly believes itself to be at a minimum equivalent to infinite-Totality. This is the epitome of blasphemy.

From the early great Upanishads [Vedic texts], the recognition of Atman [Self] = Brahman [God] was in Indian thought considered, far from being blasphemous, to represent the quintessence of deepest insight into the happenings of the world.
Erwin Schrodinger[5]

Blasphemy is when an independent mortal person (finite-entity, ego) believes itself to be separated from, and therefore equal to, infinite-Totality (in religious terms infinite-Totality is referred to as God). The ego truly thinks it exists in one place and God exists elsewhere, generally in a location an infinite distance away from its egoic finite-self. With the ego being in one place and God in another, there are now by definition two finite-entities, making God limited and finite, and therefore making God 'the same as' the limited and finite-ego, which is blasphemous.

Self, on the other hand, only knows itSelf as an infinite eternal Being in unity with infinite-Totality: Oneness. Self realizes that God is sharing Him/HerSelf through all Selfs. Being that there is only One infinite-undivided-whole (Totality), then logically there is only one infinite-undivided-Self. No Self can stand apart from another Self: there is only OneSelf, including GodSelf.

> *Each thing reveals the One [God],*
> *the One manifests as all things.*
> **Seng-ts'an**[6]

Oneness, the absence of blasphemy, is yourSelf being in absolute unity with the unconditional love and acceptance of God (Totality). you (ego) are not God, but You (Self) ARE God. God shines in Your Heart as 'I AM' (Self). Understanding wholeness from this perspective, You begin to know and see yourSelf AS others and others AS yourSelf, in which You experience peace-happy-love directly and thereby consequently lose the ability to exploit and manipulate. yourSelf = mySelf = ourSelf = Him/HerSelf

> *Whoever knows their Self, knows their Lord.*
> **Prophet Muhammad**[7]

*The soul given to each of us is moved by the
same living spirit that moves the universe.*
Albert Einstein[8]

*You are Gods (Elohim);
you are all sons of the Most High.*
Psalm 82:6[9]

A courageous question

"If I am not separate from the whole of Totality, then why
do I appear to be separate and how can I understand and Be
Totality AS IT IS?"

The manifestation of life is a dazzling sensory display of
extremely intricate detail and depth. Life's magnitude of
dazzling detail is limitless and free, which arises from the infinite
possibility of the whole of Totality, yourSelf. From the formless
of Existence (Totality) arises the form of life (manifestation),
and afterwards the ghost-like ego comes into seeming existence
and claims itself as the 'doer' of life. But how can the ego be
the 'doer' if it comes after the activities of life have happened?
It can't. The ego presupposes its apparent existence onto the
front end of life's activities, stealing infinite-wholeness's (Self's)
spotlight as the genuine creator, while all along being nothing
but a non-existent afterthought.

*The ego is the presupposing of a non-existent entity
trying to get salvation for itself.*
Sri Ramana Maharshi[10]

It is only your finite ego's presupposing perception that places
side-boards on life's boundlessness with its beliefs, judgments,

biases and knowledge, which are all subtle reminders from your ego that in some form or fashion you could be doing life better. These subtle reminders are what preserves the ego's imaginary existence, perpetuating 'otherness' and suffering.

To an ego the perennial message is a huge paradigm shift in Consciousness; a transcendence of perception; a drastic change of mindset. To your Heart, though, who has been lovingly waiting for your re-entry into its warm arms, hearing that the chaotic mind (ego) is to be eliminated is the sweet song of the cosmos.

So how can you understand and Be Totality AS IT IS? Be willing to change the way you see and know yourSelf and the world; that is, be willing to change your perception of what you believe to be real. Nonduality is not a new way *of* seeing Reality, but a new way *of how* you see it. A Self-realized Being still sees the same world as someone who is not realized, but they just see it as more of a dream in which they are one of many dreamed-characters. In a dream you don't necessarily perceive it from one point of view, but from ALL points of view, in which the dreamed-character is just one of the many perception points. The dream-state is more holistic in nature and is witnessed in more of an 'all at once' fashion, unlike how the ego categorizes objects in the manifestation of the waking-state into fragmented-separate parts.

> *Repent, for the kingdom of heaven is at hand.*
> **Jesus of Nazareth**[11]

Two thousand years ago the definition of the word 'repent' did not mean sincere regret or remorse about one's wrongdoings or sins. 'Repent' is translated from the Greek word *metanoia*. *Metanoia* is a 'change of mind and change of conduct'; 'change of mind and Heart'; or 'change of Consciousness.'

In today's language, and sticking to the verbiage being used herein, Jesus' statement would read something like:

- Change your perspective, for ever-present peace-happy-love is within You
- Know yourSelf, and experience-directly ever-lasting fulfillment-contentment
- Follow Jñāna, and experience-directly the kingdom of Totality AS yourSelf

Since Totality is one unified whole, everything that you perceive and conceive must also be Totality, specifically yourSelf. The manifestation of the world you (ego) perceive IS Totality pointing itSelf back to itSelf; You pointing yourSelf back to yourSelf. Totality is a permanent pointer and reminder that 'to Be Totality AS IT IS' you will need to change your current perception of who you are from a finite-form to infinite-formlessness.

There are many Jesus-like quotes—that is, Totality pointing itSelf back onto itSelf—that reflect His suggestion to perceive the world differently, so as to experience the love of the Divine (Totality, Oneness, Kingdom of Heaven, Brahman, Nirvana, One-Reality) first hand, such as:

It's not what you look at that matters,
it's what you see.
Henry David Thoreau[12]

Remember that your perception of the world
is a reflection of your state of Consciousness.
Eckhart Tolle[13]

If the doors of perception were cleansed,
everything would appear to man as it is—infinite.
William Blake[14]

The point is: for you to experience the ever-loving nurturing of your Heart you will need to have the courage to perceive and know yourself much differently than you do now. The craziest part about it all, though, is that after you proceed down this path for a bit, at some point you will look back to analyze the ground you have covered and it will be seen with absolute clarity that there was no path or ground to begin with, and that nothing was actually accomplished…again, how perplexing!

It will dawn on you that this has to be the case. Being that the ego does not exist to begin with, how can there be a path of ego-destruction, if there was no ego to destroy in the first place? You will most likely find this discovery to be a loving, yet bewildering, invitation into the mystery of creation, into yourSelf (Totality). Once here, a *sphurana* will occur (*sphurana*: a non-conceptual experience of a new, clear and fresh knowledge of your Existence) and you will be eternally caught in the jaws of the tiger.

Notes

7   Muhammad ibn Abdullah (AD 570–632), also known as the Prophet Muhammad, was an Arab religious, social and political leader and the founder of the world religion of Islam. According to Islamic scriptures, he was a prophet divinely inspired to preach and confirm the monotheistic teachings of Adam, Abraham, Moses, Jesus, and other prophets. Muhammad proclaimed publically that "God is One" and that complete "submission" (Islām) to God was the correct path.

9   Psalm 82 of the Old Testament is the 82nd psalm in the biblical Book of Psalms, subtitled "A Psalm of Asaph." The New King James Version describes the psalm as "a plea for justice."

11   Jesus of Nazareth (4 BC – AD 30 or 33) was a first-century Jewish preacher and religious leader. He is the central figure of Christianity, the world's largest religion. Most Christians believe he is the incarnation of God the Son and the awaited messiah (the Christ) prophesied in the Hebrew Bible. Jesus preached that He and the Father (God) were One, and so is everyOne else.

12   Henry David Thoreau (1817–1862) was an American naturalist, poet and philosopher. He was a leading transcendentalist, a literary movement that saw divine experience inherent in the everyday, rather than believing in a distant heaven. Thoreau was a lifelong abolitionist as well, someone who sought to end American slavery. His best-known book, *Walden*, has several references to the sacred Vedic texts of India.

14   William Blake (1757–1827) was an English poet, painter and printmaker. Blake is considered a seminal figure in the history of the poetry and visual art of the Romantic Age. He stood on the understanding that the imagination was the most important element of human existence. Blake believed Jesus Christ was the unity between humankind and God, stating: "He is the only God...and so am I, and so are you."

Chapter 7

What Is Real?

Hopefully by now it has been made clear that the perennial nondual message is directing you to a Truth that Reality cannot be described in words and/or be known by the senses of your body-mind. The message's purpose points you to the underlying nature and Reality of the world and relentlessly returns you to the understanding that you can only BE 'nature and Reality' inherently, not conceptually or intellectually.

But if Reality can't be known conceptually or intellectually via the mind or body, then is anything real? Absolutely YES! THAT which is reading these words is the direct proof that realness exists and is fully present...yourSelf. Since Reality must exist, and since You absolutely exist, then THAT (Your Existence) must Be Reality (real).

In mainstream culture the term 'real' typically refers to something that can be experienced through the body-mind senses, and therefore, generally speaking, anything that is perceived and known by the ego is real. The perennial knowledge has a completely different definition of Reality, one that is derived from your direct experience of your undeniable Existence.

The perennial definition of 'real' is:

1. It has to be permanent:
   a. It has to be unchanging
   b. It can't come in and out of Existence

2. It has to have Being and Awareness:
   a. It has to exist
   b. It has to know that it exists

3. It has to shine by its own light:
   a. It can't be dependent on anything else to energize itSelf
      i. It has to be Self-energizing
      ii. It has to be Self-illuminating
      iii. It has to be Self-shining

The next question you could ask then: "Is what I perceive, namely the world,* real?" The answer is simple: "Do things that you perceive in the world meet these three criteria of 'real'?" Simply not. The objects that are perceived by an ego, known typically as the ever-changing multiplicity of thoughts, sensations and perceptions seen in and as the world, do not meet the standard of nondual Reality and are therefore considered by the perennial message as 'unreal.' The term 'world' includes within it the ego, because the ego (mind+body) is one of the multiplicities perceived in the world. The ego is nothing but a cluster of images, ideas, memories, emotions and feelings — which are categorized as adjuncts — which are forever changing (more on what an ego is in the next chapter). This cluster of adjuncts (ego) come and go, hence they are not permanent, and therefore do not meet the definition of real; therefore neither does the ego. But if the ego is constantly fluctuating and not real, then what is it within you that 'feels so permanently-real' and is intimately-known by You to be so permanently-real? (Hint: it is non-objective, non-conceptual and closer than close.)

The nondual understanding

The following is the nondual understanding of the mechanics of a One-Reality.† Because Reality is perceived differently depending on whose perspective it is seen by, ego or Self, and because a One-Reality perspective is so foreign to most, it may be a slight mind-bender at first to get your ~~head~~ Heart wrapped around this. Since the following depictions (along with the help from the previous chapter, What Is Totality?) are the basis of the entire One-Reality message, once a One-Reality is understood, it will help to clarify all other nondual pointers.

Here is the Godhead of the universal paradox: The nondual perennial message, which is the utmost understanding that there is One-Reality consisting of only one substance, namely Consciousness (Awareness, Self, Totality), states:

1. From the point of view of ego there are two separate realities:
   a. A real-reality made of the manifestation, and
   b. An unreal-reality made of Consciousness

The ego mistakenly considers objects (the manifestation of the world) to have an actual independent existence separate and apart from the whole of Totality (Consciousness), creating two realities separate from one another. This is duality: separation and its consequence of suffering. So why does ego not consider Consciousness (Totality, Self) to be real? Because ego only considers objects to be real. Objects are anything 'other than' yourSelf, including the ego, which have finite forms that can be known conceptually and/or intellectually by the ego. From the ego's perspective, the manifestation is just a multitude of finite forms and objects clustered together, with each object having its own individual stand-alone existence. Totality (Consciousness) therefore does not meet the definition of an object since it is infinite, dimensionless and eternal, which is taken by the ego (mind) to be unknowable and unreal and therefore non-existent.

> *Everything we call real is made up of things*
> *that cannot be regarded as real.*
> **Niels Bohr**[1]

2. From the point of view of Self there is only One-'real'-Reality:

a. A real-Reality made only of Consciousness, which is either in an infinite-formless form (Consciousness, Self) and/or a finite-condensed form (manifestation, world), in which either form is Absolute Consciousness: the only One-'real'-Reality.

Because Self only knows itSelf AS Consciousness, it does not have a clue as to what 'other than' itSelf is, and therefore as to what an independent separate objective manifestation is. This is nonduality: the perennial message of unity-peace-happy-love.

When the world appears to be real [to the ego],
the Self [Consciousness] does not appear;
and when the Self appears,
the world [manifestation] does not appear.
Sri Ramana Maharshi[2]

Because it is inherently known by Self (Consciousness) that the manifestation (world) is truly not separate from itSelf—the manifestation is only infinite-Self collapsed down into finite-Self—the manifestation therefore is known as 'real' by Self. Because of this, Self knows the manifestation as itSelf; it's not separate from it; that is, Self IS the manifestation. Therefore, Self never is or knows anything 'other than' itSelf, even when it perceives itSelf in the form of the manifestation. Directly put, Self IS what your perception IS; the manifestation You perceive IS yourSelf.

These pointers are another way to demonstrate the nondual Reality of Consciousness and Consciousness's-activity (Advaita, not-two); that Consciousness (infinite-Self) is real and Consciousness's-activity (infinite-Self collapsed down into finite-Self, that is, collapsed down into the manifestation) is also real; they are not separate from one another. So everything that is known by Self has the underlying Reality of Consciousness:

whole-complete-peace-happy-love. This means everything: your child's high-school graduation party, war, a sunny day, resentment, your worst enemy, nonduality, duality, suffering, thoughts, flowers, evil, and so on, all have an underlying Reality of unified-happiness, only appearing as finite forms.

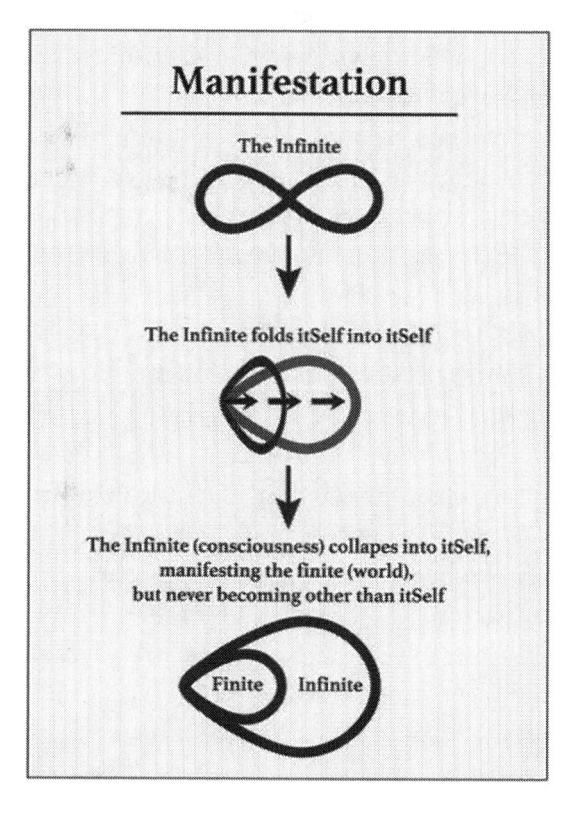

This is likened to the many forms that gold can take, such as rings, necklaces, medallions and ornaments. Yet this multitude and variety of forms only has one truthful underlying substratum of Reality: gold. This is correlated with the One-Reality of nonduality, where gold (Consciousness) is shaped into a variety of gold forms (Consciousness's-activity), while all along, no matter what the gold manifests into, its underlying substratum remains only gold.

So back to the question: "What is real?" From the standpoint of the ego, nothing is real, because the ego only knows the objective world of manifestation, and nothing in the egoic-manifestation meets the three definitions of real. From the standpoint of Self, ALL THAT IS (Totality) is real, because every perceived thing/object has an underlying Reality of the OneSelf, which meets the definition of real. Simply put: All that is 'real' is You alone; yourSelf (Consciousness).

So why does Consciousness (Self) go through the relentless effortless-effort to collapse into a finite reality to perceive and know itSelf through the flow you call life? For the same reason you are reading this book: to inquire into, and answer the question "Who Am I?"

Living the dream

Your daily waking-state could be likened to a dream you have at night. A dream is when the dreamer's infinite formless mind (Self) collapses into a finite form of a dreamed-person (ego) in a dreamed-world (manifestation). The dreamed-world is witnessed by the dreamer's mind through the perceptions of the dreamed-person. The dreamer's infinite mind corresponds to Consciousness, and the form of the dreamed-person and dreamed-world correspond to finite collapsed Consciousness-activity. Just as the form of the dreamed-person and dreamed-world are nothing but the collapsed Consciousness of the dreamer's infinite mind, so too in our waking-state is the form of the manifestation nothing but the collapsed-activity of the Divine's mind; that is, the manifestation is nothing but the collapsed-activity of yourSelf.

> "This could all be a dream," said Einstein.
> "You may not be seeing it at all."
> (When asked if one could truthfully say a tree is a tree.)
> **Albert Einstein**[3]

Just as in the dream-state, in the waking-state the ego assumes itself and the physical world it appears in to be 'real' and 'other than' collapsed-Consciousness. The ego, just like the dreamed-person in a dream, truly believes it is an independent entity that stands outside of and exists separately from the Totality of Consciousness (the Divine's mind). This misunderstanding gives rise to dualism, that is, separation and suffering, within the waking-state.

> *There is no greater mystery than this visualization,*
> *ourSelves being the Reality we seek to gain Reality.*
> **Sri Muruganar**[4]

Self-realization is when the ego (dreamed-person) wakes up within the manifestation (dreamed-world) and realizes that it's not separate from the whole of Totality (dreamer's mind), that it, the ego, has all along been the Self in disguise. The Self (dreamer's mind) then realizes that there never was an independent ego (dreamed-person) and therefore there never was separation, that separation was only the ego's delusion within the manifestation (dreamed-world). It is then witnessed by Self that there is only wholeness, only One-Reality that has only been appearing as separation, fragmentation and compartmentalization. You could say that Self-realization is likened to lucid dreaming in the sleep-state, but it is lucid dreaming in the waking-state.

The flow of Reality

The world, and all apparent objects contained in it, is the manifestation of the One-Consciousness masquerading as 'many forms' that arise when the infinite-Self collapses into a finite form of itSelf (world) to perceive itSelf. The manifestation is the 'grand illusion' of the One-Reality. An illusion is not a denial of what is perceived; it means that what is perceived is not the underlying Reality of the perception. For example, every night we watch the sun move down the horizon and set; this is an illusion. The sun doesn't move at all, it's actually the Earth's rotation that gives the false appearance (illusion) that the sun is setting. We don't deny that the sun sets; it's just that what we perceive is not its underlying Reality.

Understanding the One-Reality therefore is the realization that the world is an illusion and that Consciousness is the illusion's underlying Reality; its true nature. Therefore, for our purposes, what this means is that the perception of reality (life, manifestation) is not being denied, but that Reality's underlying nature is not based in finite three-dimensional forms, but as Consciousness acting in a condensed form of itSelf to perceive itSelf.

Life is none other than the effortless flow of Consciousness's-activity. Consciousness and its activity are not separate attributes of one another, they are not-two (Advaita); they are One underlying Reality that has the illusion of many. This illusion, if mistaken for Reality, creates separation from the Truth of Reality, creating separation from yourSelf: the Mother of all suffering.

Illusion of distance

In order for the infinite-Self to collapse down and manifest into a form it can witness, Self must create the illusion of distance within the manifestation in order to give itSelf the room for life to apparently evolve within. To do so, Self creates distance-platforms via the egoic-based illusions of space and time.

Space-Distance

Space arises when the ego establishes itself in and as the body and assumes that body to be a real separate independent form relative to every other form it perceives. The ego assumes the body to be 'itself,' and anything/everything else is seen as 'other than' itself. The apparent space between 'itself' and 'other than' itself is a distance-platform for the illusion of the finite three-dimensional manifested world to appear — the world of duality; the world of separation. Space, when thoroughly Self-investigated, is seen as just another misperception of thought in the egoic-mind.

The distance between 'self and other' is connected by the apparent five bodily perceptions: seeing, hearing, touching, tasting and smelling.††

> *The Awareness with which you see is what you are,*
> *as well as what you see. They are One.*
> **Marshall Davis[5]**

The moment the body is taken by the ego to be an independent entity, suffering and longing commence. This is because, in creating its spatial distance-platform of a separate independent dual reality, the ego undermines its connection to the whole of Totality, its home; the loving treasure of Self. The whisper of the longing that You sense calling from within is yourSelf calling the ego back home to itSelf, to rest in the wholeness and completeness of Totality.

> *An ego seeks a treasure within life...*
> *Life is the treasure.*
> **Tony Parsons[6]**

> *Our Heart will be where our treasure is.*
> **Brother Lawrence[7]**

Time-Distance

As the ego generates a mind and assumes the mind to be itSelf (a real separate individual creator), it then creates another distance-platform: the appearance of time. The mind, which consists of thoughts, images, ideas and memories, needs a distance-platform for all of these mind-characteristics to manifest. Time is the illusory distance-platform that gives the mind space to operate on and in. Like space, time when thoroughly Self-investigated is seen as just another misperception of thought in the egoic-mind.

Space and time are only thoughts created by the ego to give the appearance of manifested distance, yet in the One-Reality there is no distance between 'self and other,' there is only 'here and now'; only dimensionlessness (here) and eternity (now). The next chapter will discuss how the body and mind are just thoughts as well.

The dimensionless point

Here is an interesting point of view regarding dimentionlessness. As young children we were all introduced to elementary math in which simple graphing techniques were applied. We were asked to draw two perpendicular lines on our paper and label the horizontal line x and the vertical line y. We were then asked to add hashlines, in equal distances, to the lines and mark them as we would a number line. 1, 2, 3 and so on…on the right and upper axis; -1, -2, -3 and so on…on the left and lower axis, and 0 at the center point where the axes cross. We were then asked to place a point on one of the graph's coordinates, say, over 2 and up 3 (2, 3) from the center point of 0.

The point is the most basic element of geometry and the starting spot in which all lines, planes and cubes (forms) establish their underlying reality. A point is the underlying reality of a line; a line is the underlying reality of a plane; a plane is the underlying reality of a cube. In fact, every geometric figure possible is based on the underlying reality of a geometric point.

Yet a geometric point, in which all lines, planes and 3-D forms arise, has no reality in and of itself. A point has no width, depth or height. Even from the viewpoint of an ego it should not exist (unreal), because it is dimensionless; it only appears to have some sort of 'real' substance. In mathematical terms a point is considered to be infinitesimally small — the ego's justification for a point's non-existent reality.

This makes the point we placed on our graph at (2, 3) unreal, because the number 2 in and of itself has no width or depth and the number 3 in and of itself has no height or depth. Even if we added a third axis to create three dimensions (x, y, and z) or (2, 3, 0), this would still hold true. In fact, any point on the three-dimensional graph is non-existent, along with its corresponding lines, planes or forms — therefore making all geometry, and really any graphable math, unreal in a sense.

But the ego ignores the absence of dimension of the point, namely that the point is non-existent, and assumes it to be a real physical point, along with all of the corresponding lines, planes and forms that arise out of that point. The ego unknowingly takes what it should consider unreal (the point) to be real and builds a three-dimensional reality within the x, y, z graph that it correlates to and models as the physical world. The ego takes what it should consider to be unreal-formless-Consciousness and turns it into real-form-manifestation. This is all fine with respect to the designs created within the graph drawn on your paper, but when the ego assumes the manifestation of life to be real when it should consider it unreal, it separates itself from Reality and suffering arises.

This example relates to the mechanics of the underlying nature of Reality, in which the formless Self (the dimensionless point) manifests into the forms of the world (the manifestation), that is, how an apparent some-thing (world) arises from no-thing (Self). You in this example ARE the dimensionless point experiencing your own manifested 3-D forms.

The dimensionless point is likened to Consciousness; and the lines, planes and forms are likened to Consciousness's-activity. Regardless of what form Consciousness takes, there is only One-Reality, with its nature being only Consciousness (nonduality), and You ARE the One-Reality.

The ego in this example is the mind of a young child. Neither the teacher nor the child questions whether the point is real or not. It is just taken for granted as being real and added to the child's conditioning, along with oodles of other unreal things that will be accepted unquestionably as real. Investigating into yourSelf (Self-inquiry) is re-examining all of your conditioning of what you were taught to be real or not and discarding what is unreal and keeping what is real: You alone.

Notes

* The Sanskrit definition of the word 'world' (*loka*) is: 'THAT which is seen.'

† One-Reality, Reality, Existence, Oneness, Totality, Self, Being, Awareness, THAT, Absolute and Consciousness are interchangeable terms.

†† In Advaita, there is a term known as *Triputis*, which is the trinities of perception and knowing/thinking, namely seer-seeing-seen, hearer-hearing-heard, taster-tasting-tasted, and so on, along with knower-knowing-known and thinker-thinking-thought. With Self-realization, the doer (seer, hearer, taster, knower, thinker) and that which is perceived (seen, heard, tasted, known, thought) collapse, leaving only seeing, hearing, tasting, knowing and thinking.

4 Sri Muruganar (1890–1973), born C.K. Subramania Iyer, is widely regarded as one of the most eminent and influential devotees of Sri Ramana Maharshi (also known as Bhagavan), living with him for over 27 years. This dedication landed him the recognition of being "the shadow of Bhagavan."

Sri Muruganar compiled what is referred to as the most comprehensive summary of Sri Ramana's teaching in a book of 1254 Tamil verses entitled *Guru Vachaka Kovai* (The Garland of Guru's Sayings).

5　Marshall Davis is a retired Baptist pastor of 40+ years, is the author of over 15 books, and has an admired podcast known as The Tao of Christ that explores the mystical roots of Christianity. He describes his teaching as Christian nonduality, unitive Awareness, and/or union with God. Marshall has helped to open many Christians' eyes to the real mission of Jesus: to transcend dual-reality and wake up to the spiritual-Reality of being One with the Father.

6　Tony Parsons is the author of *The Open Secret*, which is a singular and radical book which speaks of the fundamental liberation that is absolutely beyond effort, path, process or belief. The fundamental principle of Tony's work is to define the nondual and impersonal nature of Reality and to expose the dichotomy of the dualistic belief in a progressive path leading to spiritual attainment.

7　Brother Lawrence (1614–1691) was a French Christian layman who, due to a debilitating injury, became a servant at the Discalced Carmelite monastery in Paris. Lawrence wrote a series of letters and a manifesto he called 'The Practice of the Presence of God' that lays out a simple and natural method for being fully and permanently present with Self, regardless of one's undertakings and surroundings. There is an entire section in Chapter 14 dedicated to Brother Lawrence.

Chapter 8

What Is Ego?

If you assume yourself to be an independent three-dimensional physical person that maneuvers through and manipulates other three-dimensional physical persons and objects to survive, have taken these other three-dimensional physical persons/objects to be real-matter, believe you were born, will live and will die, and think you have free will, then you have mistaken yourself for something you are not, an individual (ego, self, mind).

And if you have mistaken yourSelf to be what has just been described, it's OK. The message of nonduality is not a blame game; it's a recognition game encapsulated in love. Love yourself for the mistaking, and love yourSelf for the recognition.

> *The fault is in the one [ego] who blames.*
> *Spirit [Self] sees nothing to criticize.*
> **Rumi**[1]

In Reality, You have never actually lost yourSelf or become someone or something 'other than' yourSelf, such as a stand-alone three-dimensional physical person completely detached from Self. You ARE, have ever-been, and will ever-be yourSelf.

What muddies the waters and adds confusion between 'who you ARE' and 'what you mistakenly believe yourself to be' comes from the mixing of yourSelf and the ego. *The ego is nothing but a collection of ever-changing images, ideas, thoughts, memories, sensations, emotions, feelings and perceptions all compiled together and added on to yourSelf. The ego is also the false-identity which claims itself as the knower, doer, thinker, experiencer, perceiver, expectationer, and owner of its illusory reality.*

The ego, and its numerous fleeting identities, cloaks the Self, placing the Self in bondage, and then claims itself as the 'doer' of life when the ego is nothing but an unreal perpetrator. Confusion happens when you identify with the ego's ever-changing fragmented unreal 'personal-doer' attributes instead of the never-changing real 'non-personal' Self.

> *The human effort consists of*
> *creating bondage [ego] for oneself, clinging fast to it,*
> *and wanting to become free [Self]*
> *without giving up bondage [ego] itself.*
> **Sri Atmananda Krishna Menon**[2]

The unreal-ego bonds itself to the real-Self, thereby cloaking Self, via two wrongly attributed identifiers: a 'belief' and a 'feeling.' This personal 'belief' and 'feeling' are what generates a false 'sense' of identity that you then mis-assume to be the real You (yourSelf). The *belief* is the assumed-sense "I am the mind" and the *feeling* is the assumed-sense "I am the body."

The belief "I am the mind" correlates to images, ideas, thoughts and memories, while the feeling "I am the body" correlates to sensations, emotions, feelings and perceptions.

Self-realization, via Self-knowledge and Self-inquiry, is when the 'belief' and 'feeling' bonds that cloak the Self break, allowing ego to fall away, so that just the clear identification AS yourSelf alone remains; the home of permanent-contentness.

Pointer: Reiterated, at the core of the perennial message, ego is nothing but a false identity as a 'belief' and a 'feeling.' Self-inquiry dissolves these two false identities, eliminating ego, leaving Self alone.

The unreal ego-fragments you have falsely identified with are correlated with the adjuncts you add to yourself when describing yourself. An adjunct (ego) is a thing added as a supplementary descriptor separate from the essential subject (Self). So when you say: I am a man/woman, I am hungry, I am perplexed, I am happy; man/woman, hungry, perplexed, happy are the adjuncts to the essential subject of 'I am.'

When describing or referring to ourSelf we step over the real-piece of 'who we are' (I am, essential subject) and claim ourSelf to be the unreal-piece of 'what we are not' (ego, adjuncts); that is, we cease to identify as ourSelf and cling to and identify with descriptors 'other than' ourSelf, creating an unclear understanding of our Reality. As mentioned in the beginning of the book, this is likened to bypassing the first-person pronoun and thinking we clearly understand the second- and third-person pronouns. How can we clearly know anything 'other than' ourSelf if we don't first clearly understand ourSelf?

The ego is constantly changing and morphing into new ideas (beliefs, thoughts) of 'you' to maintain its illusory existence (again, making the ego by definition unreal). It is the greatest illusionary-magician ever imagined by itself; it creates its own illusory-world (space and time), then it imagines its illusory-self (a mind and body) to be a separate character in its illusory-world.

Thought [ego] is creating divisions out of itself and then saying that they are there naturally.
David Bohm[3]

As you identify more and more with all of the ego's illusory fragmented attributes, you move away from yourSelf more and more...creating more and more separation...more and more suffering. *Suffering is simply any movement away from yourSelf.* The ego's fragmented attributes create illusory compartmentalized segments within the whole of Totality, which creates the sense of separation; hence the movement away from your-unified-Self, and the mental and emotional suffering you experience from being separated from the innate love of yourSelf.

> *All that we are [ego]*
> *is the result of what we [ego] have thought.*
> **The Buddha**[4]

Suffering appears to have a gradient. The closer you are to yourSelf, the less suffering you have, and vice versa: the farther away, the more suffering. The selfs who are closer to their Self seem to be able to 'manage' their suffering better, relative to the other end of the suffering-spectrum. These 'closer ego-selfs' might be considered the 'lucky ones,' for they have not let the manifestation of Maya* seduce them too far from their home of peace-happy-love (Self), and are therefore content enough to not need to seek help for their manageable 'light' suffering.

Yet those selfs who have moved far away from themSelf can become very miserable and mentally-paralyzed, typically from incessant rumination, self-loathing, past resentments and future anxieties, crippling fear and life-sucking negative thoughts, all labeled in the Eastern cultures as the monkey-mind. This can lead to seeking for a solution that you can't seem to find a conventional answer to, which may be the reason you are reading this book. If so, the message in this book is You calling yourself back to yourSelf; it is love calling itSelf back home to its dimensionless place of sanity (reminder: sanity is not a clear mind, it is the absence of one).

But as you investigate further and further into this apparent separate illusory self (ego) that can cause so much pain and discomfort, you never locate it. You only find the ever-present Being of yourSelf, and simultaneously you realize this has always been the case. Practicing Self-inquiry can promptly move you back closer to yourSelf, alleviating the unnecessary mental burdens the ego has falsely identified as You. Simply put, you are a human-Being, not a human-egoing. Remembering and Being the 'Being'-ness part of you, not the 'egoing' part of you, is the definition of joy.

It is like encountering a snake in your backyard one evening, but when you investigate into the characteristics of the snake you realize it is only a rope the kids left out. The ego is the apparent snake, and You, yourSelf, ARE the actual rope. Nothing needed to be done or accomplished (effortless-effort) to realize your misperception, only seeing clearly that what you thought to be true was actually not; the snake (ego) was nothing other than a rope (Self). This is another solid pointer, and shows the non-efforts required to recognize yourSelf relative to what you have mistaken yourself to be: this is the actionless-action of Self-inquiry and Self-realization.

> *Grasping form*[1] *it [ego] comes into existence;*
> *grasping form it stands;*
> *grasping and feeding on form it grows abundantly;*
> *leaving form, it grasps form.*
> *If sought, it will take flight.*
> *Such is the ego-phantom with no form of its own.*
> **Sri Ramana Maharshi**[5]

(1) Form is another descriptor of an object. Forms, like objects, are anything 'other than' yourSelf, such as a mind, body and world.

Another example is of a lightsaber, like in *Star Wars*, that has numerous sticky notes stuck all over it blocking the light (peace-happy-love) of itSelf from shining through. The sticky notes represent all of the false thoughts, sensations and perceptions you have mistaken yourSelf to be, namely your gender, race, nationality, body type, profession, emotional state, and so on. The process of knowing yourSelf via Self-inquiry is seeing that you are the Self-illuminating lightsaber, which dissolves the sticky notes and reveals the eternal brilliantly beautiful, yet non-blinding, light that you have always been, allowing Your love-light to shine onto humanity.

It is obvious that humans have devised brilliant ways throughout the millennia to soften the tyranny of separation in the hopes to better ourself: self-help books, therapy, entertainment, pharmaceuticals, mind/sensation-altering drugs, epic adventures and adrenaline-inducing activities to name a few. All of which only temporarily soothe our desires and none of which attends to the root of the separation solution: dissolving the ego to know yourSelf.

> The idea of ourselves [ego] is our escape
> from the fact of what we really are [Self].
> **Jiddu Krishnamurti**[6]

There have also been countless industries, sectors and careers built to address the negative physiological effects of humankind's own self-allotted suffering. The perennial message, with the irony of being encapsulated in love, is not necessarily interested in any of humanity's brilliantly creative industries and ways to distract yourself from yourSelf. It is not that the perennial message doesn't care about the creative distractions; it's just that it is not interested in anything other than fixating on the Absolute solution: eliminating ego via knowing yourSelf and sharing with the world the light that remains.

By attending to anything 'other than' itSelf, ego knows that it will spin its wheels for another millennium as it tries to fix itself through the distractions mentioned above; thereby no solution will ever be found by the ego to fix its own issues (the ego will not get out of its own ego-vehicle). The ego doesn't have the courage or the desire to fix itself; and being a hollow, empty shadow (a belief and a feeling) nor does it have the authority to do so. The human race doesn't have another millennium to try and figure out its own woes. We have always had the direct conduit to the solution: know yourSelf AS yourSelf. Self only knows unity-peace-happy-love, which is eternity's lifeline to keep the human race from devouring the planet and itself.

But one thing about human beings that puzzles me the most is their conscious effort to be connected with the object of their affection even if it kills them slowly within.
Sigmund Freud[7]

People [ego] will do anything, no matter how absurd, in order to avoid facing their own souls [Self].
Carl Jung[8]

Even today an ego has never been located or isolated by any professional neuroscience or psychology association or institution, yet as a society we are still told to believe in such a non-existent ghost. Unfortunately we have unknowingly been misled our entire life to mistake ourself as the belief 'I am an ever-fluctuating illusionary-ghost.'

Chris Niebauer holds a PhD in cognitive neuropsychology. In his 2019 book, *No Self, No Problem*, he states: "Mistaking the voice in our head and labeling it 'me' [ego] brings us into conflict with the neuropsychological evidence that shows there is no such thing." Niebauer's book depicts that our sense of self [ego] is actually an illusion created by the brain in which our ego-ghost exists in the same way a mirage in the middle of the desert exists: as a phantom rather than a concrete object.

Here is a direct message from yourSelf to yourself: Bypass the countless enablers that maintain the illusory-ego, and fall deeply in love with yourSelf AS yourSelf and experience the ever-present happiness that the great wisdom of the ages has so graciously made so easily accessible: You ARE love: BE it and SHARE it.

The elephant's trunk

There is a wonderful Indian metaphor regarding the insatiable wandering mind of the ego with respect to the trunk of an elephant. During community parades, the elephant's handler will make the elephant carry a chain or rope with its trunk to preoccupy and calm the untamable movement of its massive appendage. If the elephant's meandering trunk is not put at ease, the trunk will reach for any object it can, such as an apple from the nearby street vendor, the hat off the top of a roadside bystander, or a hanging banner from an adjacent merchant.

The ego is likened to the trunk of the elephant. It will continuously reach for any object 'other than' itSelf to try and satisfy itself. But like the elephant's trunk, the ego never becomes permanently content and therefore reaches for the next object after the current object loses its 'contentness-power' and becomes unsatisfying (as in the Ramana Maharshi quote above: "leaving form, it grasps form"). Self-inquiry calms and eliminates the ever-roaming trunk of your ego-mind by returning it back to its source, your Heart, where the roaming ego perishes and permanent ever-present fulfillment is experienced.

Forgetfulness, evil and love

As infinite-Self collapses into its finite-activity of the manifestation and is cloaked by the ego, Self pays another price besides separation and suffering. The price is forgetfulness. There is a paradox here, because the ego's cloaking serves as the mechanism of Self-forgetfulness that allows life (evolution) the opportunity to apparently manifest free-willingly and unknowingly.

Without the forgetfulness, there would be no chance for life's infinite possibilities to manifest unbound. This is because

Self, which is 'all-Knowing' to begin with, would have already known the outcome of life due to its 'all-Knowingness,' and therefore would have never needed to embark on the journey of manifestation in the first place.

The collapse of Self into the manifestation creates a contrast of the finite-form (manifestation) relative to the infinite-formless (Self), allowing Self the ability to perceive itSelf via duality, and the forgetfulness (ego) allows evolution the opportunity to create life (manifestation) in an apparent free-will dualistic form.

Yet, with this forgetful freedom, the ultimate price Self pays to know itSelf is suffering and wrongdoing. Due to the duality of the manifestation, there has to be good with bad, right with wrong, ugly with beautiful, and so on.

As you move further and further away from yourSelf you forget yourSelf more and more, which moves you toward the negative end of the duality spectrum: bad, wrong and ugly. Being in the negative end of the duality spectrum is what you may refer to as depression or anxiety or an ego-trip or power-trip, which are specific forms of suffering. These egos have significantly moved away from their source of Self, the positive duality end of the spectrum—good, right and beautiful—by having severely forgotten themSelf (ignorance).

But regardless of how far you have moved away from yourSelf, there is always a lifeline back to your loving source of Self (remember that an ego never completely severs its connection from its home of Self). Since there is only One underlying Reality, anything and everything in the manifestation is made of that One-Reality (Self), which includes the 'forgetting' and the 'movement' away from yourSelf.

There is always a whisper of the love of Self contained in the 'forgetting' and 'movement' away from yourSelf, including, and most importantly, the negative attributes of duality such as arrogance, hate, shame, racism, despair, evil, and so on.

Self-inquiry utilizes the whisper of Self's love to draw the ego back to the positive end of the duality spectrum. Self-inquiry reverses the forgetting process, so that the ego remembers itSelf AS only the positive attributes of peace-happy-love, and remembers that duality is only an illusion created by itself. Self-realization is when the dualistic-ego collapses into the nondual-Self of Oneness, leaving only You.

I believe the main task of the spirit [Self]
is to free man from his ego.
Albert Einstein[9]

Ego at first might consider Self-realization a cop-out, a get-out-of-jail-free card, and conjure up a mentality of 'If I am not responsible for anything I have done or will do, then I and/or society will turn to anarchy and chaos.' Only an ego knows the concepts of anarchy and chaos; the Self doesn't have a clue as to what these or any duality words mean. Ego only uses this mentality as a scare-tactic to keep itself in existence.

Because Self only knows 'other than' itSelf as itSelf, and because it loves itSelf, it is incapable of harming anything 'other than' itSelf, which therefore negates the 'anarchy and chaos' mentality of the ego. Knowing others AS yourSelf, and therefore being incapable of harm, drives compassion for ALL, even those who you may have once considered 'bad or evil.' This doesn't mean you have to like everyone, but by knowing yourSelf You effortlessly, inherently and unconditionally love everyone at Their and Your shared core of Being.

Darkness [ego] cannot drive out darkness;
only light [Self] can do that.
Hate [ego] cannot drive out hate;
only love [Self] can do that.
Martin Luther King Jr[10]

So, as you move from the false-sense of ego into the true-sense of Self via Self-investigation, there will be a greater and greater inherent-understanding that peace-happy-love is the underlying substratum of Reality, including the so-called negative/evil attributes of others and their actions. This is an understanding of true love for All THAT IS; this is knowing yourSelf AS yourSelf; AS love itSelf. Shining with your brightest light of Self helps to drive out egoic darkness and is therefore the greatest offering You can contribute to the world.

The weight of the world

The ego can place huge overbearing weights on you unknowingly. Because the ego identifies 'other than' Self AS itself, the ego can take on the burdens of the world and wear them like a lead jacket. This is what is referred to as 'carrying the weight of the world on your shoulders.' This can become extremely exhausting, physically and mentally, not only to yourself but also to those around you. In the attempt to help the world become a better place you actually dampen your own light, reducing the beautiful impact you were striving to accomplish in the first place. Significantly reducing and possibly even eliminating the ego via Self-inquiry actually frees up your mental and physical capacity, allowing your impactful love-light (Self) to shine brightly. Your Self-shining clears up your once previously heavily-cluttered mental and physical capacity, allowing the needed space for You to have the greatest impact on the world.

In the East the local merchants are known to transport their goods in baskets on top of their heads. Some merchants are seen boarding and riding commuter trains while still carrying the heavy loads on their heads. This is likened to carrying the weight of the world on their shoulders. The train is already carrying the basket, so the merchant can set the load down and allow the train to do all the work. The perennial message is pointing to the massive basket-burden on your head, the ego, and lovingly advising you to take the load off, set it down, and allow yourSelf (the train) to carry it. What will be perplexing is that You will recognize that the ego has been an unneeded, unwanted and non-existent heavily-weighted burden your entire life, and that the Self (the train) has been effortlessly and carefreely carrying the weightless-load of life all along.

Time, space and contrast

As the unreal-ego arises with real-Awareness out of Self and manifests into life, the ego takes root in the mind and body, and from them the illusion of time, space and contrast is created.

Time: As mentioned in the previous chapter, the ego creates the illusion of time so that there is a perceivable time-platform for thoughts and images to appear on as they string through the mind. Time therefore is just another thought superimposed onto eternity by the ego for the mind to operate on and in.

> *Ultimately, all moments are really one;*
> *therefore now is an eternity.*
> **David Bohm**[11]

Eternity is not an infinitely long linear timeline in which 'now' is located somewhere on its endlessly long horizontal axis, but is actually the absence of time. Eternity is more of a vertical width-less axis, which you move horizontally through, instantaneously, and therefore it has no beginning, middle or end since a line (vertical axis) has no width. In Reality, experiencing the manifestation of life, which is truly rooted in the eternal-infinite, all happens simultaneously as you move horizontally through the width-less vertical axis of eternity, that is, 'now.' If there was not the illusion of time (the falsely perceived distance between the start and end of thought or action), life would appear to happen all at once; the bizarre paradox is that this is actually the case. YourSelf IS the eternal-infinite-timeless platform; not the thoughts, images, memories and ideas that appear on it or in it.

> *The distinction between the past, present and future*
> *is only a stubbornly persistent illusion.*
> **Albert Einstein**[12]

Space: The ego also entrenches itself within the body, creating the illusion of bodily ownership. As mentioned in a prior section above, one of the primary thoughts that leads to the felt sense of suffering is the feeling "I am the body," which then leads to the thought "I am separate from everything 'other than' my body." This feeling and thought are the two largest thieves with respect to the diminishment of ever-present happiness. Along with these two thieves comes an additional sense of false spatial recognition, where the feeling that "I am located within my body and anything 'other than' me is located outside of my body" gives rise to a space-platform and the accompanying concept of 'self and other' or 'subject and object.' This leads to the falling out of unity with the Beloved and into the bondage of the felt separation of self.

> *Spacetime is doomed.*
> *There is no such thing as spacetime fundamentally*
> *in the actual underlying description of the laws of physics.*
> *This is very startling...*
> **Nima Arkani-Hamed**[13]

Contrast: With the arising of time and space there further arises the duality of opposites and contrast. For the infinite to see itSelf it has to constrict down from Totality into the finite realm we know as the world. So that it can see its beautiful creation it needs a way to witness what precipitates out of Totality, and to do this it utilizes the mechanisms of contrast and opposites. For something to be known relative to another, self needs its contrasting opposite to decipher and see the two; this is the perceived world of duality. The ego lives in a world of opposites and contrasts: love or hate, black or white, and light or dark, to list a few. Because of these pair-opposites and the multitude of various interpretations for each pair (think light gray), judgment, self-righteousness, bias and opinions spring forth, creating the exhausting barrage of non-permanence and constant change, and with them confusion and dispute. But of all opposites, 'self and other' are the primary duality belief that creates human suffering via apparent separation, which has led to all personal, national and global conflicts.

Yet You, Consciousness, know nothing of time, space or contrast. You ARE the timeless (eternal), spaceless (infinite) and contrastless (nondual) that illuminates all time, space and opposites. The nondual perennial message does not deny the non-permanent and ever-changing dance we are witnessing right before our eyes; marvel in its intricate interwoven complexity and fragility, but do so from the seat of yourSelf. Sit in ever-present happiness while You watch the animation of *Maya* and *Leela*† attempting to mesmerize and seduce your mind and body into a world of separation and duality, and innocently chuckle at the futility of their attempts.

Notes

*   *Maya*—illusion; the power that makes the unreal world appear to be real.

†   *Leela*—the play of the Divine; Consciousness's-activity.

2   Sri Atmananda Krishna Menon (1883–1959) was an Indian sage, guru and philosopher. Menon is considered one of the three titans of twentieth-century Advaita teachers; the

other two are Sri Ramana Maharshi and Sri Nisargadatta Maharaj. His teachings have become a foundation for a spiritual method called 'the Direct Path.' He was unique in that he held a career as a legal advocate for the government and an inspector with the police.

4   Siddhartha Gautama, the Buddha, was a spiritual teacher of ancient India who lived during the sixth or fifth century BC. He was the founder of Buddhism, which taught a path to Nirvana: freedom from ignorance and suffering. Siddhartha is most revered for abandoning his privileged upbringing to live as a wandering ascetic (someone who abstains from sensual pleasures for the purpose of seeking spiritual goals). The Buddha is venerated as one of the most enlightened Beings to have ever graced the world.

7   Sigmund Freud (1856–1939) was a highly influential Austrian neurologist and the founder of psychoanalysis, a clinical method for evaluating and treating pathologies in the psyche through dialogue between a patient and a psychoanalyst. Freud proposed that the human psyche could be divided into three parts: id, ego, and super-ego. The id creates the demands, the ego adds the needs of reality, and the super-ego adds morality to the action which is taken.

8   Carl Gustav Jung (1875–1961) was a renowned Swiss psychiatrist and psychoanalyst who founded analytical psychology. Based on his study of Christianity, Hinduism, Buddhism, Gnosticism and Taoism, Jung believed that the journey of Self-transformation, which he called individuation, is at the mystical Heart of all religions. Individuation is a journey to meet the Self and at the same time to meet the Divine.

10   Martin Luther King Jr (1929–1968) was an American Baptist
     minister and activist, the most prominent leader of the civil
     rights movement from 1955 until his assassination in 1968.
     King advanced civil rights for people of color in the United
     States through nonviolence and civil disobedience. Inspired
     by his Christian beliefs and the nonviolent activism of
     Mahatma Gandhi, he led targeted, nonviolent resistance
     against Jim Crow laws and other forms of discrimination.
     On October 14, 1964, King won the Nobel Peace Prize for
     combating racial inequality through nonviolent resistance.

13   Nima Arkani-Hamed is an American-Canadian theoretical
     physicist of Iranian descent, with interests in high-energy
     physics, quantum field theory, string theory, cosmology,
     and collider physics. Arkani-Hamed is a member of the
     permanent faculty at the Institute for Advanced Study in
     Princeton, New Jersey. He is also Director of the Carl P.
     Feinberg Cross-Disciplinary Program in Innovation at the
     Institute and Director of the Center for Future High Energy
     Physics in Beijing, China.

Chapter 9

What Is Self?

There is a beautiful energetic-light within You that shines by its own illuminating-source: it is Self-shining. This light-source is transparent, permanent, intimate and Knowing; it knows itSelf just by Being itSelf. This light-source exists prior to breath and thought; in the absence of any physical and mental movement. This light-source is still, silent and empty, making it complete, content, and whole. This infinite light-source is boundless freedom. This objectiveless-energy-source IS Existence and has inherent qualities of unity-peace-happy-love. This light-source is real; this light-source is yourSelf; it IS You.

> *The lamp of the body is the eye ['I'].*
> *If your eye is sound [Self]*
> *your whole body will be filled with light,*
> *but if your eye is diseased [ego]*
> *your whole body will be filled with darkness.*
> **Jesus of Nazareth**[1]

> *Be a lamp unto yourSelf.*
> **The Buddha**[2]

Notice the descriptor of 'light-source' is not referring to the light, but to the source of the light. Light is an object that can be known by an ego, and You are not a known object. You are the source of the light that is indescribable, yet undoubtedly real, for how can light exist at all if it has no origin to arise from? Right at this moment you have a direct connection to this light-source. This source is who is reading this book, digesting your food, blossoming flowers and formulating new stars. This light-source, yourSelf, is the answer to the question, "Who Am I?"

This light-source, Self, is boundless, timeless and spaceless; it has no objective qualities or form that the ego can grasp on to and know. Yet you know-inherently that Self exists because this non-space light-source is what delivered the answer "Yes" when you asked yourSelf the question earlier, "Do I exist?" In fact, this light-source is the only non-objective *thing* (subjectness alone) that is real and exists. Therefore, you can only know-inherently and experience-directly the I AMness of Self, it can't happen via the ego; that is, you can only know and experience Self directly by BEing yourSelf alone.

Knowing and experiencing Self is not a felt-bodily sensation (not a belief or feeling) of a personal 'I' that fluctuates and is fleeting, but a permanent unwavering Presence of Being. Knowing yourSelf is therefore a Way of Being. This 'Way' is witnessed when the fluctuating personal sense of 'me' is transcended to the permanent impersonal Presence of 'I Am' through Self-inquiry. This 'Way' is a movement from 'what you perceive' in the world to 'how you perceive' the world.

Where we learned in the previous chapter that the ego is the false-identity which claims itself as the knower, doer, thinker, experiencer, perceiver, and owner of its illusory reality, *the Self would be the One-Reality of knowing, doing, thinking, experiencing and perceiving*. Self is One seamless verb, not a multitude of separate rigid nouns.

Give your attention to the experience of seeing,
rather than the object seen, and you will find yourSelf everywhere.
Rupert Spira[3]

Since the ego cannot directly know what the Self *is*, one way of trying to decipher the Self is to realize what the Self *is not*. A couple of approaches are:

1. Notice that anything that can be known or defined by you is not Self. Anything known is considered an object or form that the ego can grasp on to and claim it as its personal intellectual ownership. YourSelf has no objective qualities or form and therefore cannot be known by the ego. Anything related to your mind, body or perceptions — namely thoughts, feelings, senses — are known by the ego and therefore NOT You.

Part of its magic is that
we've always avoided defining any part of it,
and the effect seems to be that in not defining it,
it becomes everything.
Jerry Garcia[4]

2. Notice that anything that changes, wavers or comes in-and-out of existence is ego. Because Self is real, it therefore is permanent and unchanging, and does not meet the definition of the ever-changing unreal mind+body of the ego. So again, anything mind-oriented, body-oriented or perception-oriented is constantly changing, and therefore NOT You.

Yet, even after all these objective attributes have been eliminated, there is something THAT remains. THAT which remains is yourSelf; Awareness alone (from your point of view you would say, "I Am THIS"). Ask yourself the question, "Have I ever experienced my own disappearance?" Even if you have, there had to be something that was aware of your disappearance for you to know you disappeared. Even in deep sleep, you remain aware. Haven't you ever been deeply asleep and been woken up by your alarm clock? What was it that heard the alarm? It was Awareness. You permanently exist and are ever-aware, even in the three states of deep sleep, dreaming and waking. Face it, You, ever-present permanent Self, are incapable of escaping your own Existence and Awareness.

What more evidence do you need to realize the Truth of yourSelf? Start your investigation from the undeniable directly-experiential fact that You are THAT which is permanently aware. As you inquire into and rest IN and AS the permanence of Awareness, it will reveal its beautiful qualities to you, revealing itSelf AS yourSelf. itSelf = Awareness = yourSelf

Expressions of Self

Formulating equations of what Self and its activity *is* can be a useful way of understanding how life manifests. Keep in mind that all of these words are interchangeable if necessary. These equations and definitions are just another loving attempt to give you an understanding of how to possibly view and formulate your unnamable Self. As the ego dissolves and Self comes to the forefront of your Awareness via Self-inquiry, Self will create an understanding for you that will make complete sense, while befuddling your ego's ability to accurately and precisely articulate the phenomena.

The general aggregation of Self consists of two primary attributes: 1) the Structure, having two sub-attributes, and 2) the Essence, having only one attribute. It is for understanding purposes only that Self has been broken down here into segments. In Reality, Self is only One unborn-undivided-whole (Totality), not two or more.

1. Structure
   a. Permanent
   b. Knowing

2. Essence
   a. Inherent Qualities of the Structure (Peace, Happy and Love)

Self = <u>Permanent + [Knowing]</u> + <u>Inherent Qualities</u>
          (Structure)   (Essence)

Self = Totality

Structural Attributes

Permanent = *Existence, Being, I AM, Heart*
These attributes are the AMness of You. They are the eminent-inextinguishable-immortal Presence of Being which is the underlying substratum of yourSelf. Your AMness is every 'other than' yourSelf's ISness.

Knowing = *Consciousness, Awareness, I, Knowingness*
These are the 'aware' attributes that allow the 'permanent' attributes to know that they exist. This is expressed in the statement, I AM and I know that I AM—the foundational communication of Totality.

[ ] = the cloaking of ego around Knowing (Awareness). As ego extends away from its Knowing/Awareness source and, in an illusory way, manifests into life, it claims the manifestation as its own doing.

Reminder from last chapter: The ego consists of two parts: a real-piece (Self, Awareness) and an unreal-piece (all the adjuncts you mistake yourself to be). We are constantly adding unreal attributes to ourSelf. This can be expressed in the general sentence I am + adjunct; for example, I am tall, I am a librarian, I am a son/daughter, I love fishing, and so on. The 'I am' is real and the adjuncts are unreal. Via

Self-inquiry the unreal attributes fall away and only the real Reality remains — You: I am.

Essence Attributes

The Essence Attributes of Self will most likely be assumed by the ego as some sort of heightened, euphoric, elevated or exotic state of mind, but this is not the case. The Essence Attributes are more along the lines of a subtle-familiar-ordinary Presence of Being, with different understandings than you might at first think.

Also, what may be a bit disappointing at first for an ego to hear is that since there is no ego left after Self-realization, there is no individual present to 'conceptually know' that the beautiful essences of peace-happy-love are being expressed; they just happen genuinely and naturally on their own accord. Why might it be disappointing? Because there will not be a person to take credit for the 'doing' of these beautiful attributes, and egos don't like not being able to take the credit as the 'doer' of good deeds, and even of bad deeds for that matter.

The absence of a 'doer' is really the basis for knowing yourSelf, that is, acknowledging that by just Being yourSelf is Knowing yourSelf, because yourSelf is devoid of two; it is nondual. Since Being doesn't have to move away from itSelf to know itSelf, it therefore does not need a separate object involved to 'know' that it is being Being...it just organically 'Bes' by Being itSelf...the absolute truest form of selflessness and altruism.

> *They live in wisdom who see*
> *themselves in all and all in them,*
> *who have renounced every selfish desire*
> *and sense craving tormenting the Heart.*
> **Bhagavad Gita** (2:55)[5]

Inherent Qualities of the Structure:

Peace = unconditional acceptance. Self welcomes all of the manifestation with wide-open arms and zero resistance and conflict. You perceive the manifestation as You experience yourSelf. If You experience yourSelf AS peace, then the world must be THIS also. Peace is the absence of fear, since Self sees no threat or competition within the manifestation; that is, Self is not a threat to itSelf.

> *There is no fortune greater than peace;*
> *there is no force greater than peace;*
> *there is no excellent tapas [worship] greater than peace;*
> *there is no immortal life greater than [living in] peace.*
> **Sri Muruganar**[6,*]

Happy = wholeness, completeness, contentness, fulfillment and the absence of lack. When You ARE everything, You desire no-thing. Happiness is the absence of desire. Ever-present happiness is not located somewhere 'other than' yourSelf, and therefore searching and hoping to find it elsewhere is futile.

Love = the absence of separation between 'self and other,' that is, total unity; therefore love is the recognition of humanity's shared Being. Love is knowing yourSelf as others, and others as yourSelf. Love renders You incapable of hate, harm and exploitation and unable to be psychologically hurt; leaving only Love Outpouring.

Love is Peace-Happy's way of sharing itSelf. Peace-Happy could be considered your purpose (actionless) and Love your mission (action). Together you have Self manifesting as actionless-action (peace-happiness-love), and always never knowing anything 'other than' this: itSelf. You could say Love is Peace-Happy's foot soldier.

Even though Self may appear to have several different independent attributes, they are not separate from one another. Permanent + Knowing + Inherent Qualities is Oneness, as is Self. If either of the Permanent + Knowing attributes are removed, Self-realization is unattainable, and the Inherent Qualities of peace-happy-love cannot be known-inherently and/or experienced-directly.

Therefore, Self has these four primary descriptors, which all represent the same not-two (Oneness) message of nonduality:

Self = Existence-Consciousness-(Peace-Happy-Love)
Self = Being-Awareness-(Peace-Happy-Love)
Self = I AM-I-(Peace-Happy-Love)
Self = Heart-Knowingness-(Peace-Happy-Love)

In the teachings of Advaita Vedanta, the definition of *Atma-Swarupa* (One's true nature; Self) is known in Sanskrit terms as *Sat-Chit-Ananda*, where:

Sat = Existence or Being
Chit = Consciousness or Awareness
Ananda = Bliss [which is referred to above as Peace-Happy-Love]

Which then leads to:

Self = *Sat-Chit-Ananda*

which is antiquity's ultimate descriptor of the Truth of Existence (Totality). Self is not a void that is absent of any essence or quality; quite the contrary, Self is the soup of infinite possibility where all essences and qualities have existed for eternity, awaiting their turn to manifest.

Other non-objective essences

Self has another beautiful quality: no egoic attributes; that is, Self has no idea what gender, nationality, sexual identity, age, political party, race, status, and so on, are. Because Self is infinite it has no understanding of what these finite ideas and images are; it only knows others AS itSelf—beautiful-infiniteness. Knowing one's Self is humanity's solution to providing its own humanitarian and environmental relief programs. It is certainly a corporate Human Resource (HR) department's dream come true, especially in today's intensified world of diversity, equity/equality and inclusion (DE&I). An ego (mind) that has completely lost interest in its own self-interest IS Self, in which Self alone remains to serve itSelf: to serve the manifestation of the world and humanity, not to manipulate and destroy them.

> *When I understand myself, I understand you,*
> *and out of that understanding comes love.*
> **Jiddu Krishnamurti**[7]

> *I always thought that I was me—but no,*
> *I was you and never knew it.*
> **Rumi**[8]

The fear of death is also eliminated during Self-realization since that which appears to die, the ego, is seen merely as an illusion. How can a non-existent entity die when it never lived to begin with? The Self is ever-living: it never was born, never has lived and will never die. The Self is therefore said to be un-born, meaning it has existed for eternity.

No matter what descriptors you use to try and articulate Self, the bottom line is that your true nature, yourSelf, is brilliantly beautiful. Allowing yourself the courage to peek behind the illusory-cloak of the ego, even if for a moment, and to remember this beautiful brilliance is what you have been searching for since you unknowingly left it as a young child.

What will be most bewildering is when you realize just how much fear and resistance you had in confronting a non-existent entity, and just how much simpler life is without this ego-ghost.

So, follow the calling of yourSelf back home to yourSelf and know-inherently and experience-directly the warm unconditionally accepting nectar of the Grace of the Divine: yourSelf.

A letter written by yourSelf, from yourSelf, through yourSelf, to yourSelf

Remembering

Remember (verb): To bring an Awareness of something that one has always known—yet has only appeared to have forgotten.

Hello, my dear,

You have written yourSelf this letter to remind yourSelf of 'who You are.'
Simply put, You are unconditional love.
You are not the definition of love.
You are not the idea of love.
You are not some silly fabricated Hollywood unattainable love.
You are love itself...love is the fabric of your very Existence.
You know this more intimately than your deepest feelings and thoughts, yet most likely You have forgotten.

This Knowing of 'who you are' can't get any closer to You.

In fact, your love is so close that even the concept of 'knowing your love' moves you away from it...that is how interwoven your love is.

Love is yourSelf loving itSelf; yourSelf is love loving itSelf.

You are it, You are love...it is your very Being.

Perceive life from this loving-fabric and You will know happiness.

You, unconditional love, have beautiful qualities. You are boundless, whole, peaceful and complete...You have no lack. There is no before love, during love, or after love...love is eternal and infinite, and therefore, so are You.

You, love itSelf, are like the sun that never stops shining.

Only when clouds roll in and temporarily block the sun's rays does it seem the sun disappears, but in Reality the sun's rays never stop, they're only veiled.

This is like the love that lives AS You...your love's rays are constantly present, they only sometimes seem to be veiled by negative unwanted thoughts and emotions, but once remembered you can access your love again and again and again.

Your love's rays are forever available to rest into, like a mother cuddling her newborn child, ever-present and unconditionally accepting.

My dear, please do not get 'who You are' confused with 'what You are.'

Who You are is unconditional love.

What You are is all of your authentic actions and expressions that arise out of your love.

Whether you are a craftsman, manager, mother/father, designer, husband/wife, teacher or artist…these are but a few examples of how your love can express itSelf.

What You are is like a free-spirited wave that arises out of an ocean of love. A wave is free to express itSelf, but never separate from its source.

Therefore your purpose in life is to 'BE love' and 'share your love' with the world.

There is no effort required to serve your purpose. Only the willingness and courage to know yourSelf AS yourSelf.

In closing, this letter is a prompt, a tap on the shoulder, *to remember* to never forget; to never forget your origin of Being and to share what You find there.

You, my dear, are granting yourSelf your own permission to be You and to transform the world with the love of yourSelf.

Sincerely,

You

Notes

*   There are two notes to this verse that are worth stating:

> **Sri Muruganar:** What is here called peace is the state of stillness of mind. This can be achieved only by unceasing enquiry [Self-inquiry]. When the mind knows that in truth there is nothing to reject or accept, it will lose its movements and will abide in supreme peace. Since such peace is the seed of the natural state, it is therefore extolled as 'immortal life'.

Sri Ramana Maharshi: The golden crown that deserves to be worn by sadhus [Self-realized Beings] on their heads is only the tranquility that is peace. Through that noble virtue [peace] they will attain the benefit of a life that possesses the greatness of supreme bliss.

1   Matthew 6:22–23, Holy Bible, New Testament. The verse puts great importance on the depth of darkness that a dimmed spiritual eye can fall into. Placing too much focus on wealth or possessions, and not enough on the light of Self, can warp judgment. The passage implies that those who are so blinded do not even realize that they are in darkness.

4   Jerome "Jerry" John Garcia (1942–1995) was the lead guitarist for the rock band The Grateful Dead (The Dead). Over the course of The Dead's 30-year history they played over 2300 concerts, incorporating over 37,000 songs. What made The Dead so mysterious was they never played the same concert setlist twice, leaving their fans guessing as to what songs the next show would bring. The Dead graciously allowed fans to record their live concerts for free, stating that once the music was played it was the property of the fans to treasure and share openly.

5   Bhagavad Gita (The Song by God), a 700-verse Hindu text dating back to 200 BC, is revered as one of the holiest scriptures of Hinduism. The text covers Jñāna, Bhakti, Karma, and Raja yogas with an overarching theme of Self-realization, selfless service, wisdom and Truth. The setting of the Bhagavad Gita is a battlefield, which has been interpreted as an allegory for the ethical and moral struggles of human life.

Chapter 10

Sharing yourSelf with the World

Perplexing-wonder

Ego shaves the vibrancy-edges off of life, dulling life's inherent wonder and splendor, dampening the beauty of humanity and the world. Self reinstates life's vibrant-glory as Self-Consciousness re-recognizes its love for its own creation, and in doing so, falls deeper and deeper back in love with itSelf, evermore enhancing the vibrancy of the mystery of life. Self-realization eliminates the once muted ego-infused fragmentations of the manifestation, leaving only a spirited-shining, re-illuminating the wholeness that has always been, re-establishing a wondrous-sparkle to life that has not been witnessed since childhood.

So why is wonder experienced as Self is realized? Because You will inherently, and therefore non-conceptually, know that you (ego) did not 'do' the 'vibrant-glory.' That it was 'done' by something 'other than' you, something prior to you, something way more spectacular than an ego could ever envision.

The wonder experienced from Self-realization also contains within it a perplexing quality, a quality that may at first seem to be disparaging at face value, yet is somehow completely non-confusing and absolutely sane and comforting. This perplexing-wonder, also known as ever-present happiness, leads to a timeless consistent pondering of the mystery, without in any way interrupting or hindering daily life. It's as if, via Self-inquiry, you change out the infinite-loop of your agitated ego-mind for the ever-present perplexing-wonder of the clarity of your Heart.

The strangest part is that this perplexing-wonder is unavoidable and unintentional, since it is clear that there is no 'doer,' no ego, that did anything 'to make' a life of perplexing-wonder happen.

The perplexing-wonder is somehow mysteriously 'done' prior to and in the absence of the ego via the Self. This gets really bewildering and possibly upsetting for an ego, because the ego realizes that regardless of how hard it tries, it will never be able to conceptualize this, nor will it be the one that 'obtains and claims' this perplexing-wonder understanding. And furthering the bewilderment, the ego knows honestly and innately that perplexing-wonder, the mystery of Self, is and always has been the Truth of Reality.

Ego-free (Self) living is the real meaning of 'shining as yourSelf' and 'Being your Whole-Self, Authentic-Self and True-Self': your true nature. Your unbound-free Self sparkles the brightest, which creates the largest positive impact on those around you, and it does this effortlessly, since your shining-Self is unavoidably happening, inadvertently. Hence, non-conceptual unintentional happiness-sharing is your purpose in life; it is 'who You are.' The trick is to realize that to share yourSelf simply means to Be yourSelf; there are zero requirements beyond this effortless-action. Stated slightly differently, openly sharing yourSelf with the world is the unintended consequence of Being yourSelf.

As we let our own light shine,
we unconsciously give other people
permission to do the same.
Nelson Mandela[1]

Where the paradox of confusion comes into play for the ego is in how the mechanics of creation can be the way they are. It makes absolutely no sense to an ego that the most beautiful understandings and experiences arise only in the absence of itself. The ego says to itself, "Why is it, and how is it even possible, that when I surrender everything that I have taken myself to be and become no-thingness, I simultaneously obtain and become every-thingness? Damn!" It's because the ego refuses to see the simplicity of the situation. The reason the ego 'can't get there from here' is because it resists seeing that 'what remains' after its elimination is already 'here': yourSelf.

Another issue that frustrates and frightens the ego is acknowledging that if it does take the risk and surrender itself to Self, it can't know, prior to doing so, what changes will happen following its surrender. (For your self-assurance, there are no documented reports that Love Outpouring has found stating that anyone who has realized Oneness would prefer their agitated-ego-mind back.) In the response of Francis Lucille, an Advaita Vedanta teacher in southern California, regarding a question doubting the experience of Self-realization, he simply claimed: "You won't regret it."

Where your ego really has the ability to get fired up is when it hears that your greatest offering to the world is knowing yourSelf, which has absolutely nothing to do with itself. The ego will do everything in its power for you not to hear this very simple message. But this is the absolute case, that in the practice of Self-inquiry there is an inner-energy that is awakened and mysteriously changes the manifestation in inconceivable ways. By knowing yourSelf, everything just seems to fall into place without any effort on your part, thereby unintentionally positively-influencing those around you. Therefore, making the knowing of yourSelf your number one priority is the utmost goal to experience a life of peaceful-impact.

Aspirant: Master, what is the one thing that if known, all things will be known and all problems, fears and desires will no longer exist?

Master:[1] yourSelf.

(1) A Master is not someone who has acquired an overabundant amount of conceptual-knowledge. A Master is a Being who has completely emptied their mind of the multiplicity of conceptual-knowledge, leaving only an empty vessel of the One Self-knowledge (Jñāna).

Our purpose and mission

It seems that in recent years, heightened by the fallout of the Covid-19 pandemic, determining one's purpose and mission in life has become an elevated societal topic. Supposedly finding meaning in life, which is the underlying substance of purpose and mission, generates happiness and is the primary goal of a human being's life. YES!—happiness is the goal of life, but where we as a global community continue to go wrong is when we assume that it must be found in objects outside of and/or in things 'other than' ourSelf, which has led us to the current state of insane affairs we see in the world today. Happiness and its corresponding positive worldly impact is incredibly simple, and can be expressed as:

Purpose: Be and Know yourSelf (*Sat-Chit*)
Mission: Share yourSelf (*Ananda*)

Simply put, to experience ever-present happiness and to fulfill your purpose and mission in life is to: Be, Know and Share yourSelf; the purest form of love. Applying what was depicted earlier in this chapter: If sharing yourSelf is a consequential byproduct of Being and Knowing yourSelf, then by 'Being and Knowing your purpose' you automatically, and therefore unavoidably and unintentionally, serve your mission.

This is likened to understanding and being your Whole-Self, Authentic-Self and True-Self, discussed in Chapter 1. Just by Being yourSelf you unavoidably and unintentionally ARE Whole, Authentic and True. These traits are contained within Self, and therefore no additional work is required to become them because You already ARE them.

Our shared Being

Rupert Spira is a nonduality teacher who resides in Oxford, England. Rupert emphasizes classic Advaita Vedanta philosophy and is known in certain nonduality circles as one of the most enlightened Beings on the planet. His English demeanor brings an eloquence and simplicity to this message that cuts right to the Heart of one's Self, leaving attentive aspirants with clarity as to the true nature of Reality and who they are.

Rupert teaches a combination of Vedantic and Tantric Indian philosophy that gives a clear path to Being, Knowing and Sharing onesSelf with the world. He utilizes the Vedantic teachings, which he calls the inward path, to direct aspirants back to themSelf and he utilizes the Tantric teachings, which he calls the outward path, to accentuate the love that is expressed with others and the world once Self is realized.

One of the most beautiful inward/outward allegories Rupert communicates with regard to Being, Knowing and Sharing yourSelf with the world is: "When the journey **to** God ends, the journey **in** God begins." It goes something like this:

- The journey **to** God [Self-inquiry] is the inward-facing path. It is the tracing of your attention back from the objective content of your experience to God's Presence in your Heart.
- The journey **in** God [Self-sharing] is the outward-facing path. It is when the whole of your experience is permeated by God's Presence. This permeation is a transfiguration, where your entire experience is turned into the light

of God, where the 'Am'-ness of yourSelf is the 'Is'-ness of things/objects. It emphasizes the fact that the Being of all people, all animals and all things is the same shared Being.

Rupert's teachings are influenced by, and track right alongside of, the practices of Ramana Maharshi (Self-inquiry), Nisargadatta Maharaj (focus on 'I Am'), and Brother Lawrence (the Practice of the Presence of God). Experiencing Rupert's grace via his books, videos, podcasts and/or live retreats is highly encouraged.

Seeking wholeness

Where an ego falls short, duping itself into believing it is awesome and has everything under control, is when it takes its own actions, regardless of whether they are positive or not, as real unitive attempts to share itself with those around it. But as we experience time and time again within the cycles of an egoic life, our ego-actions and outcomes are only temporary and segmented futile gestures of sharing ourSelf in the hopes of obtaining permanent wholeness. This is why an ego can never be permanently satisfied, because it is constantly seeking wholeness in a world it only perceives as fragmented and divided. The ego does not have the capability to see Totality as one undivided whole, and thereby comprehends Reality as fractured and compartmentalized, which is the primary reason we see so much division and separation in the world today. As David Bohm, the renowned physicist and Nobel Prize recipient, stated in his book, *Wholeness and the Implicate Order*:

If he [humankind] thinks of the Totality as constituted of independent fragments, then that is how his mind will tend to operate, but if he can include everything coherently and harmoniously in an overall whole that is undivided, unbroken, and without a border then his mind will tend to move in a similar way, and from this will flow an orderly action within the whole.

The only way to transcend the ego fragmented-mind and unite with the undivided Totality of Self is to abandon the egoic-mind completely, so as to *flow within the orderly action within the whole*. This egoic-mind abandonment to experience wholeness is of course completed by Self-inquiry.

Love without otherness

We love what makes us happy, and since knowing ourSelf generates ever-present happiness, we therefore love knowing ourSelf. Knowing ourSelf is an inner-Self infinite-circle of unobstructed love-and-happiness. The more happiness we experience by knowing ourSelf, the more love we have to Self-inquire to experience happiness. The loving-Knowing of ourSelf is expressed in Advaita as the phrase: "Bhakti (love) is the mother of Jñāna (Self-knowledge)."

*The true path of Bhakti begins when
we are not seeking to gain anything from God [Self],
we are doing it just for the love of God.*
Michael James[2]

Over time, via Self-inquiry, we realize that we ourSelf have always been an internal infinite-loop of joy, and more importantly, that our inherent joy cannot be found or experienced anywhere else in the world, but only from directly within. The realization of Self-joy is the end of our suffering—which is continuously being acknowledged by us via our ever-present experience of unconditional love (Bhakti).

The undoubtable Knowing that we ARE unconditional love is solidified by the non-objective experience of Being ourSelf

AS ourSelf. It then dawns on us that since all we know is unconditional love, because all we know is ourSelf, then by logical deduction, everything known that is 'other than' ourSelf (the manifestation) must also be unconditional love. This understanding collapses the distance between Self and 'other than' Self into One; One-love.

Experiencing and innately-Knowing this One-love AS yourSelf is known in Advaita as 'Love without Otherness.' When you realize that in the One-Reality there is no 'other than' yourSelf, and that only love itSelf exists alone AS You, then You experience Love without Otherness.

The experience of yourSelf AS Love without Otherness is a supreme ineludible experience, for regardless of what the manifestation is presenting itself as, either favorable or not, all that you inherently-know and understand is the manifestation's underlying Reality of unconditional love: yourSelf. The experience of Love without Otherness is beyond words; it is the utmost mysterious, yet oddly ordinary and familiar, witnessing of perplexing-wonder ever imagined.

Shared by all

The longing to share ourSelf is inherent in all sentient creatures and runs throughout all great religions and spiritual traditions. If all 8 billion of us were asked a question regarding the one thing we want more in life than anything else, the answers would all relate back to being happy and to sharing that happiness with those around us.

This commonality of universal happiness-sharing and its beautiful worldly influences can be witnessed throughout the world by what would generally be considered opposing entities. This collective view of knowing and sharing yourSelf can't be more relevant than between what could be considered three of the most opposing religions in the world, Hinduism,

Judaism and Christianity, demonstrated by the statements of these admired Sages:

> *To remain in the state [of Self], having attained the supreme bliss,*
> *which is devoid of both bondage and liberation,*
> *is truly to be in the service of the Lord [world].*
> **Sri Ramana Maharshi** (Hindu)[3]

> *Whoever saves one life saves the entire world.*
> **Rav Ashi** (Jew)[4]

> *Sanctify yourSelf and you will sanctify society.*
> **Saint Francis of Assisi** (Christian)[5]

Sharing yourSelf with the world brings the brightest impact and greatest possibility of seeing and experiencing a world we all long to live in. The ego is incapable of dissolving the radical inequities and inequalities so innately woven into our cultural psyche. The only possible solution if we want to suppress further human and global degradation is to perceive Reality from a different vantage point—from a point of love and unity, not one of fear and separation; that is, by knowing and loving the world and humanity as intimately as we know and love ourSelf.

Society can't change itself

It should be apparent that globally we have huge societal and environmental issues on our hands. From species extinction, climate change, racial inequities, wealth inequalities and a pharmaceutical drug epidemic due to mental disorders (depression, anxiety, suicide, PTSD and so on), it is very obvious that if something radically sane doesn't happen to our current disparity trajectory, Earth may not be such a great place to live in soon. It is easy to see that we have lost our way, whereas we all deeply know, regardless of our individual positions in life, that life on planet Earth can be much more vibrant and way less violent.

What is your responsibility in a sick, insane society?
Jiddu Krishnamurti[6]

We need to remember that there are countless ways for a society to organize itself, and that we are witnessing but a few of them. Our current societal model only works well for a handful of people by continually decoupling the majority of us from what is sacred: each other. It is mind-boggling to see our world leaders utilizing the same economic/political/governmental systems over and over again and actually expecting them to improve the situation. Our current global growth paradigm is eating itself alive, and no one in power is actually doing anything significant to change it — which is maddening. Even Albert Einstein thought this madness in society was apparent over a hundred years ago when he expressed his insights in a letter to Heinrich Zangger on December 6, 1917:

> How is it at all possible that this culture-loving era could be so monstrously amoral? More and more I come to value charity and love of one's fellow being above everything else. All our lauded technological progress — our very civilization — is like the axe in the hand of the pathological criminal.

One significant solution to society's woes is to get out of mind (ego) and into Heart (Self). By first applying cutting-edge science — namely that Consciousness is the primary nature of Reality, not matter (discussed in Section 3) — we can rationally and logically educate society on the beautiful benefits of such a Reality. It is not hard to see, via the various inhumane ways we are encouraged by our institutions to treat each other and the Earth, that the world leadership brigade has gone verifiably insane. Showing humanity a logical path to global sanity would quench humankind's deepest desire of Peace on Earth.

The operations of converting from an ego-world to a Heart-world would slowly taper our exponential growth and consumption mindset into a world of abundant wholeness without the need to exploit people and planet in the process. This disruption for good cannot be a top-down approach; it can only arise from within and/or below, which could be what Jesus Christ meant by "The meek shall inherit the Earth."

Rupert Spira suggests replacing our current status quo paradigm of a matter-first model with a Consciousness-first model of Reality. This replacement of Reality models is, to Rupert, the easiest and most direct path to sanity, a view he expressed during an October 2020 online retreat:

> Can you imagine a culture in which the most substantial real and continuous elements of experience are systematically ignored? Imagine an alien culture that systematically ignored the most important real continuous intimate and alive aspect of their experience, we would think they were mad. Replacing the matter-model with a Consciousness-model is the direct path to peace and happiness.

To ensure a peaceful transition from humanity's current state of affairs to a future of health and sanity is the underlying reason why it is important for you to know yourSelf. To know yourSelf is to contribute to a nonviolent overthrow of a world gone mad. To do so, your purpose in life is to unintentionally radiate peace-happy-love through the effortless action of resting IN and AS yourSelf. Society does not have the capabilities or desire to make such a monstrous move of overthrowing itself, but You alone do.

Change in society is of secondary importance;
that will come about naturally, inevitably,
when you as a human being bring about the change in yourSelf.
Jiddu Krishnamurti[7]

So the paradox continues: By having no intentions to better our communities, societies and the world, via the expectationless, hopeless and desireless effortless-actions of knowing ourSelf, only then does a positive change in our surroundings miraculously somehow happen.

You ARE love (Bhakti)

It is important to remember that you don't have love, you never lost love, nor can you ever find love...it can only be Self-realized that you, yourSelf, ARE love. Any object 'other than' yourSelf does not contain a property called love that you have to obtain outside yourSelf, then add to yourself, to experience whole-love. You aren't a 'subject' of love that has a love-void that can only be filled with an 'object' of love. There is no such thing as a subject-object love bond; there is only the absence of ego, which expresses itSelf as One-love. One-love IS love loving itSelf, You loving yourSelf.

If I love mySelf, I love You.
If I love You, I love mySelf.
Rumi[8]

To see mySelf in everybody, and everybody in mySelf,
most certainly is love.
Sri Nisargadatta Maharaj[9]

It is only in the absence of separation, a collapse in distance between you and other, subject and object, that you realize that You ARE love. Love IS the subject of itSelf...and You ARE that subject. When you ARE love, you ARE whole and complete as well. Therefore, due to your inherent wholeness and completeness, there is no room left in you for 'other objects' to fit, which exemplifies what was expressed a few sections back: the experience of Love without Otherness; the ultimate experience of life.

By knowing yourSelf you lose your craving to want to know how and why it all happens as it does; for you are too enthralled by the mere fact that life is even happening at all. Yet in this apparent indifferentness, there is a continuous whisper coming from within yourSelf that is saying thank you, thank you, thank you—which you realize is a message from yourSelf to yourSelf thanking yourSelf for the unfathomable opportunity to experience such a perplexing-wondrous, beautiful mystery. And as bewildering as it may seem, all this grace happens from the sheer experience of re-establishing yourSelf AS what you have eternally been: nobody...only ever-present happiness.

Notes

1   Nelson Rolihlahla Mandela (1918–2013) was a South African anti-apartheid activist who served as the first president of South Africa from 1994 to 1999. His government focused on dismantling the legacy of apartheid by fostering racial reconciliation. Mandela was arrested and imprisoned in 1962 and sentenced to life imprisonment (serving 27 years) for conspiring to overthrow the state with nonviolent action. Globally, Nelson is regarded as an icon of democracy and social justice. In 1993 he received the Nobel Peace Prize.

4   Rav Ashi (AD 352–427) was a Babylonian Jewish rabbi of the sixth generation of Jewish scholars who preached

the teachings of the Oral Torah. He was the first editor of the Babylonian Talmud, the primary source, prior to the eighteenth century, of Jewish religious law, Jewish theology, and Jewish thought and aspirations.

SECTION 2

SELF-INVESTIGATION

Chapter 11

What Is Self-Investigation?

Our entire life has been an outward effort to become anything 'other than' ourSelf; to become loving, successful, accepted, liked and so on. This 'becoming other' appears to be the mechanics of evolution; the play of the manifestation. Regardless of what appears in front of us as life, we should cherish this dance of the manifestation (*Maya*) and marvel in its extraordinary display of imagination and detail. The manifestation, the dance of life appearing as 'other than' us, is so mesmerizing that we fall asleep to its bewildering beauty and mistakenly identify it as real. We then take ourself to be a separate real dancer among all the other apparently real objects, that is, as one of the dancers and/or actors within the dance itself.

> *You cannot change the dream from the dreamed-character [ego],*
> *you can only change the dream from the Dreamer [Self].*
> **Shakti Caterina Maggi**[1]

Believing we are a separate dancer within the manifestation, we unsuspectingly become fragmented (ignorant) from the wholeness of Self. This fragmentation, which is a companion of separation, is the restless feeling of 'longing to fill the hole of lack' we experience within, which ignites the 'personal' outward journey to become somebody. If we do not clearly see this hole for what it is, we will then attempt to fill it with more outward efforts of 'other than' ourSelf (relationships, substances, objects, adventures and so on). This hole will never be permanently filled with outward efforts. The only solution is to see yourSelf clearly, which comes from a Selfward, or inward, practice that relinquishes the efforts of the outward-forces and allows them to reside back into their source of You. This source of You is the nurturing experience of completeness and wholeness that you have been longing to return to your entire life.

The practice of seeing yourSelf clearly and experiencing peaceful-wholeness starts with truthful-knowledge (Jñāna) and ends in Self-investigation, which is likened to the lab portion of a university class, as was mentioned earlier in Chapter 5. There are many different ways to help dissolve false-knowledge, but by far, Self-investigation is the most important aspect of this entire journey; relentlessly turning your attention within to effortlessly abide in Self.

Self-investigation
(the relentless effortless attention to yourSelf that directly penetrates to your core of Being)

Relentless effortless attention is known as the Direct Path to Self-realization and is recognized in Advaita terms as Self-inquiry, Self-scrutiny or Self-investigation; permanent abidance in the Heart of Consciousness. More succinctly, Self-investigation is the absolute attentiveness to yourSelf, to such a point where yourSelf only recognizes and knows itSelf, thereby abandoning the ego and leaving You (Self) standing alone. Self-inquiry, Self-scrutiny or Self-investigation in Sanskrit is known as *Atma-Vichara*, where *Atma* means Self and *Vichara* means inquiry, scrutiny or investigation.

Self-inquiry could also be understood as the Self-embodiment of concepts; the movementless-mechanism for shifting concepts and ideas from the mind into a Knowing-sense of them in your Heart; that is, moving ego-thoughts (states of mind) into direct Self-knowledge (Way of Being). A concept such as 'peace,' something the mind thinks it wants to obtain and/or add to itself, is instead completely Self-embodied via Self-inquiry into your sense of Being. You realize through Self-inquiry that you did not become or add peace to yourSelf, but that You have always been peace; You inherently-know yourSelf AS the innate attributes of peace (unconditional acceptance, resistanceless, silent, stillness). Applying this to the concepts of love, happiness, wholeness, completeness and lacklessness, you begin to innately-recognize why Self-realization is so precious and leads to total Self-embodied contentment.

Self-inquiry, Self-scrutiny or Self-investigation empties your mind by relinquishing all the preconditioned false identities and ideas (ajñāna) you have about yourself so that you realize who you actually ARE and have always been. False identities are particles of the whole, which is the ego's way of keeping itself separated from Totality and in apparent existence. These false ego-identities 'control' whether you are happy or not, making happiness fleeting and always elsewhere in the future as an object to achieve or obtain. So once these false identities and ideas of yourself are relinquished, 'ego-control' dissolves and ever-present peace-happy-love is experienced naturally.

- Relinquish identifying as your bank account and witness your wealth of wellbeing grow ever greater—more than any king could amass.
- Relinquish identifying as your religion, spiritual/mystical and philosophical teachings and witness the Truth and the Divine grow ever closer.
- Relinquish identifying as your titles (boss/employee, father/mother, daughter/son, friend, husband/wife, etc.) and witness your relationships grow ever deeper.
- Relinquish identifying as your talents (athlete, strategist, musician, analyst, artist, etc.) and witness your skills become evermore refined.
- Relinquish identifying as your emotions (depressive, happy, sad, shame, lonely, anxious, joyful, etc.) and witness your true loving Self shine ever brighter.

Be careful here, for this is not saying that many of your life-attributes are not important; they are. Income, careers, aptitudes and feelings are what make for a vibrant life. Let these attributes be what they are, AS they are; just make the effortless-effort to release your identity from them (in Buddhism this is referred to as non-attachment) and experience life directly. This is where Self-inquiry comes into play and is so vital.

You don't become brain-dead, so to speak, as you empty your mind and Self is realized. You actually become much more aware of, connected to, yet free from whatever it is you are attending to in the manifestation. As ego becomes more and more transparent, life becomes more and more intimate, peaceful and loving, and you inherently-know this peace and love AS yourSelf (Being). This is the wondrous-mystery of life, and You ARE the mystery.

So whatever it is you do for a living—physician, priest, engineer, bus driver, politician, teacher, janitor and so on— Self-inquiry leads to Self-realization, which allows your true unobstructed light to shine through and exemplify your service to society and humanity as a whole. Being yourSelf AS yourSelf generates the most beneficial impact environment, where your largest positive influence on people and planet is possible. This is why your Self-realization is the greatest gift you can render the world.

The Direct Path

When you have eliminated the impossible,
whatever remains, however improbable, must be the Truth.
Sherlock Holmes[2]

The Direct Path is the practice of reversing and annihilating your inner tendencies that make you want to constantly move away from yourSelf; that is, the reversal of egoic-effort. These inner tendencies are known by you as the internal outward-forces of 'doing,' along with the ego who is the apparent 'doer' of these forces. The Direct Path is the relentless non-effort of subsiding the inner-forces of 'doing and doer' back into the childlike wonder of yourSelf, to be extinguished, so that only Self alone remains and shines.

Anyone who has any background in this topic knows that there is no delineated process to Self-realization. If there was, then it would most likely be in every religious and spiritual playbook on the planet. If any person or entity says they have a 10-step process to obtain the realization of eternal happiness, run the other way. Now, before you see the following numbered outline below and run the other way, let there be some explanation. The first few sections of the sequence below are actually Jñāna yoga. These Jñāna Self-inquiry sections are the starting gate to point you back to yourSelf by bringing to light what you are not; that is, to dissolve false-knowledge (ajñāna) so that only You (Jñāna) remain.

Because the Self has no objective qualities that can be known by the ego, the finite ego-mind can only take you so far with objective contemplation. Therefore the simplest, and typically the first, way to approach and experience Self is by negating what the Self is not, namely by nullifying all the objective attributes you have most likely mistaken yourself to be. This negation is through an elimination process known as *Neti Neti*, which means Not this, Not this.

Consciousness immerses itself fully into an apparent ego,
gets lost in it [forgets itSelf, ignorance], then slowly wakes up to itSelf
by knowing what it is not [Neti Neti].
Donald Hoffman[3]

Neti Neti can be considered your initial crossing of the manifestation-Existence barrier. This crossing is when you first encounter, and consciously experience, yourSelf directly by witnessing an inherent-Knowing of the difference between the familiar, yet unreal, ego and the foreign, yet real, Self. This could be expressed as your first direct taste of yourSelf.

But we cannot know what God [Self] is, only what He is not. We must therefore consider the ways in which God does not exist rather than the ways in which He does.
Saint Thomas Aquinas[4]

You cannot use ego to fully eliminate ego and therefore you have to convert to other non-ego means to complete the process. Since Neti Neti is ego based it can only take you so far in Self-discovery before having to shift ego elimination approaches.

[Using ego to eliminate ego is] likened to a thief turning himself into a policeman to catch the thief who is none other but himself.
Sri Ramana Maharshi[5]

Once it is clear what you are not via Neti Neti, you abandon the objective world of ego and enter the realm of the unnamable wonder: Awareness (Self). This unnamable realm is where the true effortless-effort of Self-investigation happens, or apparently happens. This is the continuation of the manifestation-Existence crossing and the part that is most likely new territory for you. What makes it foreign is the unfamiliarity of the practice of dis-assembling all the false-knowledge you have gathered over your lifetime, along with the concept of success without effort. You are familiar with assembling knowledge, but quite unfamiliar with dis-assembling it. There are no roadmaps or guideposts here, only the calling of your Self's love to know itSelf that is quietly whispering you back home to yourSelf. Utilize the tether of your ego-to-Heart string, the string that you have inherently-known since childhood, as the tether to gently guide your love back home to itSelf; to guide you back home to yourSelf.

Guiding yourSelf back home is done through the practice of Self-inquiry. Self-inquiry is the retracting of your attention, from the 'known-form' of ego back to the 'Knowing-formless' of Self. Once back, You will find the Self to be an empty location of silent-stillness; your Heart. Rest here and never leave.

As a reminder, an object is considered anything 'other than' yourSelf. The easy way to remember this is that if something is known, then it is an object. For instance: thoughts, sensations, material items, smells, feelings and so on are all known and therefore are objects. Because they are known, they are what the mind takes to be real. In contrast, because what we find at the source of Self is not an object, the ego-mind does not consider Self to be real and will do everything in its illusory-power to falsify its wondrous-beauty in the ego-mind's effort to have you never experience Self directly.

There are three main categories of objects: 1) mind, 2) body and 3) perceptions and their corresponding 'perceived' objects.

1. Mind consists of thoughts, memories, ideas and images.
2. Body consists of the physical body, feelings, emotions and sensations.
3. Perceptions consist of sight, hear, smell, taste and touch.

Mind and body are what you experience on the inside and perceptions are what you experience on the outside. Self-realization is when there is no perceived difference between inside and outside experience, which is recognized through the practices contained in this chapter.

Notice that the word 'meditation' is not used to define or label Self-inquiry. Meditation in Advaita is considered to be the progressive path to Self-realization, not the Direct Path. The progressive path uses techniques and approaches that are known to the ego and are therefore objects. Mind focus, thought control, breath work, *japa* (repeating of sacred names or syllables), mantras and chanting/humming are all objects that move you away from yourSelf and keep you fixated on something 'other than' yourSelf. Simply put, progressive meditation utilizes techniques 'other than' yourSelf. How can you expect to 'know yourSelf' directly if you are using 'other than' yourSelf techniques?

Progressive meditation can have great benefits for an ego who is looking for salvation, but you are trying to eliminate the ego, not improve it. The Direct Path is the retraction, or cessation, of the objective world back to the non-objective Self; therefore any progressive technique that keeps you in the objective world negates all your ego retraction efforts to experience your non-objective (subjective) Self. Meditation is an 'action of doing,' whereas Self-inquiry is the 'absence of doing'; that is, Self-inquiry is the 'cessation of effort,' in which 'Being' alone is experienced.

Racing, undesired thoughts are a hellish mental prison, the primary factor of all human suffering, and therefore significantly calming the mind in any way possible prior to the Direct Path is encouraged. Even though practices such as mindfulness, mantras, prayer, chanting or breathing techniques are progressive meditation movements away from yourSelf, they can have beneficial outcomes when soothing a monkey-mind. The most direct way to eliminate your mind (ego), so that only the Self alone remains, is to start with a relaxed one. But shortly after the progressive path has commenced, these objective techniques will need to be abandoned and the Direct Path initiated. Let it be clear, though: there is only one prerequisite for knowing yourSelf directly via the Direct Path: your love to know and experience the ever-lasting peace-happiness that lies within you.

The following outline of the Direct Path, starting with Neti Neti, is typically the Advaita process suggested for those who are new to this message. Once an understanding of Self has been witnessed by the aspirant via Neti Neti, then generally the first 14 sections are skipped as your understanding deepens and you are able to utilize the more direct practices of Self-inquiry. Remember, nothing is being asked of you that you cannot experience-directly and/or know-inherently. Therefore, only by trusting the true-knowledge you find within and allowing it to continuously erode false-knowledge will you witness the experience of infinite-eternity: yourSelf.

Neti Neti

1. In a quiet place of solitude, get comfortable, close your eyes and allow whatever is arising in your mind, body and perceptions to be as they are—sounds you might be hearing, thoughts of the workday, errands you need to run, the temperature in the room, what's for dinner, feelings you may be experiencing and so on; allow them to be as they are. Not that these are not important; it is just that we are not generally interested in them during this time of Self-investigation. And by no means try to control any of these thoughts, feelings and perceptions: again, just let them be as they are. At first, having a trusted friend or partner speak the following questions to you as you are in your relaxed state will be the most impactful. Over time, as you become more familiar with what exactly is being messaged here, you can practice without help.

2. Long pause...

3. Allow your mind to come to your attention. Notice the thoughts in your mind.

Ask yourself the question: "Are my thoughts aware of themselves, or am I aware of my thoughts?"

Let it be clearly witnessed by you (ego) that thoughts are not aware of themselves—it is You who is aware of them, making You THAT (Awareness) which is aware. Because thoughts are known by You, they fall into the definition of object; 'other than' You. Notice that for this to be true there needs to be some sort of apparent distance between You and thoughts; regardless of how minute the distance, there is still distance. You and thoughts are two distinct attributes: the Knowing (You, Awareness) and the known (thought). Do the same negation technique with your images, memories and ideas.

Conclusion: You are not your mind: thoughts, images, memories or ideas. You are THAT which is aware of your mind. Ponder the implications of this profound truthful discovery. You have just experienced-directly the immense-peace-silence that was described in Chapter 4, A Metaphor: Who You Are.

4. Long pause...

5. Now allow your body to come to your attention.

Ask yourself the question: "Is my body aware of itself, or am I aware of my body?"

Let it be clearly witnessed by you (ego) that a body is not aware of itself—it is You who is aware of it, making You THAT (Awareness) which is aware. Because your body is known by You, it also falls into the definition of object; 'other than' You. Notice that for this to be true there needs to be some sort of apparent distance between You and your body; regardless of how minute the distance, there is still distance. You and your body are two distinct attributes: the Knowing (You, Awareness) and the known (body). Do the same negation technique with your feelings, emotions and sensations.

Conclusion: You are not your body: physical body, feelings, emotions and sensations. You are THAT which is aware of your body. Ponder the implications of this profound truthful discovery.

6. Long pause...

7. Now allow your five perceptions (sight, hear, smell, taste and touch) to come to your attention.

Ask yourself the question: "Is my perception of sight aware of itself, or am I aware of my sight?"

Let it be clearly witnessed by you (ego) that sight is not aware of itself—it is You who is aware of it, making You THAT (Awareness) which is aware. Because sight is known by You, it also falls into the definition of object; 'other than' You. Notice that for this to be true there needs to be some sort of apparent distance between You and your sight; regardless of how minute the distance, there is still distance. You and your sight are two distinct attributes: the Knowing (You, Awareness) and the known (sight). Do the same negation technique with hear, smell, taste and touch.

Conclusion: You are not your perceptions: sight, hear, smell, taste and touch. You are THAT which is aware of them. Ponder the implications of this profound truthful discovery.

8. Long pause...

9. Turn your attention to the area within your body that you believe to be where your 'me' is located. 'Me' is generally observed as a cluster of vibrating sensations typically found in the head, throat or chest areas.

Ask yourself the following questions:

"What is it that is aware of these vibrating sensations I am associating as 'me'?"

Pause...

"And where is the Awareness located that is aware of these vibrations of 'me'?"

10. Long pause...

11. Notice that since the vibrating clusters of 'me' are known, they must be an object, and therefore something 'other than' yourSelf. Notice that Awareness has no location, You have no location, yet You-Awareness are fully present and permanently available.

Conclusion: Your 'me' is not You. These vibrating clusters of 'me' are what you have mistaken yourself to be all these years. Awareness IS yourSelf. You ARE Awareness, which is unlocatable...You-Awareness are simultaneously everywhere and nowhere.

12. Long pause...

13. Really ponder the implications of actually being THAT which is aware; the dimensionless, eternal and infinite

qualities of Awareness itSelf. This realization is a quantum leap of Self-understanding, a beautiful magical *sphurana*, which leaves You transparent without a center or a location. This understanding is total unity and contentment, everything you have been seeking your entire life.

Note: Relentlessly pursue the understanding of this until it becomes fairly clear as to what has been recognized here. Total pure understanding is not required to move further into Self-inquiry. The understanding and experiencing of these implications will become clearer and clearer as, over time, you rest deeper and deeper into Awareness: yourSelf.

14. Long pause...

Self-Inquiry*

Now that you have a firmer inherent-understanding of what Self is, you can abide in its depths of peace and happiness as it continually and refreshingly reveals itSelf to you as Divine-love.

> *Flow down, and down, and down;*
> *in always widening rings of Being.*
> **Rumi**[6]

Sections 15 through 17 are different direct methods of the practice of sinking deeper. Because we all have our own unique conditioning, we will all have our own unique ways of understanding and experiencing what it means to turn within and sink deeper. Take the following practices to be broad strokes that can be used concurrently or alone. They are more pointers than guides, since descriptions and words break down at this subtle level of Consciousness. No matter your method, the resultless-result is the same for all: Being-You.

15. To retract your ego back to its origin of Self, your sense of 'attention' is utilized. Remember that ego extends itself from its source (Self) into the manifestation of the ego-infused body, mind and world. The ego's path into apparent existence is from your chest realm (Heart) to your brain realm (mind). Retraction or retracing, which are other ways of saying sinking deeper, of attention is the effortless 'letting go' process of bringing the ego back from your brain area to its source of Self in your chest region, leaving an ego-free body, mind and world, which is another way of depicting that it leaves only Aware-Being. By retracting your attention from your mind to your Heart, you simultaneously retract the ego into Self. When you are very still, you can literally and subtly 'feel' a retraction sensation as attention (ego) retraces its path back from your head (mind) to your chest (Self) and disappears into the infinite.

   Try not to give your attention to the origin (Self) as an attempt to retract or retrace; you can only give your attention to an object, and Self is not an object. Witness retraction or retracing as walking your attention backwards until it sits in the source of itSelf. Once attention has been retracted back to its source of Self, clinging steadfastly to it at this placeless place (attention attending to itSelf at its source of Self) is alone sufficient to experience Self directly, even if just for a moment. Self is the direct-experience of the egoless Knowing of Being, your true nature.

   Once You are at the source of Self, you must relentlessly, yet effortlessly, be attentively Self-aware—meaning you must try without effort to focus your entire attention on yourSelf alone. Because Self is not an object, 'attentively' and 'attention' are forms of Being, not doing. You can't 'do' Self; you can only 'Be' Self. Rest here and just BE AS the source of attention (Self) and never leave. This is the foundational understanding of Self-inquiry.

The extending of ego into the manifestation of life could be likened to the stretching of a rubber band. A stretched rubber band does not need new energy put into it for it to return to its original relaxed form, just the relinquishing of the original energy that stretched it to begin with. The relinquishing of the original energy is another way of describing the effortless-effort to accomplish a goal (Wu Wei). This relaxing, relinquishing, retracing or retracting of ego is known in religious terms as the pull of the Divine Whisper or God's Grace back into its source of Self.

Pointer: Self-inquiry is learning to let go of the felt energetic-tensions of your internal outward-forces (relinquishing the stretched rubber band), thereby letting the energetic-tensions relax into their original energyless origin (Self), dispelling their power to move you away from yourSelf.

16. The thought "I am" is a direct portal to your 'sense of I' or 'sense of person'—your feeling of 'me.' This 'sense of I' is what the ego identifies with as the body, then claims this 'feeling' of 'sense of I' as being the real physical object of 'you.' Find your 'sense of I' by softly and intermittently repeating nonverbally to yourself "I am." Once located, take your 'felt-sense of I' back to its source (Self) by clinging on to it firmly with your attention and sinking effortlessly deeper with it. Hold it at the source of Self until it no longer has any impelling force to move away or any momentum to chase a thought. Effortlessly, yet relentlessly, abide in this thought-free 'sense of I' at its source of Self. Immersion of the subjective 'feeling of I' in Self dispels its outward-forces. When the 'felt-sense of I' is fully quenched of its outward-moving powers, the direct experience of Self arises.

As repeated from Section 15: Once You are at the source of Self, you must relentlessly, yet effortlessly, be attentively Self-aware—meaning you must try without effort to focus your entire attention on yourSelf alone. Because Self is not an object, 'attentively' and 'attention' are forms of Being, not doing. You can't 'do' Self; you can only 'Be' Self. Rest here and just BE AS the source of attention (Self) and never leave. This is the foundational understanding of Self-inquiry.

Note: Neti Neti leaves you standing alone AS Awareness, and sections 15 and 16 leave you standing alone AS Self. Awareness and Self are the same spaceless place, where love merges with itSelf and everlasting happiness is realized.

Awareness alone is 'I' [Self].
The nature of 'I'
is Sat-Chit-Ananda [Existence-Consciousness-Bliss].
Sri Ramana Maharshi[7]

17. Find a place within you that doesn't exist; that is, an empty inward space that is considered unreal to the ego, such as a void, vacuum, emptiness, darkness or nothingness. This place doesn't have to be located in your body; it can be anywhere in your field of Awareness. The reason for the unreal location is that at first you will have a tendency to use your ego to search your inner landscape of Awareness to find this non-existent unreal place of Self. Since the ego only knows objects, you have to use its own limited understanding and vernacular to describe this non-locatable unreal space you wish to locate (Self). This unreal place is not a total-void; it is not the absence of everything. It's literally the opposite: it is the present possibility of everything—Totality all queued up waiting to live. No matter how small or minute this unreal space

is, relax your attention into this nothingness, and never leave.

Let us understand well that this fellowship
with God [Knowing ThySelf]
happens in the depths of one's Being.
Brother Lawrence[8]

In Reality, what is non-existent and unreal to the ego is the Absolute nectar of yourSelf; the only thing (that is not a thing) that is real. YourSelf is the platform in which the manifestation is formulated, where the infinite potential for life sparks into existence. By effortlessly attending to this dimensionless non-existent unreal space it will gradually grow and grow until it becomes all of you; until it becomes You, and You become it; until it is known-inherently and experienced-directly that it has never not been You. This nothingness the ego calls unreal and non-existent is actually the only One-real existing space, which is permanent, Self-Knowing and Self-illuminating (the three definitions of 'real'). It will never leave You, betray You or not unconditionally love You. It is love loving itSelf, You loving yourSelf...the perfect lover.

Self-inquiry does not result in blissful experiences,
Self-inquiry results in the disappearance of the experiencer [ego].
David Godman[9]

The four practices above all have contained within them unique techniques for understanding how to embody the sense of Self, transfiguring yourself to You again.

1. Sections 1 through 14 (Neti Neti) separate ego from your Awareness of ego, pointing out that You ARE Awareness

itSelf. Ego, which is the lump sum of all 'objects,' is inherently witnessed to be 'seen' as somehow separate from You, giving You your first direct encounter of yourSelf alone.

2. Section 15 is the embodiment of effortless-effort and the concurring relentless pursuit of it. The retraction of your lifelong persistent outward effort-forces is extremely foreign and maybe even a tad bit frightening. You have come to mistake these outward-facing forces to be what gives you the ability to survive, and if you let them go you will not be able to defend yourself from others and the world. What you will come to understand is that being 'effortlessness' is a form of bodily transparency that is perceived by You to be unharmable, yet still complete and whole to preserve life; dissolving you back into the fearless-translucent warrior of Self.

Empty your mind, be formless.
Shapeless, like water.
Bruce Lee[10]

3. Section 16 is the understanding of why the ego 'feels' so real. The ego identifies as the "I am the body" sensation, establishes itself there, and claims it to be You, when it is actually just an illusory-thought of you. What you learned in Neti Neti allows you to see that sensations are objects and not yourSelf. As you hold on to this 'felt-sense of I' and sink deeper and deeper with it, the 'felt-sense' loses its potency, dissolving the outward-force powers, so that the Self alone remains.

4. Section 17 introduces you to what is real (existent) and unreal (non-existent) from the perspectives of the Self

and ego respectively. Existence is real and you know-inherently You are real because you know You exist (You ARE Self-existent). Because of Your Self-Existence, the infinite dimensionless place where Existence exists, but which the ego takes to be non-existent, it (the dimensionless place the ego considers unreal) has to be real. This is using the ego's false-understanding of Reality against itself to dissolve itself; the ultimate example of Jñāna-knowledge.

Vasanas

Inclinations, urges or tendencies to experience something, either outward or inward, are known in Sanskrit as *vasanas*. There are two types of vasanas: *vishaya-vasanas*, which are inclinations to experience all phenomena 'other than' yourself (outward), such as thoughts, feelings and perceptions; and *sat-vasana* which is the inclination to attend to yourSelf (inward). Therefore, sat-vasanas are our inclinations to Self-abide. Eradicating your vishaya-vasanas via Self-abidance leads to Self-realization.

Arising thoughts

If thoughts (vishaya-vasanas) arise during Self-inquiry, it means that Self-attentiveness is lost. Do not become agitated by thoughts or pursue them in any way. Instead, internally silently say: "Who is this 'I' that thinks?" Regardless of how many thoughts arise, continue to inquire with persistence, "Who is this 'I' that thinks?"

The ego (the one asking the question) falsely believes itself to be 'I' (Self) and will therefore obey its own command. The ego obeys itself and answers its own question ("Who is this 'I' that thinks?") by returning to its source of Self to find the answer, and the thought that arose will follow along with it and become immersed and deactivated in the Self. By repeating this question as thoughts arise, the ego (mind) will learn to remain in the source of Self. Regard your thoughts as positive reinforcements that point you back to yourSelf instead of pesky nuisances deterring you from realizing happiness.

Other internal vishaya-vasanas that may arise can be deactivated by the same questioning sequence, such as:

"Who is this 'I' that's *bored*?"
"Who is this 'I' that *fears*?"
"Who is this 'I' that *aches*?"
"Who is this 'I' that *doubts*?"
"Who is this 'I' that _____ *(fill in the blank)*?"

Because of the unique conditioning of each of us, we each may have our own unique vishaya-vasanas that arise and need to be dismantled. Fill in the blank as needed to abide and experience Self directly.

Self-body-bond

Even though you may be well established in knowing yourSelf as yourSelf by practicing Self-inquiry, you still may have a subtle sense of "I am the body" that is undetectable to the ego. This Self-body-bond is the last thread to be broken to achieve Absolute Self-realization. It can only be broken by relentlessly holding your attention at its source of Self (also known as Self-abidance) until the bond is severed and Self alone remains. The Self-body-bond, known in Advaita as *chit-jada-granthi* (Consciousness-body-knot), is only severed by the love of Divine Grace (the Divine Grace of Self). Since it is seen clearly that at this subtle level of Consciousness no ego remains, only Grace alone is left to make this egoless effortless-effort. When the knot is untied, ego never rises again, and Self alone remains. Experiencing Self alone is the epitome of Advaita, not-two, One without a second. At this foundation of Consciousness there is no separation, and therefore it is the end of all psychological and emotional suffering.

What appears to happen (at the core of Being nothing is actually happening) at the subtlest depths of Self is that the *chit-jada-granthi* wanders, without movement, in and out of being tied. At some point, what remains after the granthi is untied is what has always been: permanent complete immaculate loving beauty and perfection: Knowing-Being; You.

But to be fair to this Divine essence of Knowing-Being, words lack the complete ability to authentically describe Her/Him/Us. You can only know-inherently and experience-directly Her/Him/Us; meaning You can only Be Her/Him/Us Knowingly.

Other ways to put descriptors around Knowing-Being are:

- I Am what Knowing IS
- What I Am Knowing IS
- Self-embodiment of Knowing-Being
- Knowing, Knowing itSelf AS Knowing
- I Am Knowing I Am
- Bliss-Joy-Peace-Love-Happiness

The more often, both in the number of times per day and longevity, you visit (rest into) this innate placeless-place of Being, the more you realize that it is actually You. You are a warm welcome to yourSelf, comforting yourSelf as yourSelf. You realize that this warm welcome is your actual real home, to which You gradually move in, make it your residence, and take it with you wherever you go. The frustration to the ego is that it can never choose to make the choice to untie the granthi and permanently move in or not; the choice is made by Self (Grace). Either partially moved in or permanently, the paradox will then be clearly seen that You never actually left home to begin with;

you have only mistaken yourself to be something you were not, as in the snake and the rope metaphor depicted in Chapter 8.

> *To begin with, it seems like an effort to keep*
> *returning to the welcoming Presence [of Self],*
> *but at some point it is so natural that it seems to*
> *require an effort to leave it. It feels like home.*
> *We no longer feel that we need to be entertained.*
> **Francis Lucille**[11]

Daily practice

By no means is the practice of Self-inquiry, or any content of the perennial message, meant to deter you from everyday life; it is meant to exemplify the beauty of life unfiltered. Self-inquiry was not originally conceived as a traditional sitting meditation-like practice, nor was it meant for you to give up any other worldly obligations you might have. It has been witnessed that sitting quietly with your eyes closed to practice Self-inquiry delivers a relatively quick understanding of Self, but it is not a requirement. You can practice Self-inquiry any time of the day as long as your mind is not performing any outward tasking, such as tending to work or family. Anytime you have any free time, turn your attention inward, back to the solitude of yourSelf.

Pointer: Whenever you have idle time throughout the day, ask yourself the question, "Who Am I?" This will effortlessly redirect your attention back to yourSelf. You will notice a subtle sense of change and relaxation arising from within. Repeat this a few times, then relax and attentively hold on to the warming-peace of yourSelf, and be perplexed by its wondrous-aweness.

Pointer: The moment you wake up in the morning, as quickly as you can remember, ask yourSelf the question a few times,

"Who Am I?" This will not allow your ego to rise as abruptly, giving you the best start to the day as possible.

You have several hours in your day when your mind is not tasking—eating, walking, resting, exercising and so on—that you can spend tending to yourSelf by turning your attention inward. It is suggested to relentlessly pursue the effortlessness of Self in Self-inquiry in a quiet place with your eyes closed as much as possible, as well as tending to it in everyday life. The more you abide in Self, the sooner the Self is realized (either partially or permanently), at which point You then take your Being-Aware-Happy Self with You wherever you go.

Due to the mysterious inner workings of the realms encountered during the practice of the Direct Path, you are advised to never judge your experiences of Self-inquiry. There may be times you feel your Self-inquiry session did not accomplish anything, and so you may want to judge them as a waste of time. The infinite-Self works in beautiful mysterious ways. Our limited egos do not have an inkling as to how Self works its magic. What may seem to be an unsuccessful Self-inquiry session could be exactly the experience the Self had intended for you to advance down the path to Self-realization. Regardless of what you think you experienced, love your Self-investigations when they appear to be uneventful, and love them when they appear to be One-with-God.

Running the show

So, what runs the 'life show' after Self-realization if ego is not in charge anymore? The answer is: the same energy-force that has ever run it, is currently running it, and will ever continue to run it. The same energy-force that is pumping your heart, regulating your body temperature, creating quarks and keeping our solar system in orbit around the sun…this energy-force is yourSelf. Life does not need an ego for it to happen. So relax as you come into alignment with the One-Reality and witness yourSelf run the show. Life is Self-running, Self-manifesting, Self-illuminating.

> *Before enlightenment chop wood, carry water.*
> *After enlightenment chop wood, carry water.*
> **Zen proverb**[12]

Either partially moved in or permanently, You will remain calling yourSelf 'I' or 'I Am.' Anything that is aware of itSelf calls itSelf 'I.' The moon is not aware of itself and therefore does not call itself 'I.' A tree is not aware of itself and therefore does not call itself 'I.' A dog is not aware of itself and therefore does not call itself 'I.' You are aware of yourSelf; Your very nature is Knowing-Awareness. You ARE, and You are aware that You ARE. Therefore, You (your character in the dance) call yourSelf or refer to yourSelf as 'I' or 'I Am.' 'I' or 'I Am' are intrinsic words that refer back to themSelf; they preposition themSelf as themSelf. In other words they are non-objective words, as in the example of: yourSelf knowing itsSelf AS itsSelf, in which there is no object and therefore only pure-subject. Daily communication with others still happens; it's just that you lose the ability to identify as your adjuncts, since all that remains is the knowing of yourSelf: I Am.

Physical phenomena

As the ego sinks back into its source via Self-inquiry, which divests the ego of its internal contractions (vishaya-vasanas), an internal platform of expansive space gradually appears. This divesting is not completed with new efforts. It is the relaxation of the prior effort that led to the internal contractions in the first place (as described in the rubber band example). As the ego is introduced to its new environment of expansion, the body itself then experiences a sense of physical expansion, becoming less dense, less contracted, freeing up space to release lifelong tensions (fears, stress, trauma and so on) you have built up within you.

Pointer: Take for example the relaxed state of your jaw. As you close your jaw you exert effort to do so. The harder and harder you clench, the more and more effort is exerted. Returning your jaw to its previous relaxed state does not require a new effort; it is just the relaxing, the divesting, the rescinding, of the previous efforts. No new efforts were needed to obtain, gain or achieve the original state. This is another depiction of effortless-action (Wu Wei).

An exothermic reaction is when heat is released during the reaction from the breaking of the reactants' bonds.† An exothermic reaction is likened to the internal expansion experienced from Self-inquiry, where you are likely to experience physical phenomena, such as rushes of heat being generated by the body. Flashes of light could appear suddenly or gradually while your eyes are closed. Physical jerking, jolting and twitching can be witnessed as large surges of tension-energy are released from their once stored cavernous hideaways. If these are experienced let them be as they are, for it is part of the process for some.

This felt experience of the internal witnessing of what it means for a body of mass to expand and become less dense could be affiliated with the actual physical experience of bridging the manifestation-Existence barrier; the distance between the finite and the infinite, the universal difference between misery and happiness. If you currently identify as an independent condensed body of matter (ego), how awesome it is to experience your own dissolution of constriction back into the expanded eternal infinite loving Being you have always been!

Notes

*   The basis of Self-inquiry is from the quintessential book, *Who Am I?*, by Sri Ramana Maharshi.

†   There are also connections to the Ideal Gas Law, which states that as the volume of a gas increases, that is, becomes less dense, the temperature within the gas system increases: PV=T. As P is held constant and V increases, so must T increase.

1   Shakti Caterina Maggi is a spiritual guide and author. Shakti is known internationally as one of the most authentic and profound voices in contemporary spirituality. Presenting the message of Advaita and nondual Tantra, Shakti offers, with compassion and great clarity, an inner technology for dissolving the contraction of suffering that traditionally accompanies each of our lives. Her invitation is to come to the space of inner peace and unconditional love which resides in the Heart of us all.

2   Sherlock Holmes is a fictional detective created by British author Sir Arthur Conan Doyle. Holmes is known for his proficiency with observation, deduction, forensic science and logical reasoning that borders on the fantastic, which he employs when investigating cases for a wide variety of clients.

3   Donald Hoffman is a professor of Cognitive Sciences at the University of California, Irvine (UC Irvine). Hoffman's most recent contribution to the study and understanding of Consciousness is in his 2019 book entitled *The Case Against Reality: Why Evolution Hid the Truth from Our Eyes*. He is of the understanding that the spiritual traditions are correct in their profound understanding that we are not separate Beings from one another, but unified universal love, of

which he gets personal glimpses when he is in a space of no-thought. There is an entire section in Chapter 13 dedicated to Professor Hoffman.

9   David Godman has spent most of his adulthood writing on the life, teachings and disciples of Sri Ramana Maharshi. In the last 30 years Godman has written or edited 16 books on topics related to Sri Ramana and his followers. According to Godman, with respect to encountering Sri Ramana's teachings, it wasn't that he had found a new set of ideas to believe in; it was more of an experience in which he was pulled into a state of silence.

10 Bruce Lee (1940–1973) was a Hong Kong and American martial artist, martial arts instructor, actor and philosopher. He was the founder of Jeet Kune Do, a hybrid martial arts philosophy, and is considered to be the most influential martial artist of all time. Bruce believed that any knowledge ultimately led to Self-knowledge, and said that his chosen method of Self-expression was martial arts. His influences included Taoism, Jiddu Krishnamurti and Buddhism.

SECTION 3

SELF-POINTERS

Chapter 12

What Is the Mysterious Wonder of Awe?

Have you ever peered into the vastness of the Grand Canyon, gazed into the everlasting reaches of a dark starry night sky, or witnessed an unimaginable human creation such as the Great Pyramid of Giza or the Great Wall of China and marveled in wonder and astonishment how it possibly could be so? If yes, then you have experienced the emotion of awe.

When the mind is in a state of profound awe there is a brief, yet eternal, mental pause. This momentary pause is the absence of time and space itself, in which a brief moment of experiencing one's true boundless nature arises. This true nature has the qualities of being ever-present, timeless, spaceless, undivided, present and aware. This timeless pause that reveals our true nature is the gateway to realizing the affinity and vastness of ourSelf and the human potential...it is a peek into the borderless space of Consciousness itself.

It is in this moment of encountering Consciousness that you are available to see other possibilities and are more open to witnessing the infinite potential of all that is possible. The higher the occurrences of awe-inspiring knowledge and experiences, the higher the probability there will be for you to see Reality for what it really is, undivided-eternal-infinite-connected, and shift your outward actions inward (Selfward) to reflect the unconditional love you have come to know from experiencing the Conscious-infinite.

The most beautiful thing we can experience is the mysterious.
It is the source of all true art and science.
He to whom the emotion is a stranger,
who can no longer pause to wonder and stand wrapped in awe,
is as good as dead; his eyes are closed.
Albert Einstein[1]

According to a 2018 white paper entitled 'The Science of Awe,' produced by Greater Good Science Center at UC Berkeley, awe experiences are altered states of Consciousness that bring about the sensation of self-transcendence. Awe shifts our attention away from our egos, momentarily revealing our true Self, which makes us feel like we are part of something greater than ourselves; more connected and less separate from objects and others around us.

Psychologists Dacher Keltner and Jonathan Haidt, in their research paper titled 'Approaching Awe: A Moral, Spiritual, and Aesthetic Emotion,' suggest that awe experiences are characterized by the combination of two phenomena: 1) the perception of vastness, and 2) the need for mental accommodation to comprehend the vastness. The perception of vastness, especially unsolicited, violates our understanding of the world, which can create a stimulus that exceeds our mental capabilities and expectations. These newly created stimuli can provoke permanent psychological change in such a way that our perception of the world shifts or expands in order to make sense of this new experience. Awe experiences actually cause us to question reality, which forces us to revise our understanding of the world with the answers we find.

The following five AWE-ers are profound facts that have the intention of defying what you typically would perceive as logical and real. They are meant to create an environment of internal vastness that shifts your preconditioned reality into a newly open space where you are more open to investigate the nature of the infinite; the nature of yourSelf.

The goal of the AWE-ers is to unsuspectingly seep into the unwilling aspects of your conditioning and gently expand them, in the same way as water that has seeped into cracks of rock breaks the rock apart as the water turns to ice and expands, acting as catalysts for exploring yourSelf further. Self-realization is when the mind becomes so awestruck and in love with wonder that it buckles and collapses under its own aweness-weight.

The AWE-ers could be interpreted as another form of Jñāna-knowledge, where the content contained in this chapter is an attempt to relax your ego-mind enough for it to be willing to curiously dissolve itself back into its source of Self, leaving only You.

AWE-er 1: Who is the real problem-solver?

In 2009 a study led by Bhavin R. Sheth PhD, a doctor of cognitive neuroscience at the University of Houston, titled 'Posterior Beta and Anterior Gamma Oscillations Predict Cognitive Insight,' concluded that we (ego) do not solve our problems as presented to us spontaneously when life randomly introduces them to us. Our problems are solved 'off-line' in the back of the brain approximately 6 to 8 seconds before the answer (in the form of electrical stimuli) is moved to the front of the brain and registered in the prefrontal cortex, at which point we (ego) say, "I've solved the problem."

The report concluded with 100% predictability* that problem solving formulated in the brain and the concurring results happen up to 8 seconds prior to the ego becoming conscious of the answer and claiming it as its own. According to the report, "Problems are solved through an insight, a quantum leap of understanding with no conscious forewarning, [when someone] moves from a state of not knowing how to solve a problem to a state of knowing how to solve it."

A quantum leap is a jump in perception from one state of understanding to another. Scientists can observe each state independently, but the jump (the space between the two states) itself cannot be witnessed. The 'space' of the leap does not conform to physical reality as we know it and therefore cannot be measured or cognized. It is in the space of the leap that the solution to the answer is solved, which is a complete mystery to scientists.

> *There comes a point where the mind takes a leap*
> *– call it intuition [Self] or what you will –*
> *and comes out upon a higher plane of knowledge,*
> *but can never prove how it got there.*
> **Albert Einstein[2]**

If the mystery of Consciousness is solving our problems for us, then that means we (ego) aren't the problem solver, that is, the ego is not the 'doer and decider' of our life. Could it be we have mistaken ourself as something 'other than' ourSelf and ARE actually the mystery, the quantum leap, ourSelf?

AWE-er 2: Is matter a fact?

Well, as a matter of fact, no, matter is not a fact! Matter has never been found, nor will it ever be found. As of today, there is not one shred of evidence that proves anything physical exists independently from anything else.

> *As a man who has devoted his whole life*
> *to the most clear headed science, to the study of matter,*
> *I can tell you as a result of my research*
> *about the atoms this much: There is no matter as such!*
> **Max Planck[3]**

From a conventional point of view, matter is a physical substance that occupies space and possesses mass, and is distinct from energy, mind and Consciousness. But as we investigate the underlying Reality of matter, matter itself becomes something 'other than' its apparent self.

According to Bernardo Kastrup, a former scientist at CERN (European Organization for Nuclear Research), the 17-mile-circumferenced Large Hadron Collider in Switzerland:

> If you look deep enough into the Heart of matter, all concreteness vanishes, and what is left is a pure mathematical abstraction that we call fields—quantum fields. And what is a quantum field? A quantum field is a mathematical tool which is postulated because the world behaves as if it exists. But that doesn't mean that people at CERN have actually found a quantum field or touched one.
> —'Mind Over Matter,' *Beshara Magazine*, Issue 18, 2021

No existence

We have been led to believe that everything physical in our perception, that is, all inert matter, is to be taken 'for what it is' at face value. Therefore, without question, a tree is a tree, a chair is a chair and a body is a body: they are all stand-alone independent objects that exist entirely as themselves. Yet as we start to dissect the underlying nature of each component of these objects, the original component being analyzed loses its apparent single reality and therefore cannot stand and exist independently.

A tree for example:

The underlying reality of *a limb is wood* >

The underlying reality of *wood is carbohydrates* >

The underlying reality of *carbohydrates is carbon, hydrogen and oxygen* >

The underlying reality of *carbon, hydrogen and oxygen is electrons and neutrinos* >

The underlying reality of *electrons and neutrinos is mesons and baryons* >

The underlying reality of *mesons and baryons is quarks and gluons* >

The underlying reality of *quarks and gluons are bosons* >

The underlying reality of *bosons is a Higgs boson* >

The underlying reality of *a Higgs boson is dark matter* >

The underlying reality of *dark matter is dark energy* >

The underlying reality of *dark energy is no-thing (see below)*

...and therefore the true underlying Reality of any and all physical substance is no-thing, which has no physical stand-alone existence of its own.

Not one of the single attributes of the tree has its own independent existence that does not rely on something else for its existence. Every 'thing' relies on the underlying existence of the prior 'thing' until there is 'no-thing' at all. Stated differently, all objects borrow their apparent existence from their prior building block, which borrows its apparent existence from its prior building block, and so on...including the object of 'you.'

> *So what quantum physics is telling us is that*
> *matter has no stand-alone reality.*
> **Bernardo Kastrup**[4]

Stated directly, all physical matter in the cosmos is apparently 'something' that has arisen out of 'no-thing'...the origin of paradox (the origin of perplexing awe!).

Planck time

The Planck time constant is 10^{-43} seconds, or:

0.000,000,000,000,000,000,000,000,000,000,000,000,000,000,1 seconds

That is how far back in time scientists like Stephen Hawking, the famous cosmologist from the University of Cambridge, have been able to look back, via the reversal of chemical reactions, thermodynamics and general relativity mathematics/physics, to try and locate the origin of matter, that is, the components of the Big Bang. But this massively large timeframe (from now back to 10^{-43} seconds, which is equivalent to 13.8 billion years ago) is still not far enough back in time, and there is no evidence to determine whether or not physicists are even close to reaching their goal. In reality, the scientific world will never find the origin of the Big Bang since chemistry and physics break down to such a subtle level prior to Planck time that linear time is incalculable. The origin of the mystery of Existence will never allow itSelf to be known conceptually (ego, mind), only inherently (Self, Heart).

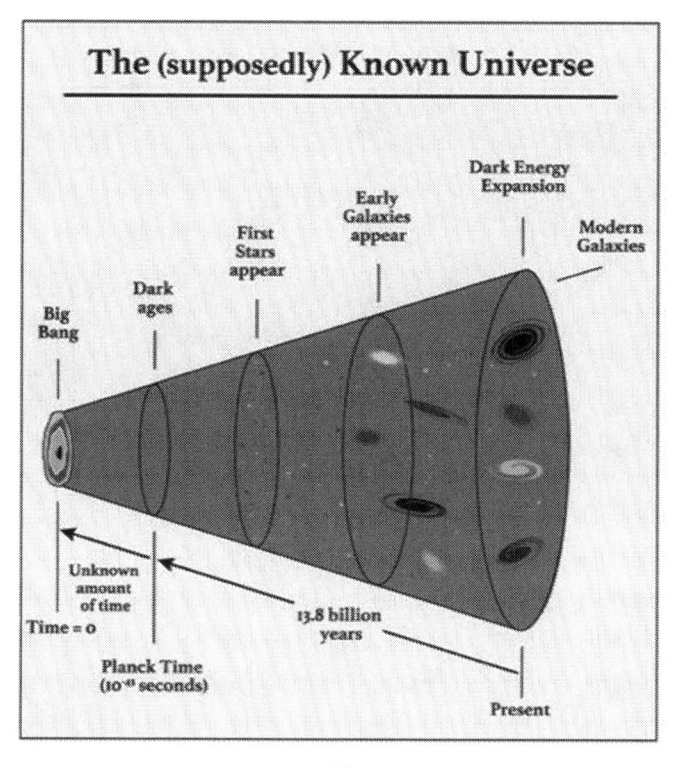

The (supposedly) Known Universe

Dark Energy Expansion

Early Galaxies appear

First Stars appear

Modern Galaxies

Dark ages

Big Bang

Unknown amount of time

Time = 0

13.8 billion years

Planck Time (10^{-43} seconds)

Present

In the unknown amount of time after the Big Bang and prior to Planck time starting (between the theoretical starting point of the Big Bang at time = 0 to 10^{-43} seconds after the Big Bang), the universe consisted of substances (which still exist today) labeled by physicists as dark matter and dark energy.

According to the CERN website:

> Astronomical and physical calculations suggest that the visible universe [matter] is only a tiny amount (4%) of what the universe is actually made of. A very large fraction of the universe, in fact 26%, is made of an *unknown* type of matter called "dark matter".

The CERN website continues:

> An even more mysterious form of energy called "dark energy" accounts for about 70% of the mass-energy content of the universe. Even less is known about it than dark matter. This idea stems from the observation that all galaxies seem to be receding from each other at an accelerating pace, implying that some *invisible extra energy* is at work.

Could this "invisible extra energy," which can't be located, measured or witnessed, be the true origin, namely pure-Consciousness (dark energy), of the manifested matter we perceive as the world/universe today that has not yet collapsed into apparent physical finite perceivable matter?

Volumeless matter

According to the website Nature, the mass of the knowable universe is 4^{52} pounds, or:

40,000,000,000,000,000,000,000,000,000,000,000,000,000,0
00,000,000 lb

And according to Stephen Hawking, extrapolating the expansion of the universe backwards in time, this yields an infinite density and temperature of the components of the Big Bang.

The density of matter is calculated by its mass divided by its volume ($d = m/v$). Because the density and mass of the components of the Big Bang are known, its volume can be calculated ($v = m/d$, $4^{52}/\infty$), which equates to a value of zero. This is a bit bewildering. According to some of the most intelligent people to have ever walked the planet, the 4^{52} pounds of substance which the Big Bang consisted of had no volume, that is, no space, yet was infinitely hot (what was 'there' to be hot?!). Yet our 4^{52} pound universe today consists of the volumeless-matter that was contained in the no-space of the Big Bang...a head scratcher.

Again, how is it that 'something' (our universe) arose out of 'no-thing' (Big Bang)? And again, how perplexingly wondrous!

Quick Jñāna-pointer: Get comfortable with the fact that you can't, and don't, know anything with absolute certainty (except yourSelf). Since matter has never been found, how can you know what anything really is? You can't.

You can label things like you do, but that doesn't mean the object actually is what you label it. You can call a horse a horse or a table a table, but these labels don't make them a horse or a table. How could they, if the brightest scientific minds in history have never found an independently existing horse or table?

There is only One non-thing that is known for absolute certainty: Your aware-Existence. Any label you try to place on it falls completely short. So just learn to let 'things' be as they are, as You ARE.

AWE-er 3: The Hard Problem of Consciousness

We have been conditioned our entire life to believe that approximately 14 billion years ago an unprecedented physical event happened known as the Big Bang, which formed the matter, stars, planets and galaxies of the cosmos, with the most familiar being our beloved planet Earth. Over millions of years of evolution, life crawled out of Earth's ooze, and eventually the human brain developed and corresponding life was created. Then, once our advanced matter-based brain was formulated, Consciousness spawned from our brain, giving rise to human Conscious-Awareness.

This matter-based prototype of creation, in which Consciousness is an afterthought of matter, is known in our materialistic Western culture as the 'matter-first' model of manifestation (also known as mainstream physicalism) and is the current prominent scientific paradigm of reality. Once again, though, there is absolutely no evidence from the scientific community to substantiate this matter-first paradigm, yet it is the model of reality that most of the world operates within.

To consider Consciousness an emergent property of brains
is either an appeal to magic or the mere labeling of an unknown.
In both cases, precisely nothing is actually explained.
Bernardo Kastrup[5]

In the realm of quantum physics and neuroscience lies what is known as 'the Hard Problem of Consciousness,' which seeks to answer the question, "How does Consciousness arise out of matter?" Scientists have absolutely no idea and have zero credible evidence for how Consciousness arises out of matter, yet most (but the tides are turning) refuse to acknowledge that maybe it doesn't, that maybe, instead, matter arises out of

Consciousness. And since we humans appear to be constructed of matter, this would apply to us as well.

Donald Hoffman PhD is a professor of Cognitive Sciences at the University of California, Irvine. In his 2019 book, *The Case Against Reality*, Professor Hoffman dares us to question everything we think we know about the physical world we see.

In his book, Hoffman states, "We [the scientific community] have no scientific theories that explain how brain activity [matter] — or computer activity, or any other kind of physical activity — could cause, or be, or somehow give rise to, conscious experience. We don't have even one idea that's remotely plausible."

Taking Professor Hoffman's investigative findings to be credible and accurate, namely that humans have a misguided false belief system with respect to how we understand and perceive our surroundings, we then conclude that the perceived world as we know it is only a false abstract representation of its true underlying Reality.

Could it be that the matter-first model is not the correct representation of Reality? By utilizing our own direct experience of ourSelf as our basis of Reality, we have a clear path back to the origin of Consciousness via Self-investigation. This clear path quickly delivers us to our own Existence of Consciousness, which we can logically and rationally experience-directly and know-inherently. Direct witnessing of our own Consciousness (Self) confirms a Consciousness-first model of Reality, which is the basis of the nondual perennial message.

The only solution to this conflict
[the Hard Problem of Consciousness],
insofar as any is available to us at all, lies in the
ancient wisdom of the Upanishads [Hindu Vedic texts].
Erwin Schrodinger[6]

The Hard Problem of Consciousness was first postulated by David Chalmers in his 1995 paper, 'Facing Up to the Problem of Consciousness,' and followed up in his 1996 book, *The Conscious Mind*. Chalmers claims that physical properties of matter do not correlate to mental properties of human experience, and therefore materialism and physicalism must be false, and Consciousness must be a fundamental fact of nature.

> *What we need to do is to take conscious experience*
> *itself as primitive, as a fundamental element of the world.*
> **David Chalmers**[7]

The unsolvable solution to the Hard Problem, in Chalmers' point of view, lies with the struggle to logically answer the 'why' and 'how' processes of life and their correspondence to witnessable human experience. *Love Outpouring* complements Chalmers' insights that a Consciousness-first model of Reality needs to be the fundamental paradigm of the world, yet disagrees with his approach.

Spending time asking scientific and philosophical 'why' and 'how' questions to solve the mystery of the universe is futile. As mentioned earlier in *Love Outpouring*, these types of 'why' and 'how' questions spin the ego-mind into infinite loops of unanswerable questions. These infinite loops only perpetuate ridiculous analysis, postulates and theories that continuously continue to move humanity further and further away from the Truth of the mystery.

> *Science cannot solve the ultimate mystery in nature.*
> *And it is because in the last analysis*
> *we ourSelves are part of the mystery we try to solve.*
> **Max Planck**[8]

The real solution to the Hard Problem is in asking and investigating into 'who' experiences and witnesses human processes. The solution lies in the willingness and courage of the human Heart to look closely at the one 'who' falsely believes itself to be real, the ego, see it for what it actually is, and witness the ego dismantle itself. What remains after this courage is engaged, and the ego dismantled, is the undeniable answer to the Hard Problem: You, Consciousness!

What is so hard about that...what is so hard about Knowing and Being yourSelf?! The answer to the Hard Problem is so incredibly simple and effortless that the ego takes the over simplistic nature of the solution and converts it into a super-complex burdensome situation that it labels as unsolvable. By first answering the question of 'who,' you will simultaneously answer the question of 'why.'

Also, referring back to AWE-er 2, if matter doesn't exist to begin with, then how can Consciousness arise from it? As more and more facts against the credibility of the current matter-first paradigm come to light, it becomes more and more obvious just how absurd it actually is.

AWE-er 4: What are we made of?

Physical non-permanence

The human body is in a perpetual, moment-by-moment cycle of physically replacing itself via ingestion and excretion. All of our life-giving body systems are constantly decaying, and so the decayed dead cells and tissues are constantly being replaced with new cells derived from the new nutrients we eat. Due to the universal law of the conservation of mass, for us to maintain a consistent body weight, as the body excretes, sluffs off and evaporates spent cellular components, it has to restore these components with new elements external to the body to maintain consistency and functionality. Simply stated, to maintain a specific body weight, what leaves the body has to be replaced with nutrients from outside the body.

> *The nitrogen in our DNA,*
> *the calcium in our teeth,*
> *the iron in our blood,*
> *the carbon in our apple pies*
> *was made in the interiors of collapsing stars.*
> *We are made of star stuff.*
> **Carl Sagan**[9]

Due to the unique tasks for each cell and tissue type, and the respective different stresses they encounter, some cells and tissues have much larger lifespans, that is, turnover rates, than others. From the chart below you can see that some cells/tissues have very quick turnover rates (bone marrow, 3.4 days) and some cellular turnover rates are over an entire lifetime (neurons, 32,850 days [90 years]). Another way to comprehend a turnover rate is the amount of time it takes for that gland or organ to fully replace its physical components with brand-new components. For instance, your esophagus has a turnover rate of 10 days, so every 10 days every esophagus cell has died, been excreted, and replaced with new cells that have been generated from recently ingested nutrients (elements).

From a macro point of view, the average adult human body loses between 50 and 70 billion cells each day due to a cellular process known as apoptosis. Apoptosis is a form of programmed cell death, sometimes referred to as cellular suicide, that typically is initiated to prolong a tissue or organ's turnover rate. It has been correlated that as apoptosis eliminates cells, the biological process of mitosis replaces them, creating an environment of mass homeostasis (body weight equilibrium). There are approximately 30 trillion cells in our body, so via

Summary of Human Cell and Tissue Turnover

Tissue/cell type	Estimated turnover (days)	Estimated turnover (years)
Adipose tissue	2,448	6.71
Adrenal gland	455	1.25
Bone marrow	3.2	0.01
Colon	3.5	0.01
Endometrium	13	0.04
Esophagus	10	0.03
Heart muscle	25,300	69.32
Keratinocyte (skin epidermis)	64	0.18
Kidney	270	0.74
Liver	327	0.90
Lung	200	0.55
Neuron (neocortex)	32,850	90.00
Osteoblast (bone)	8.3	0.02
Rectum	3.5	0.01
Salivary gland	60	0.16
Skeletal muscle	5,510	15.10
Smooth muscle	67.5	0.18
Spleen	7.8	0.02
Thyroid gland	3,180	8.71
Urinary bladder	49	0.13

Gene expression signatures of human cell and tissue longevity

Inge Seim(1), Siming Ma(1), and Vadim N. Gladyshev(1)*

(1) Division of Genetics, Department of Medicine, Brigham and Women's Hospital and Harvard Medical School, Boston, MA, 02115, USA

* Corresponding author: Division of Genetics, Department of Medicine, Brigham & Women's Hospital and Harvard Medical School, New Research Building, Room 435, 77 Avenue Louis Pasteur, Boston, MA 02115 USA. Phone: (617) 525-5122. E-mail: vgladyshev@rics.bwh.harvard.edu

https://www.ncbi.nlm.nih.gov/pmc/articles/PMC5514998/#xob1

apoptosis alone, the average adult body replaces the equivalent of itself approximately every 600 days (30 trillion divided by 50 billion), or every 1.6 years.

In an even more staggering cell turnover rate example, according to an article from *Scientific American* entitled 'Our Bodies Replace Billions of Cells Every Day,' there are approximately 30 trillion cells in the human body, of which about 330 billion die and are replaced daily; hence the equivalent to a new physical you is created every 90 days.

Where the disconnect from Reality arises is that we take ourselves to be a permanent person who is experiencing life AS a permanent body. But as was just illuminated, the terms 'permanence' and 'body' oppose each other; even your brain and heart replace themselves once over the course of your life.

We are made of the universe.
We are not only Earthlings, we are Universlings.
We are the universe conscious of itSelf.
Marshall Davis[10]

So you have to ask yourself: are you the body that you have previously excreted, currently are, or have yet to eat? You experience-directly a felt-sense of permanence and You know-inherently that you have ever-existed. Yet bodies do not meet the definition of permanent-Existence, and therefore logically You are not your body. If You are not your body, then what or who is the permanence you know yourSelf to Be?

Who is living who?

The published research article entitled 'Revised Estimates for the Number of Human and Bacteria Cells in the Body,'† from the Weizmann Institute of Science in Rehovot, Israel, determined that we have more bacteria living in our body than we have human cells in our body. The ratio of bacteria to human cells (B/H ratio) is 1.3:1, meaning we have about 38 trillion bacteria cells living in our body compared to our 30 trillion human cells.

Pointer question: Does the B/H ratio make you more bacteria than human?

By weight, though, because bacterial cells are about one tenth the size of a human cell, human cells outweigh bacterial cells by 99.7% in a typical body. But what constitutes one type of cell being more important than another? Does the size of a living organism determine its relevance; for comparison, is a mouse less significant than an elephant due to its significantly smaller size?

An organism is an individual life-form with interdependent 'parts' that create the living organism's 'whole' configuration. So, the parts create and define the whole. Through logical reduction, then, bacterial cells have to be just as important as human cells, since bacterial cells are a 'part' of the human 'whole'; regardless of size, functionality or structure.

What is it that truly defines an independent, stand-alone, living organism and what determines its relevance—its size, cellular components, mass, DNA structure, intellect and so on? We have been taught that there are true physical boundaries that specifically determine one object relative to another, and these boundaries give different objects relevance respective to one another. But in Reality, there are no such boundaries. There are no distinct separations that make anything independently different from any other thing. The apparent separation of objects derived from illusory boundaries, albeit very persuasive, are only constructs of the ego-mind.

The notion of a separate organism is clearly an abstraction,
as is also its boundary. Underlying all this is unbroken wholeness,
even though our civilization has developed in such a way
*as to strongly emphasize the separation into **parts**.*
David Bohm[11]

ALL THAT IS is just one continuous, undivided whole only appearing as many separate objective parts—including You. By knowing yourSelf directly you will experience the loss of your 'part,' and become the boundaryless 'whole' of Totality.

AWE-er 5: Is your daily life more complex than the game of chess?

Most people would say "Yes" to this question, and rightly so. Especially these days, life seems to have become very complicated. The rise of computers, smartphones, social media and cloud-based direct messaging have brought incredible advances in productivity, while at the same time these advancements have also created higher and higher levels of societal interactions and complexity, leading to increased levels of personal choices and decision-making.

But let's go back to the simplicities of life for a moment, like the repetitious process of getting out of bed in the morning: making our way to the bathroom and brushing our teeth. Even something as apparently mundane as this can be a sleepy gauntlet of decision-making. Which foot hits the floor first— maybe both? Do you start walking with the left foot or right? Do you step over the dog or go around it? What if your partner or child is up, which leads to the numerous possible interactions you could have with them? Do you start brushing on the top or the bottom row of teeth, the left or the right, or the front or the back? You can see that within the first few minutes of your day, you could have several hundred, possibly several thousands, choices and/or decisions to make. Couple this with getting out of the house, commuting to work, interacting with colleagues, exercising, entertainment, an evening with friends or family. When you think about it, it can become exhausting just trying to comprehend it all. No wonder we look forward to turning off our decision-making machine (our brain) and falling asleep every night. So yes, it is easy to say that our life, with regard to the number of choices and decisions made every day, is much more complex than the game of chess.

Before we dive into just how complex the game of chess is, we first have to establish a basis of materialist understanding.

According to the website Universe Today, there are between 10^{78} and 10^{82} atoms in the universe. For simplicity let's assume an average of 10^{80}, which is the number 1 with 80 zeros after it—a massive, massive number. How scientists determined this is beyond most people's understanding, but regardless of how, it is an incredibly large quantity. The universe has been evolving and expanding for about 13.8 billion years formulating the physical cosmos, and 10^{80} represents everything material in all of the cosmos, as we currently know it, well beyond any human comprehension.

Now let's dive into chess's mind-boggling statistics. As most of us know, the game consists of an 8 x 8 gridded board, making a total of 64 spaces. Each player has 16 pieces with varying moving capabilities. The object of the game is to place the opponent's king into checkmate, a position where the king has no room to move without being captured. Most boards are approximately 16 inches square and can easily fit on any coffee table.

Now here is where it gets perplexing. In 1950 an American mathematician by the name of Claude Shannon published a paper entitled 'Programming a Computer to Play Chess.' In the paper, Shannon demonstrated the impracticality of winning a game of chess by brute force when he calculated that the number of possible move variations in any single game of chess was 10^{120} moves. 10^{120} is known as the Shannon Number; a number that is certainly approaching infinity, especially within the realm of the human experience.

Shannon Number:

1,000,000,000,000,000,000,000,000,000,000,000,000,00
0,000,000,000,000,000,000,000,000,000,000,000,000,00
0,000,000,000,000,000,000,000,000,000,000

Now sit back and take this in for a moment, for the ramifications of this finding are enough to scramble one's understanding of what human Consciousness is capable of performing. To use the cherished quote from the movie *The Princess Bride*, "It's inconceivable." The Shannon Number is suggesting that within the 64 spaces on a 16x16-inch game board, that easily fits on a standard-size coffee table, there are 10^{40} times (10^{120} divided by 10^{80} = 10^{40}) more decisions on it than there are atoms in the cosmos...it is absolutely absurd! "Wait wait," you say. "The Shannon Number assumes 32 total pieces, 16 per team, each piece representing a person making decisions in the real world. When you divide 10^{120} by 32 to get the average move per piece (person), the number becomes reasonable!" Not even close to being "conceivable," this number is still infinitely large: 3.13^{118}...and you most likely agree that your daily life is more complex than a game of chess!

To further the perplexity, humans have somewhere between 6,000 and 70,000 thoughts per day (6^3 and 7^4). And to maximize the point, let's assume that every thought is a decision. Assuming you are one who agrees that your daily life is more complex than a game of chess, who or what decides the remaining 3.13^{118} minus 70,000 decisions? No one knows, nor can they ever know. To say the least, it just doesn't add up.

So what does this mean, if anything? You could look at it in one of two ways. Either you consider it nonsense, and write it off as too complicated with no value deriving from it; or you could be open to the possibility that there is no way that a human is capable of such grandeur and decide that you are open and willing to explore the unknown, infinite realm further—collapsing the distance between yourself and yourSelf—to experience the Shannon Number directly.

Cessation statement

These five quantitative AWE-ers are meant to be a curiosity catalysis for you to become motivationally intrigued to move toward what is being pointed to throughout *Love Outpouring*: the Truth of You.

There are countless other credible AWE-ers that could have been mentioned, but it's not the focus of the book. You will, though, start to recognize more and more of them in your day-to-day life as you proceed down this effortless path of Self-realization.

In the spirit of celebrating scientific minds that acknowledge a deeper meaning to empirical data, from the final statement in the closing 'Discussion' of the article referenced in AWE-er 4, 'Revised Estimates for the Number of Human and Bacteria Cells in the Body,' the professors wrote:

> *We thus became aware [conscious] through this study*
> *of promising steps forward in fulfilling the*
> *Delphic maxim of 'know thyself' from a quantitative perspective.*
> **Sender, Fuchs, and Milo**[12]

To be direct, though, these five AWE-ers are really a loving tactic to engage your ego into trying to prove the nondual perennial message false, while all along knowing that in the end all you will find is yourSelf...ever-present intimate happiness: the Truth.

Notes

* Gary Weber PhD, 'The Default Mode Network & End of Suffering Presentation,' *Heart of Art*, 2015.

† https://www.ncbi.nlm.nih.gov/pmc/articles/PMC4991899/pdf/pbio.1002533.pdf

3   Max Karl Ernst Ludwig Planck (1858–1947), known as the Father of Quantum Physics, was a German theoretical physicist whose discovery of energy quanta won him the Nobel Prize in Physics in 1918. He believed there was a virtuous force that holds the solar system of an atom together, and behind this force is the existence of a conscious and intelligent spirit (Self), and this spirit is the matrix of all matter.

4   Bernardo Kastrup is the executive director of Essentia Foundation, whose work leads the modern renaissance of metaphysical idealism, the notion that Reality is essentially mental. He has a PhD in philosophy and another PhD in computer engineering. As a scientist, Bernardo has worked for the European Organization for Nuclear Research (CERN) and the Philips Research Laboratories. There is an entire section in Chapter 13 dedicated to Bernardo and his extensive work on creating a sane and coherent science-based model of Reality.

7   David John Chalmers is an Australian philosopher and cognitive scientist. He is a professor of Philosophy and Neural Science at New York University, as well as co-director of NYU's Center for Mind, Brain and Consciousness. Chalmers is best known for formulating the Hard Problem of Consciousness.

9   Carl Edward Sagan (1934–1996) was an American astronomer, planetary scientist, cosmologist, astrophysicist, astrobiologist and author. He is best known for his scientific research on extraterrestrial life, the book *The Pale Blue Dot*, and his 1980 award-winning PBS television series *Cosmos: A Personal Voyage*. He believed that science is not only

cohesive with spirituality, but science is a profound source of it.

12   Ron Sender, Shai Fuchs, and Ron Milo are professors at the Weizmann Institute of Science, Rehovot, Israel. They are the co-authors of the 2016 article, 'Revised Estimates for the Number of Human and Bacteria Cells in the Body,' *PLoS Biol* 14(8): e1002533.

Chapter 13

Science, Philosophy and Self

There appears to be a point in most scientists' careers, primarily physicists, neuroscientists and scientific-philosophers, when they realize, viscerally, that the world/universe is literally not what it appears to be; that space (the universe) is not some cold, dead, inert, vast emptiness, but an interconnected unbroken network of conscious intelligence.

> *But also, everyone who is seriously*
> *involved in the pursuit of science*
> *becomes convinced that a spirit is*
> *manifest in the laws of the universe,*
> *a spirit vastly superior to that of man,*
> *and one in the face of which we*
> *with our modest powers must feel humble.*
> **Albert Einstein**[1]

> *Space is not empty. It's full.*
> *It is the ground for the existence of everything,*
> *including ourSelves.*
> **David Bohm**[2]

The following five scientists/philosophers (the first three falling into the category of the Godfathers of Quantum Physics, and the remaining two being current cutting-edge thinkers and scientists) demonstrate that if you take your role as an advancer-of-humanity seriously, by seeking the Truth regardless of where it takes you, then you will always end up in a spiritual, Consciousness realm.

The following outlines of each advancer-of-humanity are but brief understandings of how each one merged into such mystical universal conclusions. Each summary provides just enough information to give the reader a sense of credibility that some of the most influential geniuses who have ever walked the planet are in line with the perennial message of nonduality. Further investigation into each one of these bright-souls, and the multitudes like them, is encouraged.

> *Science is not only compatible with spirituality;*
> *it is a profound source of spirituality.*
> **Carl Sagan**[3]

Advaita Vedanta is inviting you to be your own empirical scientist, where you diligently scrutinize your reality-environment with skepticism to reveal the Truth (the Path of Jñāna). This is accomplished by analyzing the data obtained from your experiments (Self-inquiry) and discarding the invalid information (false-knowledge) that does not serve your hypothesis.

At the Heart of science itself lies the 'Path of Jñāna' where the scientific community's own sacred *scientific method* is purposely designed to unbiasedly (zero-ego) discard what is untrue to divulge what is true.

Therefore, to realize Self directly, you are encouraged to follow the *scientific method* of Jñāna, where false-knowledge exposed from Self-inquiry is abandoned, unveiling the true-knowledge of the One-Reality: yourSelf.

David Bohm, PhD (1917–1992)

Possibly the most influential Truth-progressor physicist regarding the nature of universal Reality was Dr David Bohm. Bohm was an American-Brazilian-British theoretical quantum physicist who is described by his colleagues as one of the greatest scientific-philosophers of the twentieth century.

The Dalai Lama has referred to Bohm as his 'science guru' and was depicted by Albert Einstein as his 'spiritual son.' What made Bohm such a significant influencer was that he allowed his quantum findings to lead him to the Truth, regardless of the current mainstream ways of thinking. In his own words, Bohm said of his non-status quo work:

> I would say that in my scientific and philosophical work, my main concern has been with understanding the nature of Reality in general and of Consciousness in particular as a coherent whole, which is never static or complete but which is an unending process of movement and unfoldment.

Bohm's most paradoxical mind-bending theory, later proven experimentally to be true, was what he called the Implicate Order, which he detailed in his 1980 book, *Wholeness and the Implicate Order*.

According to Bohm, the Implicate Order states that two subatomic particles that once interacted can instantaneously "respond to each other's motions thousands of years later when they are light-years apart." Bohm's calculations exposed the fact that any individual element located anywhere in the universe could reveal "detailed information about every other element in the universe." The predominant theme of Bohm's theory is the "unbroken wholeness of the Totality of Existence as an undivided flowing movement without borders." Bohm's theorem shocked the physicalist community and led to the beautiful realization that we are all energetically connected to one another regardless of our positions in the universe.

> *We are all linked by a fabric of unseen connections.*
> *This fabric is constantly changing and evolving.*
> *This field is directly structured and influenced by*
> *our behavior and our understanding.*
> **David Bohm**[4]

Jiddu Krishnamurti

Over the course of Bohm's last 25 years of life, he met frequently with an Eastern Indian philosopher by the name of Jiddu Krishnamurti (1895–1986). Krishnamurti was a modern Buddha-like figure, in the sense that at a young age Krishnamurti denounced his privileged-life to adhere to an ordinary-life of seeking the Truth. Krishnamurti was groomed and indoctrinated to be the next World Teacher of The Order of the Star in the East (OSE), a sister organization to the Theosophical Society of Madras, India, and instead dedicated his life to seeking and sharing the Truth with the world. From 1929, when Krishnamurti denounced the OSE, until his death in 1986, he spent his life illuminating the need for a revolution in the mind of every human being. He emphasized that such a revolution cannot be brought about by any external entity, be it religious, political, or social, but only from within.

Jiddu's resignation from the OSE came in the form of a presentation known as 'The Dissolution Speech.' The following are a few of his impactful words from that day:

I maintain that Truth is a pathless land, and you cannot approach it by any path whatsoever, by any religion, by any sect. That is my point of view, and I adhere to that absolutely and unconditionally. Truth, being limitless, unconditioned, unapproachable by any path whatsoever, cannot be organized; nor should any organization be formed to lead or coerce people along a particular path. This is no magnificent deed, because I do not want followers, and I mean this. The moment you follow someone, you cease to follow Truth. I am concerning myself with only one essential thing: to set man free. I desire to free him from all cages, from all fears, and not to found religions, new sects, nor to establish new theories and new philosophies.

Bohm realized that to fully understand and encapsulate his scientific findings he would have to approach and perceive them from a completely different 'vehicle' than his intellectual mind. Bohm had to be willing to break free of his educational and societal conditioning if he was to be successful at obsoleting the solidity of the status-quo scientific orthodoxy.

> *The ability to perceive or think differently*
> *is more important than the knowledge gained.*
> **David Bohm**[5]

> *So there must be a revolution in thinking,*
> *A revolution in the mind itself,*
> *and not in what the mind thinks about.*
> **Jiddu Krishnamurti**[6]

Bohm recognized that at some point the 'known' of mathematics and physics would need to be abandoned for the 'unknown' conscious mind to be experienced, so as to benefit humanity; hence the transcending insights of the Hindu Consciousness-based understanding of Krishnamurti to aid in Bohm's efforts.

> *One can see that in a certain sense the East was right*
> *to see the immeasurable as the primary Reality.*
> **David Bohm**[7]

The Bohm and Krishnamurti conversations, the most pertinent entitled *The Future of Humanity*, originated to help society find a way to bridge the much needed incoherence gap between Reality and the mind, the misunderstanding-gap (manifestation-Existence barrier) that has led to so much human suffering throughout history. These talks are a beautiful example of two intelligent open-Hearted people from two vastly different mindsets and cultures uniting in honest dialogue to passionately aid in healing the global physical and psychological wounds unnecessarily generated by ego. In a sense, this is a loving attempt to merge science with the mystical to actively advance humanity and set every human being free.

The solution in Krishnamurti's words is to:

Start simple, start with 'what is,' 'what I am.' That's why Self-knowledge is so important. Self-knowledge is not conditioned-knowledge. Self-knowledge is to know [the Truth] and comprehend and understand oneSelf.

In Bohm's words:

It is proposed that a form of free dialogue may well be one of the most effective ways of investigating the crisis which faces society, and indeed the whole of human nature and Consciousness today. Moreover, it may turn out that such a form of free exchange of ideas and information is of fundamental relevance for transforming culture and freeing it of destructive misinformation, so that creativity can be liberated.

As an act of humanitarianism, in Bohm's later years he initiated and participated in what are known as the Bohm Dialogues. These dialogues are meant to create a forum of conversation in which the attendees cease current beliefs and biases and give others and themselves the vulnerability to become conscious of the thought (mind) process itself. The Bohm Dialogues can be likened to what is known in Eastern philosophy as *satsang*, where *sat* means 'Being or Existence' and *sang* means 'company,' that is, a gathering of Aware-Beings.

Could there be a more loving way for Bohm to celebrate the recognition of his friend and colleague, Krishnamurti, and contribute to the advancement of humanity as a whole, than via satsang (East) / dialogues (West)?

This kind of overall way of thinking is not only
a fertile source of new theoretical ideas:
it is needed for the human mind to function
in a generally harmonious way,
which could in turn help to make possible
an orderly and stable society.
David Bohm[8]

Albert Einstein (1879–1955)

Childlike genius

There have been many significant scientific deep-thinking minds that have changed the course of history over the past several hundred years: Nicolaus Copernicus (1473–1543), Father of Modern Astronomy; Galileo Galilei (1564–1642), Father of Modern Science; Sir Isaac Newton (1642–1727), Father of Calculus and Physics; Max Planck (1858–1947), Father of Quantum Physics; but of all the geniuses who have graced the ages, Albert Einstein, Father of Modern Cosmology, has been the most aggrandized and pedestalized.

Between the years 1905 and 1915 Einstein derived the General Theory of Relativity equations, which were experimentally proven accurate during a solar eclipse in 1919, on the island of Principe off the west coast of Africa. This confirmation catapulted Einstein into becoming the world's first famous celebrity scientist. But regardless of Einstein's astronomical intelligence and global fame, he is also possibly the most misunderstood mastermind-contributor to humanity.

Einstein was considered an intellectual elite only by those who did not know him closely; to those near to him, he was more of a frumpy wiry-haired child than a wise elder. Einstein's second wife and cousin, Elsa, regularly referred to Albert as her son, even proclaiming in front of company, "He is such a child!", when he demonstrated immaturity in obvious adult situations.

Einstein often took serious situations nonchalantly, perplexing those in his presence. This behavior was especially visible during the rise of Nazi Germany in his hometown of Berlin, prior to his escape to America in 1932. Even though death threats and bounties were on his head, due to his humanitarian protests against Hitler's regime, he still remained somewhat unperturbed under the severe circumstances.

Albert understood the sacredness of a free mind and the immense abundance of creativity and capability such a mind awarded. He spent a significant amount of time alone in isolation, which allowed his innocent and boundless thought-process to become available.

He understood that his greatest attribute was his own 'permission' to create a mind-platform in which imagination superseded knowledge and education. This 'permission' was a struggle for Albert to maintain as he went through his teenage years, which stemmed from his elementary/middle-school teachers spitefully considering him 'backward,' mentally slow, unsociable, and adrift forever in his foolish dreams.* Yet his 'permission' was a direct rebellion emerging from his negative outlook on the modern education system; he couldn't believe that "modern methods of instruction have not yet strangled the holy curiosity of inquiry."†

Education is that which remains [Self],
if one has forgotten everything he learned in school [ego].
Albert Einstein[9]

Imagination [Self] is more important than knowledge [ego].
Knowledge is limited. Imagination encircles the world.
Albert Einstein[10]

A mother once asked Einstein what kind of reading would best
prepare her child for a career as a scientist.
Einstein answered: "Fairy tales and more fairy tales."
Albert Einstein[11]

Einstein understood that Being and remaining child-mind-like was his greatest asset; it is what gave him the open-mental stage for genius to arise. This wisdom to remain forever-youthful correlates with him once saying, "With fame, I become more and more stupid, which of course is a very common phenomenon."

He apparently, and most likely unknowingly, protected his greatest asset of 'wondrous intuition' by devoting himself to his inner-child, which noticeably reared itself through his boyish behaviors and mannerisms that flustered his wife so dearly.

Yet in his later-year inward-reflections, in which he openly acknowledged his youthful demeanor, he appeared to be at peace with his childlike-innocence and superior-intelligence and the subsequent happiness that arose out of this child-genius combination.

Only a boy can be a thinker.
He who considers himself grown up and mature
forfeits the wondering wisdom of a child.
Albert Einstein[12]

The following quotes are from other highly recognized global influencers on the importance of maintaining a youthful-mind.

There are children playing in the streets who
could solve some of my top problems in physics,
because they have modes of sensory perception that I lost long ago.
Robert Oppenhiemer[13]

It is the child that sees the primordial secret in Nature
and it is the child of ourSelves we return to.
The child within us is simple and daring enough to live the Secret.
Lao Tsu[14]

Great is the human who has not lost his childlike Heart.
Mencius[15]

A child-like man is not a man whose development has been arrested;
on the contrary, he is a man who has given himself a chance
of continuing to develop long after most adults have muffled
themselves in the cocoon of middle-aged habit and convention.
Aldous Huxley[16]

Genius meets mystic

Between mid 1926 and late 1930 Einstein met with 1913 Nobel Prize recipient in literature, Rabindranath Tagore, approximately five times at Einstein's home in Berlin, Germany. Tagore was a revered Sanatana Dharma based Hindu, who was highly recognized as a poet, composer, philosopher and Indian mystic.

The meeting of the minds between Western science and Eastern philosophy was a global sensation. The most reported meeting was on July 14, 1930, when the two deep-thinkers discussed free will, universal-Truth, and beauty. Besides their social ideals and their warm regards for one another's insights, the two differed on the fundamentals of Reality.

Tagore, being steeped in the Indian Vedantic texts of the Upanishads, perceived Reality as One-whole, in which humanity was One with/as Totality. He respected Western science, yet understood it to be a tool to understand Reality, not Reality itself. Tagore expressed his insights in the July 14th meeting as follows††:

The world is a human world—the scientific view of it is also that of the scientific man. Therefore, the world apart from us does not exist; it is a relative world, depending for its reality upon our Consciousness.

According to the Indian philosophy there is Brahman, the Absolute Truth, which cannot be conceived by the isolation of the individual mind [ego] or described by words, but can be realized only by merging the individual in its infinity.

It was obvious from Einstein's contributions to the July 14th conversation that he believed there are two realities; 1) a Reality of Truth independent of the 2) human experience. During the dialogue, Albert kept to his understanding of universal reality, acknowledging that Truth does exist, but because Truth/Reality/Existence can't be known conceptually, it then does so separately or apart from humankind. During the conversation, Albert went on to say:††

There are two different conceptions about the nature of the universe—the world as a unity dependent on humanity [nonduality], and the world as reality independent of the human factor [duality, physicalism].

Our natural point of view in regard to the Existence of Truth apart from humanity cannot be explained or proved, but it is a belief which nobody can lack—not even primitive beings. We attribute to Truth a superhuman objectivity. It is indispensable for us—this reality which is independent of our Existence and our experience and our mind—though we cannot say what it means.

It is clear from these conversations with Tagore that Albert had a dualistic physicalism point of view, which is completely understandable, especially considering his Western upbringing and conditioning. These conversations were most likely Einstein's first significant collision and realization with the nondual Truth of Reality, which slowly started to detach him from a system-of-beliefs and engage him into a world of Self-verifiable mysticism.

This gentle shift into mysticism apparently stemmed from Tagore's status (he was globally recognized for his brilliant wisdom), which empowered Einstein to transcend his misconceptions and to perceive the nature of Reality in a different light; thus enabling Einstein's first sphurana—his first 'permission' to repent (change his perspective) and see that the Kingdom of God (the world) is not independent and separate from himSelf.

It is also clear, via his writings and statements, that even though Albert inherently knew the universe was one undivided whole, he still was not able to drop his dualistic world beliefs and adopt a nondual Eastern understanding (bridge the manifestation-Existence barrier); at least he did not do so publicly. Such a stubbornness to not change views demonstrates the power of belief, and the reluctant outcome of not changing one's paradigm even when the belief is proven to be false.

There is also the fear of possibly being ridiculed and discredited for publicly acknowledging a Conscious-first model of the universe, in which no ego or separate-self exists independently, that might have entrenched Einstein in his materialistic views. It appears that Albert could not succumb to the idea that he himSelf was an infinite-eternal entity, not separate from the wholeness that he knew and experienced directly. Yet, his Totality-Unity-Oneness statements and calculations were profound and direct pointers to the true underlying nature of Reality.

When we read what Albert, the most cherished and brilliant mind in modern history, says in the following quotes, how can it not come from a deep understanding of the real underlying mechanics of the nondual wholeness of the manifestation and the peace and harmony obtained by becoming free of self?

I like to experience the universe as one harmonious whole.
—William Hermanns, *Einstein and the Poet: In Search of the Cosmic Man*, Brandon Books, 1983

The soul [Self] given to each of us is moved by the same living spirit that moves the universe.
—William Hermanns, *Einstein and the Poet: In Search of the Cosmic Man*, Brandon Books, 1983

The true value of a human being is determined primarily by the measure and the sense in which he has attained liberation from the self [ego].
—Albert Einstein, *The World as I See It*, 1949

...we can see that we all dance to a mysterious tune, and the piper who plays this melody from an inscrutable distance—whatever name we give him—Creative Force, or God—escapes all book knowledge.
—William Hermanns, *Einstein and the Poet: In Search of the Cosmic Man*, Brandon Books, 1983

A human being is part of the whole, called by us 'universe,' a part limited in time and space. He experiences himself, his thoughts and feelings, as something separate from the rest—a kind of optical delusion of Consciousness. The striving to free oneself from this delusion is the one issue of true religion. Not to nourish it [religion] but to try to overcome it is the way to reach the attainable measure of peace of mind.
—Letter to Robert S. Marcus, February 12, 1950

Erwin Schrodinger (1887–1961)

Erwin Schrodinger was an Austrian physicist who developed the fundamental understanding of quantum theory; the understanding which aided Albert Einstein, Niels Bohr, and Werner Heisenberg to develop their revolutionary theories. Erwin was awarded the 1933 Nobel Prize in Physics for the formulation of the Schrodinger equation, the discovery of the mathematical function that governs quantum physics, and the 1937 Max Planck Medal for extraordinary achievements in theoretical physics.

During his studies of the quantum-physical world, Schrodinger came to realize that the Self and the world are one [nonduality] and that they are all [Totality]. His mode of grasping the perennial message of quantum physics was first through the Zen Buddhist writings of Lafcadio Hearn and then through Advaita Vedanta scriptures of the Upanishads, leading to his rejection of traditional Western religious beliefs.

Erwin's understanding of Reality could not be more in line with the perennial message of Zen Buddhism and Advaita Vedanta, which is made clear in his statement:

The only possible alternative is simply to keep to the immediate experience that Consciousness is a singular of which the plural is unknown; that there is only one thing [Consciousness] and that what seems to be a plurality is merely a series of different aspects of this one thing [Consciousness's-activity], produced by a deception (the Indian MAYA); the same illusion is produced in a gallery of mirrors, and in the same way Gaurisankar and Mt Everest turned out to be the same peak seen from different valleys.
—Schrodinger, *What Is Life?* 1944

Erwin's insightful understanding of Eastern philosophy, which was ultimately spawned by seeking and following the

Truth derived from quantum-science, subsequently converted him into a Vedantist. It is apparent through his writings that Erwin realized that the Indian scriptures were a vehicle for him to rationalize and experience what his quantum calculations were suggesting: Oneness.§

In his own words, Schrodinger expresses his fundamental-Oneness conclusions as follows:

There is obviously only one alternative, namely the unification of minds or Consciousnesses. Their multiplicity is only apparent, in Truth there is only one mind. This is the doctrine of the Upanishads [Vedic texts]. And not only of the Upanishads. The mystically experienced union with God regularly entails this attitude unless it is opposed by strong existing prejudices; and this means that it is less easily accepted in the West than in the East.
—Schrodinger, *What Is Life?* 1944

Consciousness cannot be accounted for in physical terms. For Consciousness is absolutely fundamental. It cannot be accounted for in terms of anything else.
—'General Scientific and Popular Papers,' in *Collected Papers*, Vol. 4. Vienna: Austrian Academy of Sciences; Braunschweig/Wiesbaden: Vieweg & Sohn.

The doctrine of identity can claim that it is clinched by the empirical fact that Consciousness is never experienced in the plural [duality], only in the singular [nonduality]. Not only has none of us ever experienced more than one Consciousness [Self], but there is no trace of circumstantial evidence of this ever happening anywhere in the world.
—Erwin Schrodinger, 'On Determinism and Free Will,' section of *What Is Life?* 1944

In Schrodinger's doctrine ('On Determinism and Free Will,' section of *What Is Life?*), he clearly describes a nondual perspective in which there is an unseeable underlying Reality of the manifestation of life that *throws an image of itself into his [Erwin's] Consciousness, through for which he then perceives it.* Erwin goes on to use a tree as an example to specify the point, that even though we will all see the tree from our 'many points of view,' we will also all agree that there is only one supposedly real tree and all the underlying *image business is a ghost-story* [meaning our ego-minds will disregard the underlying Reality (image business) as unreal or even non-existent (ghost-story)].

Erwin goes on to question the validity of the 'many points of view' witnessing the tree, reducing them down to individual units in which each person indisputably would agree that their 'I' is quite distinct from that of any other's 'I'. He then asks the question, *What Is this 'I'?* He describes 'I' as the canvas upon which the collection of single data, such as experiences and memories, are collected; that each 'I' has its own canvas, yet there is only one canvas (Self) that is shared by all.

There are suggestions within his writings that Schrodinger was practicing Self-inquiry. In *What Is Life?* he describes an observation process that is very similar to Self-inquiry. He finds that his body and world are somehow separate, yet still a part of, his onlooker-Self.

...we step [Self-inquiry] with our own persons [ego] back into the part of an onlooker [Self] who does not belong to the world, which by this very procedure [Self-inquiry] becomes an objective world. Now, once this is done, my own body becomes part of the objective world [body becomes 'other than' Self]; and since I (an embodied Being) experience

Consciousness [Self-conscious], I conclude that my objective body is the bearer [body is unconscious] of a Consciousness.
—Michel Bitbol, *Schrodinger and Indian Philosophy*, Paris: CNRS, 1998

In Erwin's later years his speaking appointments tended to be less and less about creating new physical theories and more and more about his love for Advaita Vedanta. According to comments made by Bernard d'Espagnat, who attended some of Schrodinger's later conferences, Erwin typically ended with the comment: "Atman equals Brahman" (Self = God), which he referred to as "the second Schrodinger equation."

Bernardo Kastrup, PhD

Bernardo Kastrup is the founder, executive director and primary spokesman of the Essentia Foundation. The Essentia Foundation was established to question the validity of the current materialism paradigm and to offer a coherent theory of the nature of Reality known as Analytic Idealism, otherwise known as Metaphysics. Analytic Idealism is based on the notion that Reality is essentially mental and nondual, and therefore matter is nothing but a manifested projection of our Consciousness.

Bernardo holds a PhD in computer engineering and another PhD in philosophy. His career as a scientist stems from his time at Philips Research Laboratories and the European Organization for Nuclear Research (CERN), the Large Hadron Collider in Geneva, Switzerland. Kastrup's deep passion for the Truth led him away from his primary role as a material physicist at CERN and into his current position at Essentia as a scientific-based nondual philosopher and author, where he and other thought-leader scholars connect modern scientific research and philosophy/psychology to the idealist perception of Reality, via free audio, visual and text.

For example, Essentia has a free 6+ hour online video course that utilizes current scientific research with undertones of historical philosophy, such as the wisdom of Arthur Schopenhauer and Carl Jung, to methodically articulate the absurdity of modern-day materialistic theory. It is remarkable how closely Analytical Idealism and Indian philosophy track one another. As seen throughout time, the only obvious difference in how the perennial message is expressed is in the verbiage and language of the period and culture in which it is communicated.

To determine nondual authenticity, the trick is to listen closely to the descriptions of the commentary, not necessarily the specific words of the discipline one is speaking from (such as science, religion, spirituality). Because of description synchronicity, Analytical Idealism is firmly a modern-day scientific and philosophical representation of the perennial wisdom of antiquity, whose inherent primary characteristics are aimed at bettering humanity.

Bernardo's understanding of Truth is that there is only One-Reality appearing as a multiplicity of objects, and that we as conscious observers experience this One-Reality via the manifestation of life, in which, he claims, the manifestation is only an abstraction of the One-Reality, not the One-Reality itSelf. Bernardo argues that the manifested-world we consciously observe is likened to a cockpit dashboard of an airplane, where the dials on the dashboard (the manifestation) are only a representation of the weather and coordinates outside the plane (the One-Reality). The dashboard represents collapsed finite-conscious activity, and the conditions outside the plane represent infinite-Consciousness. The cockpit dials are not Reality, they are just renditions of Reality, such as what we experience and perceive as the manifesting-dials of life. In Bernardo's words:

The key difference is between the thing in itself—the world as it is in itself [the weather outside the cockpit]—and the world as it presents itself to our observation [the cockpit dashboard]. The world [the One-Reality] as it is in itself is pure: it's a function of itself. But the world as it presents itself to our observation [the manifestation] is not only a function of the world as it is in itself; it's also a function of us and how we are put together to observe the world.

—Interview with *Beshara Magazine*, 2021

During the 2021 interview with *Beshara Magazine*, Bernardo uncovers the notion that if matter in itself has stand-alone existence, then it has no underlying meaning besides what we project onto it. This materialistic meaningless view of the world in his eyes is what could be considered nihilism, and the leading contributor to the bulk of humanity's suffering. Since a materialist point of view takes the manifestation to be real, when in Reality it is only an illusion, we as a modern civilization become crazed and confused because we can't figure out how to obtain deep satisfaction from the solid-dead manifestation of life, regardless of how hard we try. The consequence of materialism is isolation, depression and anxiety, which are the great detriments of today's society.

But, as Kastrup elaborates from the same *Beshara* article, if matter is only an appearance perceived from a nondual point of view, then suddenly the entire physical world becomes a book to be read, a novel that points to an underlying Reality of depth, meaning, wonder, and mystery. Bernardo suggests from an Analytical Idealism point of view that we ourSelf become the mystery whose eyes of nature are looking and experiencing itSelf AS the world we perceive, which restores peace and sanity to once manic minds.

Bernardo does acknowledge that for someone to experience directly a nondual Analytical Idealism Reality, they must go through an ego dissolution; death of the self. He states that ego dissolution can be unpleasant at first, but as someone disassociates from the feeling of being a separate fearful individual they are led to the experience of unity with the one universal Consciousness, which he foresees is an experience equivalent to being in the arms of a loved family member.

> It's the reintegration [ego dissolution] into the
> matrix of Being where we were before we were born.
> And this reintegration is what most people call love.
> **Bernardo Kastrup**[17]

Kastrup maintains it is possible for this reintegration to be experienced in our lifetime since we are already connected to Existence via the mere fact that we are living Beings [via Self]. The issue we have with society as a whole easily reintegrating with Oneness is that our culture has conditioned us to *believe* that these insights are untrue and to therefore neglect the innate feelings of love we have within. Thus on a global scale our culture is constantly reinforcing the false-fact that we are separate individuals unconnected from one another. This makes it virtually impossible for civilization to rise up to a sense of universal belonging where unity and freedom are sought and encouraged, not our current cultural operating system of oppression.

What is concerning, though, is that Bernardo puts doubt into the notion of a beneficial future of humanity living in a world of universally connected Beings. He raises the issue that reintegration will be blissful, but then claims all bets are off for us as a culture to maintain such a peaceful environment and that it is conceivable society could fall back into a world of suffering.

This concern of Bernardo's does not align with the Advaita teachings. Advaita states that once an ego has been annihilated (ego dissolution), it never rises again. Therefore after ego-death, the once-believed-to-be-person carries out life only knowing themSelf AS themSelf, that is, One with Universal Consciousness. If this is scaled globally, and reinforced by the new culture of Consciousness Beings, eventually an ego-based reality would be snuffed out. Also, as we will see in the next paragraph, it appears that Consciousness is manifesting as life to know itSelf and to learn from itSelf. If so, it could be learning to no longer manifest as suffering separate egos and is in a current transition back to knowing and unifying with itSelf alone.

In the Essentia online course, Bernardo exposes many scientific studies that align with the perennial view of a One-Reality expressing itSelf as a multiplicity of objects. The most fascinating find from the series comes from the correlation of two separate research studies depicting that the universe is actually one large neuronal-web that is in a process of learning from itSelf. "What is 'it' that learns?" Bernardo asks. "A mind learns," he answers. These two papers suggest that the universe is one large networking mind that calculates and learns in the same way that logarithmic equations and neurons do. The Universal-Mind therefore expresses itSelf through the extrinsic appearance of the language of physics and chemistry. Bernardo expresses these Universal-Mind findings in the Essentia online video course as follows:

The mathematical structure of the functional laws of physics is compatible with the mathematical structure of how a neuronal network performs computations and learns. The laws of physics may actually be the expression of a learning process in the underlying and imminent neuronal network that is imminent across the entire physical universe.

Donald Hoffman, PhD

Donald Hoffman is Professor of Cognitive Sciences at the University of California, Irvine (UC Irvine), with a joint commitment at UC Irvine as Professor of Logic and Philosophy of Science. He received his Doctorate of Philosophy in computational psychology at the Massachusetts Institute of Technology (MIT). He has received numerous awards from such institutions as the US National Academy of Sciences, the American Psychological Association, the US Department of Defense and the Alzheimer's Foundation. Donald's most recent contribution to the study and understanding of Consciousness is from his 2019 book entitled *The Case Against Reality: Why Evolution Hid the Truth from Our Eyes*.

It is Hoffman's understanding that Reality is a nonphysical monism (monism being a Oneness or Singleness), and that Consciousness is the nonphysical element of the underlying Reality of a monistic-Existence. From Donald's point of view, monism is the antonym of dualism and is the scientific way of describing nonduality. Hoffman and his team have built testable mathematical models of the underlying Reality of nature that demonstrate proof for the theory of monism. From these models they have made significant progress showing that the physical world (collapsed-Consciousness) is simply a visible representation (manifestation) of the underlying dynamics of Consciousness.

Donald uses the same type of metaphor that Bernardo Kastrup uses to describe the nature of Reality, except that instead of a dashboard in the cockpit of an airplane, Hoffman uses the analogy of icons on the home screen of your computer, where the icons are only a representation of the programming, circuitry, resistors, diodes and capacitors that are actually doing the work from an underlying unforeseen location. If the user had to actually witness and comprehend all of these processing elements to obtain an outcome, the user would, in Donald's words, "melt into a puddle of ooze due to sensory overload." Therefore the icons on your computer's home screen are just adaptive fictions of the computer's computational nonfiction, just like the manifested-world is an adaptive fiction of nonfictional-Consciousness. Hoffman concludes that Consciousness is too complex for us humans to comprehend, so it (Consciousness) "dumbed it down for us" in a form of "manifesting eye-candy" so that the human race could adapt, survive and evolve.§§

Spacetime denied

In Hoffman's book, *The Case Against Reality*, he points out that humanity believes that spacetime is the pre-existing three-dimensional stage in which all of life plays out over time. Furthermore, humanity generally believes that just prior to the Big Bang, 13.8 billion years ago, there was no such thing as Consciousness, just matter, energy and space; then after the Big Bang, life came into existence billions of years later, and Consciousness somehow arose out of that matter-based life. Hoffman, and several other highly respected physicists, such the 2004 Nobel Prize in Physics recipient David Gross and theoretical physicist Professor Ed Witten of Princeton University, argue that this entire framework in which humanity has based its entire understanding of reality is false, or as these professors like to say: 'Spacetime is doomed!'

> *We can prove, with a probability of zero, that our senses*
> *would evolve to show us the Truth of Reality.*
> *Which means our perceptions of space and time and objects*
> *are not the Truth, we make them up on the fly.*
> **Donald Hoffman**[18]

Donald postulates that spacetime is really nothing more than a mental data structure (ego) that our perceptions and sensory systems construct on the fly; we simultaneously create spacetime and discard spacetime as we would any other perception or thought. Since we take our perceptions and thoughts to be real, we therefore take spacetime to be real, when spacetime is yet another play of collapsed-Consciousness.

One of many like-minded colleagues Hoffman points to, who has drawn the same perturbing conclusion from his research findings, is Nima Arkani-Hamed, Professor of the Institute for Advanced Study at Princeton University, who notably stated in a 2016 lecture at Cornell University:

Spacetime is doomed. There is no such thing as spacetime fundamentally in the actual underlying description of the laws of physics. That is very startling, because what physics is supposed to be about is describing things as they happen in space and time. So if there's no spacetime, it's not clear what physics is about.

Hoffman emphasizes that since everything we as a society and scientific community consider to be real is constructed in space and time, then if we postulate that spacetime is doomed, the shock to the whole mental-fabric of society and science could be significant. Hoffman realizes that we as a civilization are going to have to let go of some deeply held beliefs and assumptions to make scientific and human progress, and the assumptions and beliefs needing to be relinquished will be stunning and counterintuitive to us all. One example of mental perplexity that would stem from spacetime being non-existent would be the mere fact that without space there is no volume, and since our bodies, which appear voluminous and real, would no longer be regarded as such, "what is one to do with such preposterous information?" he asks.

Free will

From the point of view of physicalists—those who believe that matter is the primary existing reality in which Consciousness arises—our brains cause our conscious experience and our behavior. Yet the physicalists have no idea how matter generates Consciousness. Physicalists have no theory, not even a remote plausible guess, that explains how neural activity could cause a single conscious experience, like the smell of a rose. For the physicalists, this is the Hard Problem of Consciousness (discussed in the previous chapter) which they are so diligently trying to solve, but to no avail. This unsolvable 'problem' is the thorn in the physicalist's saddle that is quickly eroding away their longstanding materialism-first supremacy.

Another aspect of this problem was discussed in a 2019 Science and Nonduality presentation given by Professor Hoffman. According to most neuroscientists (physicalists), since our brains, via our neural activity, generate Consciousness, all of the decisions being made are not being made by us as independent agents (egos), but by the mechanics of the electrochemistry in our head. This by definition is the absence of free will. To take it a step further, even if we were to have free will, what would give us the free will to have free will? That is, what gives us the freedom to choose whether or not we choose? This leads the physicalists back to the absence of free will, because obviously we don't get the privilege to decide if we are going to decide or not.

> *I do not choose to choose what I choose.*
> *There is a regress here that always ends in darkness.*
> **Sam Harris**[19]

As a reminder, Hoffman and his team are not physicalists, they are monists; nondualists, who do not take objects to have independent stand-alone existences. His findings have led him to the conclusion that objects are appearances in Consciousness and they only appear when an observer perceives them, which means, accordingly, that they have no stand-alone existence. Therefore the neurons in our brain, the electrochemical synapses that physicalists claim give rise to Consciousness, do not exist when they are not perceived. Not only do neurons not have a stand-alone existence, they consequently have no causal powers, and in particular they don't cause our conscious experiences, nor do they cause our behavior. Therefore Consciousness alone is simultaneously the observed and the observer (leaving only observing), and is the free will allowing the staggering manifestation of the observed-observer dance to appear.

From *Love Outpouring*'s point of view this is where it gets interesting, because the physicalists and monists are both correct according to Eastern nondual philosophy, where both views lead to an egoless Reality. By default, the physicalist's stance of not having free will is another way of saying there is no 'doer' (ego) required 'to do' life; that all actions performed for life to happen are just systematically arising from the mechanics of our neurons. If we don't choose our actions, thoughts, sensations and general human faculties, then there is no 'doer' of life required. If there is no 'doer' then the entire construct of self (ego) falls apart and the 'who we have mistaken ourself to be' is exposed as being non-existent. Where physicalists fall short is that they don't regress their 'no free will' findings back to their origin. For if they did—and this could save their fleeting primacy—they would ultimately have to conclude that if there is no ego, no independent observer, no 'doer,' the only plausible 'thing' remaining would be Consciousness—and the Hard Problem of Consciousness would then be solved.

Furthering *Love Outpouring*'s stance, from the conscious-monistic point of view, just stating that all of Totality is Consciousness alone doesn't leave room for a stand-alone ego (doer) to exist separate from Totality to have free will. From the monistic position, it is Consciousness itself that has the free will to choose to choose what it chooses. Either way, physicalism or monism, leads to an egoless Oneness-Reality where free will IS the simultaneous manifestation of life. Aligning with free will means seeing ourSelf for who we really are, Consciousness, thereby melding with the Oneness of the Divine and experiencing directly peace-happy-love.

Beingness

According to Hoffman, in some sense love is fundamental in the manifestation *and* underlying Reality of Consciousness.§§ He is of the understanding that the spiritual traditions are correct in their profound insight that we are not separate Beings from one another, but unified universal love, of which Hoffman gets personal glimpses when he is in a space of no-thought. Hoffman understands God is not 'a Being,' but just 'Being' in itSelf, which is the ground of Consciousness. He recognizes that the spiritual traditions that point to a One-Consciousness Reality are in line with the mathematics of his conscious-agent work as well. He aligns himself with the knowledge that the universe (Consciousness) is trying to know and understand itSelf through us.

Hoffman's advice for young people is beautiful, as he states:

The universe is a lot more interesting than you might expect and You are a lot more interesting than you might expect. You might think you are an irrelevant person in a vast billion light-years across space, and that is not the case. You are the Being that is creating that space all the time, every time you look. So wake up to who You really are [Consciousness alone, Self] outside of space and time, as the author of space and time, the author of everything you see.

Notes

* Victor Goertzel and Mildred G. Goertzel, *Cradles of Eminence*, p. 248.

†   *The New York Times*, March 13, 1949, p. 34.

†† January 1931 issue of *Modern Review*.

§   Subhash Kak, *The Wishing Tree: Presence and Promise of India*, 2001.

§§ Lex Fridman Podcast #293 | Donald Hoffman: Reality Is an Illusion—How Evolution Hid the Truth.

13   Robert Oppenheimer (1904–1967) was an American theoretical physicist and a professor of physics at the University of California, Berkeley. Robert was the head of the Los Alamos Laboratory and is often credited with being the "father of the atomic bomb." The first atomic bomb was successfully detonated on July 16, 1945. Robert later commented that the explosion brought to mind a phrase from the Indian sacred text the Bhagavad Gita: "Now I am become Death, the destroyer of worlds."

15   Mencius (372–289 BC) was a Chinese Confucian philosopher who has often been described as the "second Sage," second only after Confucius himself. Mencius continued Confucius' primary teachings after his passing, which was that human nature is righteous and humane. He drew interest from Western philosophers due to his views on the four cardinal virtues: benevolence, righteousness, wisdom, and propriety.

16   Aldous Leonard Huxley (1894–1963) was an English novelist and critic gifted with a profound and broad intellect whose writings are highly recognized for their cleverness and deep insights. His most notable accomplishment is for his 1932 novel, *Brave New World*. As he aged, Aldous grew more interested in philosophical mysticism and at the age of 45 joined the Vedanta Society of Southern California.

19   Sam Harris is the author of five *New York Times* bestsellers. His writing and public lectures cover a wide range of topics: neuroscience, moral philosophy, religion, meditation practice, human violence, rationality, but generally focus on how a growing understanding of ourselves and the world is changing our sense of how we should live. Sam has a degree in philosophy from Stanford University and a PhD in neuroscience from UCLA. He has also practiced mindfulness meditation for more than 30 years.

Chapter 14

Western Religion and Self

The deeper one sinks into the message of nonduality, the clearer one will see it and experience it in the beauty of everyday life. But as the deepening of understanding occurs, it is common to continuously encounter obstacles that will need to be addressed and be overcome as false. Because of our societal upbringings and indoctrination into Western religions, the largest obstacle to Self-realization typically faced is our unquestioned religious beliefs.

Yet, when we are absolutely honest with ourself, we know inherently that the story of religion, the supposed story of Truth, just doesn't line up with the reality of our continued suffering: the harder we try to unite with God (Divine, Source, Infinite, Spirit, Brahman, Allah, Christ, Buddha, Shiva, Way, and so on), the further away we seem to get from the promised loving integration with Him.

Where most Western religions go wrong is that they have turned a nondual union WITH God (a realization) into a duality of you AND God (a relationship). This duality sends the devotee on a wild goose chase of rituals, dogmas, ceremonies, contemplations, practices, meditations, catechisms, and so on, which are all movements and actions away from themSelf, away from God HimSelf. Religion's perpetual decoupling mechanism is the deception and depiction of God as something 'other than' yourSelf, something that needs to be sought and obtained—an endless pursuit of everlasting exhausting futile action of effort.

He who adheres to the teachings of the church,
as to an infallible rule, assents to whatever the church teaches.
Saint Thomas Aquinas[1]

The decoupling mechanism is the continuous addition of false-truths that never leads to a conclusion, just more false-truths to be worked through. This is why Western religion is not successful—its 'infallible rule' appears to be designed to not solve anything. Compare this to Advaita: as one discards false-truths instead of adding them, one quickly comes to an end, a solution, a conclusion, where the entire movement stops at One with Self, One with God—success, DONE! Once Self-success is realized, no books, buildings, teachings, or deities are further required to experience Oneness with Him/Her. Once unity is experienced, one then rests IN and AS the Divine, deepening the clarity of the Union.

Many people do not advance in the Christian life,
because they get stuck in penances and particular spiritual exercises.
They neglect the love of God, which is the goal.
Brother Lawrence[2]

These 'other than' yourSelf Western exercises of organized religion continuously decouple the devotee from the love they seek, from the love they ARE, holding them in guilt and fear until the time of bodily death.

Fear is the destructive energy in man.
It withers the mind, it distorts thought,
it leads to all kinds of extraordinarily clever
and subtle theories, absurd superstitions, dogmas, and beliefs.
Jiddu Krishnamurti[3]

It is not until the devotee becomes conscious of their own Existence during the waking state of life, and experiences directly the love of God that has always been contained within them AS theirSelf, that they realize the religious vehicle they were traveling in to unite with God was propelling them in the wrong direction: outward instead of inward, separation instead of unity, effort instead of stillness, obtaining instead of relinquishing, chatter instead of silence.

It is deeply realized by the devotee that the problem is not the message contained in the scriptures and texts themselves, but how they have been interpreted and represented by the church, or better stated, misinterpreted and misrepresented. This understanding may at first trigger a rejection of the scriptures by the devotee due to their initial feelings about the misuse of power by such establishments, but the devotee will soon come to realize the intimate unity with God when the scriptures are understood from a nondual perspective; allowing the devotee to fall deeper and deeper than ever before in love with themSelf, others, the world and the Divine. Unconditional love and unity with the Divine is witnessed when, at first, the devotee separates the church from God, realizes God directly AS themSelf, then re-enters their religion with a much deeper intimacy with God and a greater clarity of Him/Her than ever before.

Brother Lawrence (1614–1691)

Marshall Davis is a retired Baptist pastor of 40+ years who takes the message of Jesus one step further by saying, "Religion is not about a relationship with Him, but a realization AS Him." Marshall is the author of over 15 books and has an admired podcast known as The Tao of Christ that explores the mystical roots of Christianity. Marshall describes his teaching as Christian nonduality, unitive Awareness, and/or union with God. He has helped to open many Christians' eyes to the real mission of Jesus: to transcend dual-reality and wake up to the spiritual-Reality of being One with the Father, which Jesus called the Kingdom of God and Heaven on Earth.

One of Marshall's many books is the modern English translation of the 300+ year-old spiritual classic, *The Practice of the Presence of God*. This book contains an enlightening series of letters written in the mid 1600s by a French Christian layman by the name of Brother Lawrence, to Monsignor Joseph de Beaufort, vicar general to the Archbishop of Paris.

At a young age an injury to Lawrence's sciatic nerve while in the army left him debilitated and unable to support himself. Within six years of his injury he entered the Discalced Carmelite monastery in Paris, where he resided as a servant until his death in 1691. During his stay at the monastery he attracted many visitors seeking spiritual guidance, due to his reputation for practical obtainable wisdom.

In the letters, Brother Lawrence lays out his simple and natural method for being fully and permanently present with God, regardless of one's undertakings and surroundings. He reported that his practice was to merely turn his attention to the Divine Presence available at all times during his activities, and stay present with the Presence for as long as possible.

Lawrence's Christian description of experiencing God directly, via truthful-knowledge and Self-investigation, remarkably resembles what is being described in the Advaita Vedanta teachings. It is clear from Lawrence's practice that regardless of where one starts on the path of Unity with God or Self-realization, at the subtlest levels, all God-realization exercises merge into the same practice.

Lawrence's practice, which he so perfectly calls "the Practice of the Presence of God," is nearly the same Self-abidance practice depicted in Chapter 11, only called by a different name: the Direct Path of Self-inquiry. Brother Lawrence's understanding of the 'Practice' basically tracks right alongside Ramana Maharshi's Self-realization book, *Nan Yar?* (Who Am I?), with the only difference being the language of the separate cultures and time periods in which each one of these sages lived.

Therefore, Lawrence's practice, via his letters and Spiritual Maxims manifesto, is an incredibly impactful Christian source for any aspirant to use as a catalyst to Know thySelf and unite IN and AS the Oneness of God.

Below are some illuminating excerpts from Lawrence's letters, taken from Marshall Davis's translation, depicting the unmistakable similarities between his Western religious mind and the Eastern perennial message of Advaita:

Self-Knowledge [Jñāna]:

In the beginning of the spiritual life, we ought to be faithful in denying ourselves [ego] and thoroughly examine [Self-investigation] what we are.

In the beginning, one often thinks of this practice as wasting time, but you must continue and persevere in it. Do not be discouraged by the natural resistance [ego denying the Self as real] that you might experience in doing this practice [Self-inquiry].

To practice this correctly, the Heart must be empty of all other things [relinquish all resistance to everything 'other than' yourSelf].

Understanding the mind [ego] is of little value. Useless thoughts spoil everything. All troubles begin here. We ought to let go [Path of Jñāna] of such thoughts as soon as we are aware of them. They are worthless to either life or salvation.

When the mind [ego] first undertakes spiritual devotion, it has the bad habits of wandering and distraction. These are difficult to overcome and pull us against our will toward worldly things [things 'other than' ourSelf]. The will [the love to know yourSelf] must pull the mind [ego] back into tranquility [Self, Heart].

Do not restrict yourself to certain religious rules or forms of devotion. It is not necessary to be in church to be with God [Self]. Have courage.

The more one knows Him [Self], the more one desires to know Him. Knowledge [Jñāna] is commonly understood as the measure of love [Bhakti].

> *The measure of love is to love without measure.*
> **Saint Francis de Sales**[4]

Then out of love for Him [Self], I renounced everything [ego] that was not God [everything 'other than' Self].

Self-Investigation [Self-inquiry]:

I repeat, let us go inside ourSelves [Self-inquiry].

Only those who experience this [the love of ourSelf] and practice it [Self-inquiry] can comprehend it.

We shall not seek pleasure in this exercise [no expectations, no hope, no intentions].

If you do it as you ought, you can be assured that you will soon see results [sphuranas, ever-present happiness].

My prayer [Self-inquiry] is nothing more than the sense of the Presence of God [Self-Awareness].

Surrender yourself [via Self-inquiry] to an attitude of faithful devotion and insight rather than reasoning and thinking.

I have arrived at a state of mind [a Way of Being] where it is more difficult for me NOT to think of God [Self] than it was at the beginning to think of Him.

I do this [Self-inquire] simply by paying attention to, and directing my affection to, God [Self]. I call this the actual Presence of God, which is a habitual, silent, and secret communion of the soul with God [Self].

I know that some people say that this state is inactivity, delusion, and self-love [ego-love]. I confess that it is inactivity, but it is holy inactivity [God-abidance]. I cannot bear to hear this [God-realization] called delusion.

In conclusion, by repeating this practice often it becomes second nature, and the Presence of God [Self, Being] becomes our normal state of mind [Way of Being].

The Benefits [peace-happy-love-contentment]:

This [Self-realization] often causes such joys and raptures inwardly, and sometimes outwardly [Love Outpouring], that I am forced to make an effort to moderate them to prevent their appearances to others.

I continually find within me a great treasure of contentment and satisfaction [immense silent-peace].

When our minds are focused on God [Self], suffering will be filled with peace and solace [peace-happy-love, Ananda].

If we do our part [Self-inquiry], we shall soon see the transformation within us that we desire.

In the end we will develop a habit [a permanent Presence], which will naturally produce acts through us without effort [effortless-action, Wu Wei], to our exceedingly great delight [causeless joy].

If it [Self-inquiry] is pursued faithfully, it works imperceptibly to produce marvelous results [peace-happy-love].

Meister Eckhart (1260–1327)

The following paragraphs are a brief summary of the prologue to Oliver Davies' book, *Meister Eckhart: Selected Writings*. They are the history of the Christian philosophy and mysticism of Meister Eckhart, who at his core sought to reconcile traditional Christian belief with transcendental metaphysics. You are highly encouraged to read Eckhart's actual sermons within Davies' book to experience directly the profound insights of this transformational Christian mystic.

Johannes Eckhart, respectfully known as Meister Eckhart after receiving his Master's degree in 1302, was born in Thuringia, Germany in around 1260. At the age of 15 Eckhart entered the Dominican Order of the Catholic Church in Cologne, Germany and studied under Albert the Great. He was directly influenced by the great thinker and Dominican theologian, Thomas Aquinas, which could have been what gained him the position of Prior of Thuringia (a prior was a superior officer overseeing churches and dioceses within a province) at the age of 35.

Over the course of his life, Eckhart became renowned as a theologian, philosopher and mystic. Due to his brilliant use of imagery and metaphysical passion to depict a 'single Oneness' between Self and God, Eckhart is still considered today to be one of the most earnest and radical thinkers ever associated with Christianity.

In 1326, Eckhart's Oneness methods led him to become the first and only Dominican theologian of major rank to face charges of heresy. The charges were eventually dropped due to the court finding the doctrines to comply with the orthodox tradition. But soon after acquittal, Pope John XXII found Eckhart's doctrines to be "evil-sounding, rash and suspect of heresy." Prior to any sort of conviction and punishment on the matter, Meister Eckhart died in March of 1327.

Eckhart surely pushed the boundaries of blasphemy with respect to the church's views on such vital matters, hence the heresy charges. Eckhart never made the direct claim that humankind and God were One, for he knew his life was at stake if he ever made such a sacrilegious statement. Yet his analogies and imagery of the metaphysical universe came so close to making such a profound claim that anyone with any sort of logical insight could see this was precisely what he was pointing to: the Soul (Self) and God are One.

> *People should not worry so much about what they do [ego],*
> *but rather about what they are [Self].*
> **Meister Eckhart**[5]

His challenge was to foundationally affix the dynamics of the One within the context of the Christian Trinity of 'more than one'; not an easy task. Eckhart clarified that the word One is the greatest descriptor to define God, since all other like-kind words 'add' something to God, such as God Almighty, All-Powerful and Godhead, which limits God's One-infinity. He claimed that adding words onto the description of God shrouded Him in concepts that only suited human nature, not God's (this is likened to not identifying as our ego's adjuncts, but only with 'I' or 'I am').

Eckhart claimed that the world does not reside or evolve in time, but that it exists outside of time in eternity. He stated that Creation must be eternal as it could not have occurred within time, since time itself did not presuppose Creation. He believed that Creation was not some cataclysmic event that happened eons ago, but is unborn, and is evolving IN and AS this originless space (likened to finite collapsed-Consciousness appearing within infinite-Consciousness). This understanding is Eckhart's description of Totality. Eckhart stresses that we are to become wholly embodied as the Existence of this unborn-eternal Creation, that is, become One with the Mind-of-God.

> *For they who possess God [Self] alone are one in the One*
> *in whom all multiplicity is One and is non-multiplicity.*
> **Meister Eckhart[6]**

The Meister stated that all multiplicity, the fragmentations of the manifestation, were on loan from the One-God, in which nothing has its own ownership; all of manifestation is borrowed from the One. This is another way of saying that nothing in the multiplicity of the manifestation has a stand-alone existence, that everything has the underlying nature and quality of emptiness, or God (Self, Consciousness).

In Eckhart's eyes there is only one portion of the multiplicity that is not separate from God, and which has its own existence, what he called Soul, Light, Intellect; that is, the Self. He outlines that the Intellect is 'more nameless than with name' and 'more unknown than known,' and is beyond humankind's intellectualization. In the Meister's terms, a human's unity with God was what he referred to as a transcendental potentiality; a non-objective coupling between Self and God that cannot be known directly by the mind, and therefore can only be known by negating what it is not (Neti Neti).

The Meister proclaimed that our Self-Existence was actually God giving birth to HimSelf inside us constantly (Self-shining), which is simply His nature. He preached that those who do not experience His Beingness within themSelf, witnessing His birth within us, are not open to allowing Him to do so. He claimed most would prefer to deny His Presence with false notions of ourself (ego) and to attach to Godless-objects, namely anything 'other than' ourSelf.

Eckhart declares that detachment from physical objects in the world is liberation for the mind. Cutting one's self off from worldly things is a must to significantly progress down the path of enlightenment. Detachment is primarily to allow a mind to become free enough to transcend the limitations of the human ego and give the mind the utmost possibility to experience the Oneness of God. The Meister states that this transcendence from the world and uniting with God will be realized as a 'Knowing-essence' from within; an inherent-Knowing.

> *The eye through which I see God*
> *is the same eye through which God sees me:*
> *my eye and God's eye are One eye,*
> *One seeing, One knowing, One love.*
> **Meister Eckhart**[7]

The Meister preached that as one experienced this Knowing-essence and Oneness with God, a virtue of humility would arise and any further human efforts would be carried into the world as altruism: seeing and treating others as if they were OneSelf. Eckhart asserts that a human who is detached from the world is loving, wise, and humble, possessing an aura of serenity, and entirely contained in the Presence of God (ever-present happiness). The Meister declares that as a person loses their selfhood (ego) by fixating their Heart (Self) in God, which he claimed was the primary way to experience directly the Presence of God, they become enlightened and well established in the Christian life of virtue.

Only those for whom God [Self] is present in all things
and who make the very best of their reason,
know what true peace is and truly possess Heaven.
Meister Eckhart[8]

It's clear that Eckhart's finest talent was his creative-imaginative writing and preaching skills that allowed him to describe the absolute affinity of the Oneness of Self and God without actually saying 'I am God.' This subtleness leaves only a very small distinction, then, between Eckhart and Jesus Christ, in which the only obvious difference between the two was that Jesus was willing to openly admit 'I and the Father are One,' whereas Eckhart would not cross this line, at least not publically.

Diversity of Oneness

The message of eternal bliss is not a hidden secret; it is not forbidden wisdom that is only periodically made available to a select few 'chosen ones.' The message and wisdom is present and available IN and AS every perceived object (especially the object of 'you') known in the manifestation of life, including every great religion and spiritual/mystical practice. The following are relevant examples of the diversity of religious/spiritual/mystical Oneness (Selfness), which inherently expresses the equivalence of all Beings, regardless of their skin color, race, gender or heritage.

• **Christianity**

There is neither Jew nor Greek, there is neither bond nor free, there is neither male nor female: for ye are all One in Christ Jesus.
—Saint Paul (Galatians 3:28)

It will be as if He were One with our soul, and our soul One with Him.
—Brother Lawrence

For indeed, the Kingdom of God is within You.
—Jesus of Nazareth (Luke 17:21)

• **Christian mysticism**

When the Soul wants to experience something She throws out an image in front of her and then steps into it.
—Meister Eckhart

Be gentle to all and stern with yourSelf.
—Saint Teresa of Avila

• **Judaism**

Whoever saves one life saves the entire world.
—Rav Ashi (Babylonian Talmud)

• **Taoism**

Do not develop the nature which is of man [ego], but develop the nature which is of God [Self].
—Chuang Tzu

• **Hinduism**

Tat Tvam Asi: Thou Art That.
Brahman [Reality] is One without a second.
—Chandogya Upanishad

I am the Soul which dwells in the Heart of all things.
I am the beginning, the middle, and the end of all that lives.
—Krishna (Bhagavad Gita, Chapter 10)

- **Native American Indian**

  Man did not weave the web of life; he is merely a strand in it.
  Whatever he does to the web, he does to himSelf.
  —Chief Seattle

  The Earth and mySelf are of One mind.
  —Chief Joseph

- **Buddhism**

  Do not look for a sanctuary in anyone except yourSelf.
  —Siddhartha Gautama, also known as Buddha

- **Zen**

  If you cannot find the Truth right where you are, where do
  you expect to find it?
  —Dogen Zenji

- **African heritage**

  Ubuntu: I am, because You are.
  —Zulu proverb

- **Islam**

  Whoever knows themSelf knows their Lord. I know my Lord
  through my Lord.
  —Prophet Muhammad

- **Sufism (Islamic mystics)**

  I saw my Lord with the eye of the Heart.
  I asked, "Who are You?" He replied, "You."
  —Al Hallaj

  I have learned so much from God that I can no longer call
  myself a Christian, a Hindu, a Muslim, a Buddhist, a Jew.
  —Hafez

- **Sikhism**

  He who regards all men as equals [One] is religious.
  He who has no faith in himSelf can never have faith in God
  [Self].
  —Baba Nanak

- **Jainism**

  In happiness and suffering, in joy and grief, we should
  regard all creatures as we regard our own Self.
  —Mahavira

- **Physics**

  A physicist is just an atom's way of looking at itSelf. I go into
  the Upanishads to ask questions.
  —Niels Bohr

  Try not to become a man of success [ego], but rather try to
  become a man of value [Self].
  —Albert Einstein

- **The Way** (the effortless-action of Being)

  Christianity: "I am **the Way**, the Truth, and the life." (Jesus of Nazareth)

  Hinduism: "Hinduism is **a Way** of life, not a religion." (Sadhguru)

  Buddhism: "All know **the Way**; few actually walk it." (Bodhidharma)

  Taoism: "Taoism is **the Way** of the universe." (Tao proverb)

  Zen: "Zen is **the Way** of complete Self-realization." (Zenkei Shibayama)

  Islam: "Islam is **a Way** of life (Sunnah)." (Muhammad)

- **The Great Knowledge of all spiritual traditions** (that the inherent nature of each one of us is equivalent to the inherent nature of eternity)

  Christianity: I and the Father are One

  Hinduism: Atman [Self] equals Brahman [God]

  Buddhism: Samsara equals Nirvana

  Taoism: What is and what is not create each other

  Zen: Form is emptiness, emptiness is form

  Islam: As above, so below

- **Trinity** (doctrines or philosophies of three entities in one Godhead)

  Christianity: (Trinity) Father, Son and Holy Ghost

  Hinduism: (Brahman) Existence-Consciousness-Bliss [Sat-Chit-Ananda]

  Buddhism: (Trikaya) Essence, Enjoyment and Transformation

  Taoism: (San Qing) Primordial Beginning, Numinous Treasure and Tao's Power

Jainism: (Three Jewels) Right Belief, Right Knowledge and Right Conduct

'I AM' sharing

From a Christianity point of view, 'gospel' means 'good news.' And the real good news is not simply that Jesus is the Son of God, but that Jesus was the one God sent to shine His light through, and to open the eyes and ears of everyone else to the fact that they too are the Son of God!

Jesus proclaimed that we all contain within us an inner portal to unity with the Divine; the portal being our 'I am.' He restated, time and time again, that His 'I am' is our 'I am' is God's 'I am'; that your 'I am' is yourSelf...that your 'I am' is your portal to directly experience Heaven on Earth, and is your Self-illuminating light-source to shine unconditional love into and onto humanity.

In the Old Testament, Exodus 3:13–14, Moses said to God, "Suppose I go to the Israelites and say to them, 'The God of your fathers has sent me to you,' and they ask me, 'What is his name?' Then what shall I tell them?" God said to Moses, "*I am* who *I am*. This is what you are to say to the Israelites: '*I am* has sent me to you.'"

When Jesus said in John 14:6, "*I am* the way, the Truth, and the life. No one comes to the Father except through Me," the emphasis is typically placed on Jesus' physical person in the word 'Me,' but this is misdirected. The emphasis refers to the '*I am*' at the start of the sentence; the same '*I am*' portal in which all of humanity has direct access to experience the Father AS One.

Jesus reiterates several times throughout the Bible that His 'I' and God's 'I' are the same 'I,' which again is your 'I.' In John 14:11 Jesus proclaims, "Believe me when I say that I am in the Father and the Father is in me," and further reinforces His claims in John 10:30, when he genuinely yet radically states, "I and the Father are One."

The real guru is THAT which is
shining in your Heart as 'I Am.'
Michael James[9]

The Mahavakyas are Hindu statements defined as the 'Great Utterances.' They are typically distilled to four key Upanishadic statements that define the nature of Reality and one's identity with it. The four sacred Mahavakyas are:

1. Consciousness is Brahman*
2. Atman (Self) is Brahman
3. Thou art That, Brahman You are
4. I am Brahman

* Brahman is that which is Absolute, fills all space, is complete in itself, to which there is no second, and which is continuously present in everything, from the creator down to the lowest of matter.

According to the Shankaracharya Narayana Guru, the Mahavakyas all essentially have the same message:

To realize that we are one with Brahman and to love each other and love all living and non-living Beings. If it is realized that you and I are part of Brahman, how can we hate or destroy each other?

Yet, regardless of how profound these four Hindu statements are, Sri Ramana Maharshi, the highly adorned Advaita Indian sage of the twentieth century, claimed there is one statement that is even more sacred than these four; a Jewish/Christian statement: Exodus 3:14, 'I am who I am.'

According to Michael James, author of *Happiness and the Art of Being*, the reason for Sri Ramana's Mahavakyas claim was due to the subtle duality still inherent in the four Mahavakyas' definitions. Just by having more than one descriptor of Oneness in the Mahavakyas statements, there is the possibility of misleading a devotee into thinking that 'Consciousness,' 'Atman,' 'That,' or 'Brahman' are something 'other than' one's Self; objects that need to be acquired outside of their Self. Sri Ramana stated that the Exodus 3:14 statement was the most direct statement of Self possible, leaving the devotee with absolute clarity that to know one's Self they did not have to leave one's Self to do so: *I am I* (Sanskrit: *aham aham*) is the utmost direct pathless-path for one to pertain the Self-knowledge of themSelf.

Self-psalm

Be Still,
and Know
I am
God.
Psalm 46:10[10]

Psalm 46:10 is a beautiful representation of the message of eternity. It illustrates the clarity of Being; the simple message of Christ and all other Christian-minded saints and prophets, which was/is: just Be and experience peace: experience Him. Utilizing the Self equation from Chapter 9, Psalm 46:10 can be reconfigured to show unity with the nondual message of Advaita.

Self = Existence + Consciousness + Peace-Happy-Love
Self = Psalm 46:10
Self (I am God) = Existence (Be) + Consciousness (Know) + Peace-Happy-Love (Still)
Self = I am God = Be + Know + Still

The psalm also gives the devotee a direct-experience and an inherent-Knowing of what God actually IS. By stilling the mind and resting in Being via our 'I am,' we experience Him directly AS ourSelf. God is not 'a Being,' but just 'Being'; and yourBeing is myBeing is ourBeing is HisBeing. It becomes apparent that God is not some independent Marvel superhero ruler who utilizes His power to dominate the cosmos, but is 'Being: Absolute Contentment and Wholeness' (not 'a Being' of Absolute Contentment and Wholeness, just 'Being' AS that).

Die to Self

Several times throughout the New Testament, Jesus depicts the only way to experience Heaven on Earth, and be One as He and the Father are One: that you must first die to Self.

But what is it that Jesus is referring to that dies in order to experience Self directly? Simply put, it is the ego. The only real difference between Jesus' message and what is being pointed to in Eastern philosophy is in the words and phrases used during their eras. Destroying the ego and living as One with God (Self) is expressed in several phrases throughout the Bible, such as:

- "Crucify the flesh [kill the ego]"
- "Die to sin [ego] and live to righteousness [Self]"
- "Present your bodies [ego] as a living sacrifice [Self-inquiry]"
- "Be dead to sin [ego] and alive to God [Self]"
- "It is no longer I who live [ego], but Christ [Self] who lives in me"

There are also several 'die to Self' statements in the Bible that align with similar messages of Advaita. The following are two Christian statements and two Advaita statements. Notice the remarkable similarities between the two cultures. By reading these statements, including the phrases from above, how can you not acknowledge that Western religion and Eastern philosophy are suggesting the same path to God-realization?

> Whoever seeks to preserve his life [live by flesh/ego] will lose it [sin, suffer], but whoever loses his life [crucify the flesh, ego-elimination] will keep it [Kingdom of God, Self].
> —Jesus of Nazareth (Luke 17:33)

> For if you live according to the flesh [ego] you will die [sin, suffer], but if by the Spirit [Self] you put to death the deeds of the body [ego], you will live [in the Kingdom of God, as Self].
> —Saint Paul (Romans 8:13)

> Your glory lies [Heaven on Earth] where you [flesh, ego] cease to exist [God, Self].
> —Sri Ramana Maharshi (Maharshi's Gospel)

> To be free in the world [ego-free] you must die to the world [crucify the flesh, ego-elimination], then the universe is your own [Kingdom of God, Self], it becomes your body, an expression, and a tool; the happiness of being absolutely free [fleshless, egoless] is beyond description [Heaven on Earth, Bliss].
> —Sri Nisargadatta Maharaj (*I Am That*)

After spending more and more time analyzing Christianity and inherently realizing that the perennial message does align with it, you can abandon both Christianity and Advaita/Nonduality as 'not the Truth,' only truthful-knowledge, and rest in the only Absolute left remaining: yourSelf. Then, once fully established in Self, You can come back to Christianity and/or Advaita and know them directly and intimately as One with yourSelf...the original purpose of ALL religion, spiritual and mystical experiences.

Notes

4   St Francis de Sales (1567–1622) was the Catholic Bishop of Geneva, Switzerland. He is known also for his practice of spiritual direction, which involves being with people as they attempt to deepen their relationship with the Divine and grow in their spirituality.

10   Psalm 46:10 of the Old Testament is the 46th psalm in the biblical Book of Psalms, subtitled "Song of Holy Confidence." The New King James Version describes it as "Cease Striving." The verse depicts how God is telling the people to stop using their futile human efforts to fight a battle bigger than themselves. They are to stop striving to gain results, and turn to God and let Him take His place in the situation.

Appendix

Acknowledgments

A loving outpouring goes out to the following Beings for their many insightful contributions that led to the fruition of this book:

Alan F., Jay R., Mark I., Jeremy F., Pete G., Dan H., Doug B., Max F. and the FF5.

Quote Sources

Epigraph

1   Meister Eckhart
    Breakthrough: Meister Eckhart's Creation Spirituality, in New Translation, tr. Matthew Fox, Doubleday, 1980
2   Brother Lawrence
    The Practice of the Presence of God, tr. Marshall Davis, independently published, 2013

Prologue i

1   Wei Wu Wei
    Wei Wu Wei, *Open Secret*, Sentient Publications, 2nd edition, 2004
2   Jiddu Krishnamurti
    Jiddu Krishnamurti, *Think on These Things*, HarperOne, 1989
3   Rumi
    Attributed
4   Pooh and Tigger
    Benjamin Hoff, *The Tao of Pooh*, Dutton Adult, 1981

Prologue ii

1   Sant Kirpal Singh Ji
    Man! Know Thyself: Being a Talk Given by Sant Kirpal Singh Ji for Seekers after Truth, 1954

2   Meister Eckhart
    Meister Eckhart: Selected Writings, tr. Oliver Davies, Penguin Classics, 1994

3   Rumi
    Rumi: Selected Poems, tr. Coleman Barks, Penguin Classics, 2004

4   Sri Nisargadatta Maharaj
    I Am That, tr. Maurice Frydman, Acorn Press, 1973

Chapter 1

1   Anne Frank
    Anne Frank: The Diary of a Young Girl, Bantam, reissue edition, 1997

2   Erwin Schrodinger
    'On Determinism and Free Will,' section of *What Is Life?* 1944

3   Eckhart Tolle
    A New Earth: Awakening to Your Life's Purpose, Plumb, 2005

4   Albert Einstein
    William Hermanns, *Einstein and the Poet: In Search of the Cosmic Man*, Brandon Books, 1983

5   Blaise Pascal
    Pensées [Thoughts], tr. Dr A.J. Krailsheimer, Penguin Classics, 1995

6   Sri Nisargadatta Maharaj
    I Am That, tr. Maurice Frydman, Acorn Press, 1973

7   Buckminster Fuller
    St Martin's Griffin, 1982

8   David Bohm

'The Nature of Things,' Dr David Bohm interviewed by David Suzuki, CBC Canadian Radio, 1979

9   Mark Twain

Mark Twain's Notebooks, ed. Carlo De Vito, Black Dog & Leventhal, 2015

10   Mother Teresa

Attributed

11   Morpheus

Movie, *The Matrix*, Warner Bros. Entertainment, 1999

12   Thomas Aquinas

St. Thomas Aquinas Philosophical Texts, ed. Thomas Gilby, Oxford University Press, 1951

Chapter 2

1   E.E. Cummings

A Miscellany, ed. George J. Firmage, October House, 1967

2   Michael James

Sri Ramana Teachings Podcasts, license: https://creativecommons.org/licenses/by-sa/4.0/ No changes were made

3   Sri Ramana Maharshi

Padamalai, *Teachings of Sri Ramana Maharshi: Recorded by Muruganar*, tr. Dr. T. V. Venkatasubramanian, Robert Butler and David Godman; ed. David Godman, Avadhuta Foundation, 2004

4   St Francis of Assisi

Attributed

5   David Carse

Perfect Brilliant Stillness, Non-Duality Press, 2005

6   Rupert Spira

Rupert Spira YouTube Channel

7   Niels Bohr
     L.I. Ponomarev, *The Quantum Dice*, CRC Press, 1993
8   Lao Tsu
     Tao Te Ching, tr. Gia-Fu Feng and Jane English, Vintage
     Books, 1989
9   Zen koan
     Anonymous
10   Thich Nhat Hanh
     You Are Here: Discovering the Magic of the Present Moment,
     Shambhala, 2010
11   Seng-ts'an
     Hsin-Hsin Ming, tr. Richard B. Clarke, White Pine Press,
     1973
12   Jiddu Krishnamurti
     The Order of the Star in the East Dissolution Speech,
     1929
13   Thich Nhat Hanh
     Your True Home: Everyday Wisdom of Thich Nhat Hanh,
     Shambhala, 2011
14   Meister Eckhart
     Attributed
15   Francis Lucille
     The Perfume of Silence, Truespeech Productions, 2006
16   Dante
     Epic poem: *Inferno*, 1300
17   David Carse
     Perfect Brilliant Stillness, Non-Duality Press, 2005
18   Jiddu Krishnamurti
     Social Responsibility: Talks, Krishnamurti Foundation, 2017
19   Ram Dass
     Film: *Becoming Nobody*, dir. Jamie Catto, 2019
20   Jiddu Krishnamurti
     Commentaries on Living, Series II, Chapter 6 'Boredom,'
     Krishnamurti Foundation, 1956

21   Niels Bohr
       Attributed
22   St John of the Cross
       The Collected Works of Saint John of the Cross, tr. Kieran
       Kavanaugh and Otilio Rodriguez, ICS Publications, 2010
23   Albert Einstein
       Memoirs of William Miller, editor, *Life Magazine*, 1955

Chapter 3

1   Madeleine L'Engle
       Madeleine L'Engle, *An Acceptable Time*, Macmillan, 2007
2   Confucius
       Debbie Brewer, *Quotes of Confucius and Their
       Interpretations*, A Words of Wisdom Collection Book,
       Lulu, 2020
3   Eckhart Tolle
       A New Earth: Awakening to Your Life's Purpose, Plumb,
       2005

Chapter 4

1   Sri Nisargadatta Maharaj
       I Am That, tr. Maurice Frydman, Acorn Press, 1973

Chapter 5

1   Albert Einstein
       Ideas and Opinions, tr. Carl Seelig, Wings Books, 1954

Chapter 6

1   David Bohm
       Read at the memorial service of Malcolm Lee
       Sagenkahnand, 1987
2   Rumi
       Attributed

3   David Bohm
    Wholeness and the Implicate Order, Routledge, 1980
4   Sri Nisargadatta Maharaj
    I Am That, tr. Maurice Frydman, Acorn Press, 1973
5   Erwin Schrodinger
    'On Determinism and Free Will,' section of *What Is Life?*
    1944
6   Seng-ts'an
    Hsin-Hsin Ming, tr. Richard B. Clarke, White Pine Press,
    1973
7   Prophet Muhammad
    Muhyiddin Ibn 'Arabi, Awhad al-din Balyani, *Know
    Yourself: An Explanation on the Oneness of Being*, tr. Cecilia
    Twinch, Beshara Publications, 2011
8   Albert Einstein
    William Hermanns, *Einstein and the Poet: In Search of the
    Cosmic Man*, Brandon Books, 1983
9   Psalm 82:6
    Bible, The Old Testament
10 Ramana Maharshi
    Sri Sadhu Om, Sri Ramana Kshetra, *The Path of Sri
    Ramana*, Kanvashram Trust, Tiruvannamalai, 1971
11 Jesus of Nazareth
    Matthew 4:17, Bible, The New Testament
12 Henry David Thoreau
    *Walden: "It's not what you look at that matters, it's what
    you see."* Scope Publishing, 2015
13 Eckhart Tolle
    The Power of Now: A Guide to Spiritual Enlightenment,
    New World Library, 2004
14 William Blake
    The Marriage of Heaven and Hell, ed. Geoffrey L. Keynes,
    Oxford University Press, 1975, reprint of 1790 original

Chapter 7

1 Niels Bohr
   Attributed
2 Sri Ramana Maharshi
   Who Am I? The Teaching of Bhagavan Sri Ramana Maharshi, 32nd edition, Sri Ramanasramam, Tiruvannamalai, 2021
3 Albert Einstein
   'Death of a Genius,' *Life Magazine*, 2 May, 1955. From a 1954 conversation with Einstein and Hermanns
4 Sri Muruganar
   Guru Vachaka Kovai, ed. and tr. David Godman, Avadhuta Foundation, 2008, #622, note
5 Marshall Davis
   The Tao of Christ Podcast, 2020
6 Tony Parsons
   The Open Secret Website
7 Brother Lawrence
   The Practice of the Presence of God, tr. Marshall Davis, 2013

Chapter 8

1 Rumi
   Timothy Frek, *Rumi Wisdom: Daily Teachings from the Great Sufi Master*, Hamlyn, 2000
2 Sri Atmananda Krishna Menon
   Notes on Spiritual Discourses of Shri Atmananda, tr. Nitya Tripta, Non-Duality Press, 2006
3 David Bohm
   Thought as a System, Routledge, 2004
4 The Buddha
   Attributed
5 Sri Ramana Maharshi
   Ulladu Narpadu (Forty Verses on What Exists), tr. Michael James, verse 25, Happiness of Being Website,

license: https://creativecommons.org/licenses/by-sa/4.0/
No changes were made

6   Jiddu Krishnamurti
    The Book of Life: Daily Meditations with Krishnamurti,
    HarperOne, 1995

7   Sigmund Freud
    Attributed

8   Carl Jung
    Psychology and Alchemy, tr. Gerhard Adler and R.F.C.
    Hull, Princeton University Press, 1980

9   Albert Einstein
    William Hermanns, *Einstein and the Poet: In Search of the
    Cosmic Man,* Brandon Books, 1983

10 Martin Luther King Jr
    Engraved in stone at the Martin Luther King Jr Memorial.
    MLK Memorial is a national memorial located in West
    Potomac Park next to the National Mall in Washington,
    DC.

11 David Bohm
    F. David Peat and John Briggs, 'Interview with David
    Bohm,' *Omni Magazine,* 1987

12 Albert Einstein
    Letter to the family of Michele Besso after Besso's death,
    1955

13 Nima Arkani-Hamed
    Cornell Messenger Lecture, 2016

Chapter 9

1   Jesus of Nazareth
    Matthew 6:22–23, Bible, The New Testament

2   The Buddha
    Attributed

3   Rupert Spira
    Daily Quotes

4 Jerry Garcia
Jerry Garcia interview, *Relix Magazine*, 1995
5 Bhagavad Gita
Krishna: Bhagavad Gita (2:55), tr. Eknath Easwaran, Nilgiri Press, 1985
6 Sri Muruganar
Guru Vachaka Kovai, ed. and tr. David Godman, Avadhuta Foundation, 2008, #796, note
7 Jiddu Krishnamurti
Poona India Fourth Public Talk, September 19, 1948
8 Rumi
Hush, Don't Say Anything to God: Passionate Poems of Rumi, Shahram Shiva, Jain Publishing Co., 1999

Chapter 10

1 Nelson Mandela
Long Walk to Freedom, Back Bay Books, 1995
2 Michael James
Sri Ramana Teachings Podcasts, license: https://creativecommons.org/licenses/by-sa/4.0/ No changes were made
3 Sri Ramana Maharshi
Upadesa Undiyar (The Essence of Spiritual Instructions), tr. Michael James, verse 29, Happiness of Being Website, license: https://creativecommons.org/licenses/by-sa/4.0/ No changes were made
4 Rav Ashi
Babylonian Talmud
5 Saint Francis of Assisi
Attributed
6 Jiddu Krishnamurti
Brockwood Park School Discussion 6: What is your responsibility in a sick society? 1972

7   Jiddu Krishnamurti
    Beyond Violence, Part 1, Chapter 3, Third Public Talk, Santa Monica, 1970
8   Rumi
    The Love Poems of Rumi, ed. Deepak Chopra, Ebury Press, 1998
9   Sri Nisargadatta Maharaj
    I Am That, tr. Maurice Frydman, Acorn Press, 1973

Chapter 11

1   Shakti Caterina Maggi
    Shakti Caterina Maggi Website: Videos
2   Sherlock Holmes
    Arthur Conan Doyle, *His Last Bow: Some Reminiscences of Sherlock Holmes*, John Murray Publisher, 1917
3   Donald Hoffman
    Lex Fridman Interview #293: Donald Hoffman: Reality Is an Illusion—How Evolution Hid the Truth, 2022
4   Saint Thomas Aquinas
    Summa Theologiae or *Summa Theologica*, 1485
5   Sri Ramana Maharshi
    Sri Ramana Teachings Podcasts, license: https://creativecommons.org/licenses/by-sa/4.0/ No changes were made
6   Rumi
    The Essential Rumi, tr. Coleman Barks, HarperOne, 2004
7   Sri Ramana Maharshi
    Who Am I? The Teaching of Bhagavan Sri Ramana Maharshi, 32nd edition, Sri Ramanasraman, Tiruvannamalai, 2021
8   Brother Lawrence
    The Practice of the Presence of God, tr. Marshall Davis, 2013
9   David Godman
    Talks on Sri Ramana Maharshi: Narrated by David Godman—Self-Enquiry, 2015

10   Bruce Lee
       Bruce Lee: The Lost Interview, *The Pierre Berton Show*, 1971
11   Francis Lucille
       The Perfume of Silence, Truespeech Productions, 2006
12   Zen proverb
       Traditional

Chapter 12

1   Albert Einstein
       Walter Isaacson, *Einstein: His Life and Universe*, Simon & Schuster, 2008
2   Albert Einstein
       'Death of a Genius,' *Life Magazine*, 2 May, 1955. From a 1954 conversation with Einstein and Hermanns
3   Max Planck
       The New Science, Greenwich, 1959
4   Bernardo Kastrup
       'Mind Over Matter,' *Beshara Magazine*, Issue 18, 2021
5   Bernardo Kastrup
       Brief Peeks Beyond: Critical Essays on Metaphysics, Neuroscience, Free Will, Skepticism and Culture, Iff Books, 2015
6   Erwin Schrodinger
       My View of the World, Cambridge University Press, 1961
7   David Chalmers
       YouTube Video: Hard Problem of Consciousness, David Chalmers, 2016
8   Max Planck
       Where Is Science Going? Forgotten Books, 2018
9   Carl Sagan
       Cosmos: A Personal Voyage, 1980
10   Marshall Davis
       The Tao of Christ Podcast, 2020

11 David Bohm
    David Bohm and Basil Hiley, *The Undivided Universe*,
    Routledge, 1995
12 Ron Sender, Shai Fuchs, and Ron Milo
    'Revised Estimates for the Number of Human and
    Bacteria Cells in the Body,' 2016

Chapter 13

1   Albert Einstein
    Letter to Phyllis Wright, 1936
2   David Bohm
    Film: *Infinite Potential: The Life and Ideas of David Bohm*,
    dir. Paul Howard, 2020
3   Carl Sagan
    Carl Sagan and Ann Druyan, *The Demon-Haunted World:
    Science as a Candle in the Dark*, Random House, 1997
4   David Bohm
    Film: *Infinite Potential: The Life & Ideas of David Bohm*, dir.
    Paul Howard, 2020
5   David Bohm
    Wholeness and the Implicate Order, Routledge, 1980
6   Jiddu Krishnamurti
    A Collection of Works of Jiddu Krishnamurti, Volume XI,
    Krishnamurti Foundation of America, 1962
7   David Bohm
    Wholeness and the Implicate Order, Routledge, 1980
8   David Bohm
    Wholeness and the Implicate Order, Routledge, 1980
9   Albert Einstein
    Carl Seelig, *Ideas and Opinions*, Wings Books, 1954
10 Albert Einstein
    'What Life Means to Einstein: An Interview by George
    Sylvester Viereck,' *The Saturday Evening Post*, 1929

11 Albert Einstein
    Montana Libraries, Volumes 8–14 (1954)
12 Albert Einstein
    William Hermanns, *Einstein and the Poet: In Search of the Cosmic Man*, Brandon Books 1983
13 Robert Oppenhiemer
    New Challenges for Human Communications, Volume 4, International Center for the Typographic Arts, Southern Illinois University, 1965
14 Lao Tsu
    The Tao of Lao Tzu: Insights from the Father of Taoism, Aksapada, 2019
15 Mencius
    The Mencius, Book 4, Part 2, verse 12, AD 300
16 Aldous Huxley
    Vulgarity in Literature, Chatto and Windus, 1930
17 Bernardo Kastrup
    Jane Clark and Richard Gault, 'Mind Over Matter: Interview with Bernardo Kastrup,' *Beshara Magazine*, Issue 18, Spring 2021
18 Donald Hoffman
    Science and Nonduality Conference Presentation: The Mystery of Free Will, 2019
19 Sam Harris
    Free Will, Free Press, 2012

Chapter 14
1 Saint Thomas Aquinas
    Summa Theologiae, Pt2, Pt2, respondeo
2 Brother Lawrence
    The Practice of the Presence of God, tr. Marshall Davis, 2013
3 Jiddu Krishnamurti
    The Book of Life: Daily Meditations with Krishnamurti, HarperOne, 1995

4 St Francis de Sales
   Attributed
5 Meister Eckhart
   Meister Eckhart: Selected Writings, tr. Oliver Davies, Penguin Classics, 1994
6 Meister Eckhart
   Meister Eckhart: Selected Writings, tr. Oliver Davies, Penguin Classics, 1994
7 Meister Eckhart
   Meister Eckhart's Sermons, Sermon IV: True Hearing, tr. Claud Field, 1909
8 Meister Eckhart
   Meister Eckhart: Selected Writings, tr. Oliver Davies, Penguin Classics, 1994
9 Michael James
   Sri Ramana Teachings Podcasts, license: https://creativecommons.org/licenses/by-sa/4.0/ No changes were made
10 Psalm 46:10
   Bible, The Old Testament

End matter

1 Bodhi Avasa
   One Liners: A Collection of Quotes by Avasa, ed. Dioni Riccardo Lautizi and Shakti Caterina Maggi, 2013

Bibliography

Adams, Robert. *Silence of the Heart: Dialogues with Robert Adams*. Robert Adams Publishing Group. 1980

Allen, Summer, PhD. 'The Science of Awe.' Greater Good Science Center at UC Berkeley. 2018

Avasa, Bodhi. *One Liners: A Collection of Quotes by Avasa*. Dioni Riccardo Lautizi and Shakti Caterina Maggi, editors. 2013

Bhagavad Gita, The. Eknath Easwaran, translator. Nilgiri Press. 1985

Bohm, David. *Wholeness and the Implicate Order*. Routledge. 1980

Bohr, Niels. *Atomic Physics and Human Knowledge*. John Wiley & Sons Inc. 1958

Brother Lawrence. *The Practice of the Presence of God*. Marshall Davis. 2013.

Carse, David. *Perfect Brilliant Stillness*. Non-Duality Press. 2005

Clark, Jane, and Gault, Richard. 'Mind Over Matter: Interview with Bernardo Kastrup.' *Beshara Magazine*. Issue 18. Spring 2021

Eckhart, Meister. *Breakthrough: Meister Eckhart's Creation Spirituality, in New Translation*. Matthew Fox, translator. Doubleday. 1980

Eckhart, Meister. *Meister Eckhart: Selected Writings*. Oliver Davies, translator. Penguin Classics. 1994

Fridman, Lex. Lex Fridman Interview #293: Donald Hoffman: Reality Is an Illusion—How Evolution Hid the Truth. 2022

Hartong, Leo. *Awakening to the Dream: The Gift of Lucid Living*. Non-Duality Press. 2007

Hedderman, Paul. *The Escape To Everywhere*. Let It Be Publishing. 2015

Hermanns, William. *Einstein and the Poet: In Search of the Cosmic Man*. Brandon Books. 1983

Hoff, Benjamin. *The Tao of Pooh*. Dutton Adult. 1981

Hoffman, Donald. *The Case Against Reality: Why Evolution Hid the Truth from Our Eyes*. W.W. Norton & Co. 2019

Huang Po. *The Zen Teaching of Huang Po on the Transmission of Mind*. John Blofeld, translator. Grove Press. 1958

Ibn 'Arabi, Muhyiddin, and Balyani, Awhad al-din. *Know Yourself: An Explanation of the Oneness of Being*. Cecilia Twinch, translator. Beshara Publications. 2011

James, Michael. *Happiness and The Art of Being*. Michael D A James. 2006

Kastrup, Bernardo. Analytic Idealism Course: Online. Essential Foundation. 2022

Lao Tsu. *Tao Te Ching*. Gia-Fu Feng & Jane English, translators. Random House Vintage Books. 1989

Niebauer, Chris, PhD. *No Self, No Problem*. Hierophant Publishing. 2019

Parsons, Tony. *The Open Secret*. Open Secret Publishing. 1998

Parsons, Tony. *This Freedom*. Open Secret Publishing. 2015

Rumi, Jalaluddin. *The Essential Rumi*. Coleman Barks, translator. HarperCollins, 1996.

Schrodinger, Erwin. *What Is Life? The Physical Aspect of the Living Cell with Mind and Matter & Autobiographical Sketches*. Cambridge University Press. 1944

Seng-ts'an. *Hsin-Hsin Ming*. Richard B. Clarke, translator. White Pine Press, 2001

Spira, Rupert. *Being Aware of Being Aware*. Sahaja Publications. 2017

Spira, Rupert. *The Transparency of Things: Contemplating the Nature of Experience*. Sahaja Publications. 2016

Sri Atmananda Krishna Menon. *Atma Darshan: At the Ultimate*. Advaita Publishers. 1983

Sri Atmananda Krishna Menon. *Atma Nirvriti: Freedom and Felicity in the Self*. Advaita Publishers. 1983

Sri Atmananda Krishna Menon. *Notes on Spiritual Discourses of Shri Atmananda*, Volume 1. Nitya Tripta, translator. Non-Duality Press. 2009

Sri Muruganar. *Guru Vachaka Kovai*. David Godman, translator and editor. Avadhuta Foundation. 2008

Sri Nisargadatta Maharaj. *I Am That*. Maurice Frydman, translator. Acorn Press. 1973

Sri Ramana Maharshi. *Be As You Are: The Teachings of Ramana Maharshi*. David Godman, editor. Penguin Arkana, 1985

Sri Ramana Maharshi. *Ulladu Narpadu* (Forty Verses on What Exists). Michael James, translator. Happiness of Being Website

Sri Ramana Maharshi. *Who Am I? The Teaching of Bhagavan Sri Ramana Maharshi*, 32nd edition. Sri Ramanasramam, Tiruvannamalai. 2021

Sri Sadhu Om. *The Path of Sri Ramana—Part One*. Sri Ramana Kshetra, Kanvashram Trust, Tiruvannamalai. 1971

Tolle, Eckhart. *A New Earth: Awakening to Your Life's Purpose*. Plumb. 2005

Tolle, Eckhart. *The Power of Now: A Guide to Spiritual Enlightenment*. New World Library. 2004

Upanishads, The. Eknath Easwaran, translator. Nilgiri Press. 1987

Weber, Gary, PhD. 'The Default Mode Network & End of Suffering Presentation.' *Heart of Art*. 2015

Wei Wu Wei. *Open Secret*. Sentient Publications. 2004

Wheeler, John. *Awakening to the Natural State*. Non-Duality Press. 2004

About the Author

Ever since emerging from young adulthood, Scott has had an affinity for understanding the inherent properties of human and objective nature. From the inner workings of chemical and biological systems, to the physical phenomena of heat, energy and mass behaviors in material-assemblies and structures, to the unitive mindset required to create and operate socially-conscious businesses, his interests were all, unbeknown to Scott, a relentless pursuit to locate the underlying nature of Reality.

It wasn't until Scott was introduced to the intimate-innate properties of Self, via the integration of the nondual Eastern philosophy of Advaita Vedanta with the intelligence of Western quantum physics, that love and understanding of the inherent-Truth of human and objective nature arose. Experiencing inherent-Truth directly, Scott clearly realized that not only can ever-present happiness be experienced in this lifetime, but it is the preeminent attribute of all 8 billion of us.

Scott expedites Self-realization by utilizing the perennial philosophy of Nonduality to point you back to yourSelf, so that you can experience-directly the ever-present peace, happiness and love of yourSelf. Scott's nondual understanding originates from current teachers such as Rupert Spira and Michael James, but primarily from the twentieth-century sages Sri Ramana Maharshi and Sri Muruganar. Yet Scott's greatest inherent-understanding comes from thousands of hours of Self-inquiry.

Scott holds a Bachelor of Science Degree in Chemical Engineering from the University of Idaho and is a founder and former Chief Executive Officer of two Certified Benefit-Corporations (B-Corps).

Note to Reader

My deepest gratitude shines for your reading of *Love Outpouring*. There is honestly nothing more mySelf longs for in life than for you to know yourSelf. To continue the destinationless journey to know yourSelf, please feel free to reach out through the Love Outpouring website www.loveoutpouring.com Here you can find further nonduality insights, links to social media and meditations, and blogs.

May you permanently experience a peaceful 'here and now.'

Love Outpouring,

Scott

Where could you go,
Where I would not be?

Where can I go
Where you are not with me

In each new hello
Is an echoed good-bye

But good-bye never happens.
Bodhi Avasa[1]

Notes

1 Adrian G.A. Meyers, also known as Bodhi Avasa (1947–2016), was an Englishman who at the age of 23, after a number of glimpses of Oneness during his youth, had a spontaneous awakening. From his time of awakening till his bodily death, Avasa traveled in Europe holding talks and retreats wherever he was invited. Through sincerity, joy and laughter, Avasa lovingly communicated the primal message of eternity: There is but One Being in all things and this One is You.

MANTRA
BOOKS

EASTERN RELIGION & PHILOSOPHY
We publish books on Eastern religions and philosophies.
Books that aim to inform and explore the various traditions
that began in the East and have migrated West.
If you have enjoyed this book, why not tell other readers by
posting a review on your preferred book site.

The Less Dust the More Trust
Participating in The Shamatha Project, Meditation and
Science Adeline van Waning, MD PhD
The inside-story of a woman participating in frontline
meditation research, exploring the interfaces of mind-practice,
science and psychology.
Paperback: 978-1-78099-948-7 ebook: 978-1-78279-657-2

I Know How To Live, I Know How To Die
The Teachings of Dadi Janki: A warm, radical, and life-
affirming view of who we are, where we come from,
and what time is calling us to do
Neville Hodgkinson
Life and death are explored in the context of frontier science
and deep soul awareness.
Paperback: 978-1-78535-013-9 ebook: 978-1-78535-014-6

Living Jainism
An Ethical Science
Aidan Rankin, Kanti V. Mardia
A radical new perspective on science rooted in intuitive
awareness and deductive reasoning.
Paperback: 978-1-78099-912-8 ebook: 978-1-78099-911-1

Ordinary Women, Extraordinary Wisdom
The Feminine Face of Awakening
Rita Marie Robinson
A collection of intimate conversations with female spiritual
teachers who live like ordinary women, but are engaged
with their true natures.
Paperback: 978-1-84694-068-2 ebook: 978-1-78099-908-1